Tips and Traps
When Incorporating
Your Business

Tips and Traps When Incorporating Your Business

Jeffery A. Jensen, CPA
Brian Radford
Stephen Bulpitt

McGraw-Hill

New York   Chicago   San Francisco   Lisbon   London
Madrid   Mexico City   Milan   New Delhi   San Juan
Seoul   Singapore   Sydney   Toronto

1 2 3 4 5 6 7 8 9 0   FGR/FGR   0 9 8 7 6 5

ISBN 0-07-145786-0

This publication is designed to provide accurate and authoritative information in regard to the subject matter covered. It is sold with the understanding that neither the author nor the publisher is not engaged in rendering legal, accounting, or other professional service. If legal advice or other expert assistance is required, the services of a competent professional person should be sought.
—*From a Declaration of Principles jointly adopted by a Committee of the American Bar Association and a Committee of Publishers*

McGraw-Hill books are available at special quantity discounts to use as premiums and sales promotions, or for use in corporate training programs. For more information, please write to the Director of Special Sales, McGraw-Hill Professional, Two Penn Plaza, New York, NY 10121-2298. Or contact your local bookstore.

 This book is printed on recycled, acid-free paper containing a minimum of 50% recycled, de-inked fiber.

Library of Congress Cataloging-in-Publication Data

Jensen, Jeffery A.
    Tips & traps when incorporating your business / by Jeffery A. Jensen, Brian Radford,
    Stephen Bulpitt.— 1st ed.
       p.   cm.
    ISBN 0-07-145786-0 (alk. paper)
    1. Incorporation—United States—Popular works. 2. Corporation law—United States—
    Popular works. I. Title: Tips and traps when incorporating your business. II. Radford, Brian.
    III. Bulpitt, Stephen. IV. Title.
  KF1420.Z9J46 2005
  346.73'06622—dc22

                                                2005015221

Contents

Tips and Traps When Incorporating Your Business

1

Introduction

Have you ever wondered why the rich keeping getting richer? Tax breaks are one of the biggest reasons. These breaks are set up to benefit corporations while most hardworking Americans are stuck losing a HUGE chunk of their paycheck each year. Does that seem fair? Let us show you how you too can take advantage of the tax breaks that will increase your income.

Have you ever thought about:

- Taking your business to the next level?

- Increasing your income by paying less tax?

- Making the biggest risk in your business a thing of the past?

- Starting a home business to bring in additional income?

If you've ever thought about any of this, there's something you absolutely have to do first: INCORPORATE. The benefits are enormous. If you're bringing in money from a home business right now, or especially if you're losing money in a home business, you need to incorporate.

Here are just a few of the endless benefits of incorporating your small business, partnership, or sole proprietorship:

- Incorporating your business is like creating a new individual. It acts as a new legal entity, separate from that of its owners/shareholders.

- Incorporating almost completely eliminates the personal risk of owning a company because it separates your personal identity from that of your business. So, though the assets of your corporation will be at risk, your assets and those of your shareholders won't be.

1

- If you're a small business looking for investors, becoming a corporation will make you much more attractive because the risk of personal assets often scares investors away from partnerships and sole proprietorships.

- We all know how important image is when it comes to the success of any business. Adding that "Inc." or "Corp." to the end of the title of your business adds an enduring sense of permanence, professionalism, and authority, even if your corporation consists of just a few people or even one person.

- Transferring ownership of a corporation is also simple and effortless. It basically involves transferring shares to new stockholders, with no need for complex legal documentation.

- A corporation has the capability of continuing indefinitely. Its existence is not affected by the death or incapacity of its shareholders or directors.

- Last but not least, corporations are afforded unbelievable tax benefits, including endless opportunities for tax write-offs, income-shifting, and fringe benefits, which you will learn much more about as you read through this book.

You will be absolutely amazed at how easy and affordable it is to incorporate yourself and gain access to all the privileges that until now were only accessible to big businesses or those who could afford to spend thousands of dollars to hire lawyers and accountants to incorporate their businesses.

What Is a Corporation?

So now that you have seen some of the benefits of a corporation, what exactly is a corporation? A corporation, also known simply as a "company," is a legal entity that exists separately from its owner(s). It is empowered with legal rights that are usually only reserved for individuals. These include acquiring assets, entering into contracts, the right to sue and be sued, hiring employees, loaning and borrowing money. The primary advantage of a for-profit corporation is that it provides its shareholders with a right to participate in the profits (by dividends) without any personal liability, because the company absorbs the entire liability of the organization.

Formation of a corporation occurs when properly completed articles of incorporation (called a charter or certificate of incorporation in some states) are filed with the proper state authority and all fees are paid. The corporation is granted a state charter, which permits a group of people, as shareholders (for-profit companies) or members (nonprofit companies), to create an organization, which can then focus on pursuing its own objectives.

Common Terms When Forming a Corporation

When discussing a corporation, there are many common terms that are used. If unknown, these terms can add to the confusion for newcomers and complicate their understanding. The following are some of the most important terms and their definitions:

Articles of Incorporation.   The Articles of Incorporation (referred to as the Charter or the Certificate of Incorporation in some states) is the document filed with the state in order to create a corporation. For most states, these articles only need to include several basic statements. Usually it is more flexible to keep the articles short and put the details in the bylaws. Long-detailed Articles of Incorporation make it harder to make changes and to adjust corporate structures.

Board of Directors.   The Board of Directors is the controlling body of a corporation. This body usually meets at least once per year in order to make major corporate decisions and elect officers. In a small corporation, the officers usually serve as the Board of Directors.

Bylaws.   These are a set of rules for the Board of Directors, officers, and shareholders that govern the structure and operation of the corporation.

Officers.   The officers of a corporation run the daily affairs of the business. These positions usually include president, vice president, and secretary. In some states the same individual can hold all of the offices of a corporation.

Registered Agent.   The Registered Agent is the person designated to receive all legal papers for the corporation. This individual usually has to sign a statement that says he or she understands the duties and the responsibilities of this position.

Registered Office.   This is a location where the Registered Agent should be regularly available. It may be the corporate office, the office of the corporation's attorney, or the office of the person who is the Registered Agent.

Shareholders.   A shareholder is a person who owns stock in a corporation. For a small corporation, this may be the same set of people who are the officers and Board of Directors, but sometimes individuals other than officers, such as spouses, are listed as the shareholders. Shareholders must meet once a year to elect the Board of Directors and to make other major corporate decisions.

Why Should I Incorporate?

If you own a business or have a business idea, you may have wondered: Should I incorporate? The answer to this question may not be as straightforward as you had hoped. While there are many benefits to incorporating, you need to consider the advantages and disadvantages and all the possibilities as they relate to your business. A comforting fact may be that the form of your business doesn't have to be set in stone once you have created it. You can change the legal structure of your business as it grows or changes focus or membership.

TIP

After educating yourself about the many possibilities out there (we discuss the different options for structuring your business in Chapter 2), consult with an attorney and/or tax professional about the legal and tax ramifications before making your decision to incorporate. Once the decision has been made, this book will walk you through the necessary steps so you can incorporate on your own.

TIP

You may also wish to consult with a tax accountant to compare projected income, if you incorporate, with your personal taxes to see which one is more advantageous for you.

Advantages to Incorporating

The most common reasons for incorporating are to avoid or limit personal liability and to save on taxes. However, there are several advantages and disadvantages, and you should review each of them in light of your particular situation.

Avoid or Limit Personal Liability. The most common and possibly the key advantage of incorporating is the limited liability it affords its shareholders. Typically, shareholders are not liable for the debts and obligations of the corporation, which means that creditors will not come knocking at the door of a shareholder to pay the company's debts. A shareholder's liability is limited to the investment in the company, and as long as personal guarantees have not been given, his or her personal assets are protected. However, while personal assets are protected, a corporation functions as an individual, and thus can own property, incur liability, and sue or be sued.

In contrast, if you do not incorporate and instead form a sole proprietorship, then your personal assets—including but not limited to your house, cars, and money in your bank accounts—can be seized to pay your business debts. You are generally liable for any debts or claims made against your company.

TRAP

Many people refer to the liability protection they receive as a result of incorporating as a liability "shield." Although incorporating can protect you personally in some situations, it is important to remember that it is not bulletproof. Incorporating may not protect you in many legal battles if you are the sole owner of a very small corporation. Nor does incorporating excuse misconduct or protect you against negligence. If you are negligent, then both you (the negligent person) *and* your company will be liable. If you're concerned with liability issues, consult with a lawyer before incorporating for an explanation of specific liability details and situations that are covered in your home state.

TRAP

If you fund your company through loans and you've guaranteed the loan with the bank with a personal guarantee, then you are still personally liable.

Save on Taxes. This is a bit of a moving target right now. Many may tell you that incorporating will save you money on taxes, but with the current tax brackets, this may not necessarily be the case. It can definitely be an advantage of incorporating, but you'll have to look into it before knowing whether it will in fact be an advantage to your specific situation.

The potential savings in taxes may result from the corporation being taxed at a lower rate than your personal income tax rate. And payments may be given out in dividends, which are taxed at a different rate than personal income tax. A shareholder does not have to be actively involved with a corporation to receive dividends. Your spouse and/or children could even be shareholders, giving you the possibility to distribute dividends across those who may be in a lower tax bracket.

Another real tax advantage is that you can control when you receive income. Instead of a set interval, it's possible to control when dividends are paid out, which allows you to take your income at a time when you'll pay less in taxes.

There are other potential tax advantages as well, and we'll explain them in detail in Chapter 8. Incorporating provides the potential for tax deferrals; that is, deferring taxes until a later time, when you would be in a lower tax bracket, for instance, or after rates have fallen. You may also qualify for a small business deduction, which is an annual tax credit calculated as a fixed percentage of the first $200,000 of taxable income.

TRAP

Owners will be held personally liable if the corporation has left any unpaid taxes.

Continuance.   A corporation's life is not dependent upon its members. A corporation possesses the feature of unlimited life. If an owner dies or wishes to sell his or her interest, the corporation will continue to exist and do business.

Increase Your Business and Image.   Like a sole proprietorship, a corporation can borrow and incur debt, but a corporation also has the ability to raise capital through this selling of stock. This means it's easier to expand your company. Generally equity capital does not incur interest nor does it have to be repaid.

The addition of *Corporation, Corp., Inc., Ltd.,* and so on to your company name can also help increase your business, because your company might be perceived as larger or more stable than an unincorporated business. This perception also increases your ability to raise capital through investors.

Other Advantages.   There are many other advantages of incorporating. For one, retirement funds and qualified retirement plans—like 401(k)s—

may be set up more easily. For another, ownership of a corporation is easily transferable and management is more centralized.

You might ask: So why doesn't everyone incorporate? With all of these advantages, isn't the decision a no-brainer?

Not necessarily.

Disadvantages to Incorporating

While there are some great advantages to incorporating, there are also several disadvantages. You need to weigh both sides of incorporating before jumping into it. Let's discuss some of the disadvantages.

Double Taxation.   The primary disadvantage to a corporation is double taxation. Profits are taxed first as income to the corporation, then as income to the shareholder. All reasonable business expenses, such as salaries, are deductions against corporate income and can minimize the double tax. Further, the double tax can be eliminated by electing to file as an S corporation.

Complicates Taxes.   If you dread filing your personal taxes each year and you are used to only filing a single personal tax return, this may be a larger drawback than it sounds. You will now have to file a corporation return as well as your personal return. This means you will either have increased accounting fees or a larger headache to work through on your own. Corporate losses also cannot be deducted from your personal income taxes as they can be in a sole proprietorship or a partnership.

Liability Not as Limited as You Hope.   Limiting your liability may be weakened by personal guarantees. If lending institutions feel your corporation has not existed long enough or does not have sufficient assets to secure a loan, personal guarantees are required from the business owner(s). So technically, the owner providing the personal guarantee remains liable for any unpaid debt by the company.

Increased Paperwork.   Not only do you have to file an additional tax return, as noted above, but you now must keep separate records of your bank accounts and assets. Business licenses must be obtained. Records must be kept of corporate meetings, such as those of the Board of Directors and shareholders, as well as of Articles of Incorporation, amendments to your articles, etc. Such records may be overwhelming for some individuals, but help is available through online incorporation services.

Complexity and Expense.   Many choices and decisions have to be made when incorporating. A corporation will cost money to form, and it may increase your accounting costs as well. As a more complex legal entity than a sole proprietorship or a partnership, you will find that it is more complicated and more costly to form this type of entity.

TIP

An attorney is not a legal requirement to incorporate. You can prepare and file the Articles of Incorporation yourself; however, you need to be thoroughly versed in the laws of your state. This book will step you through the requirements to incorporate on your own and help identify the tips and traps along the way.

So, do you incorporate?   We have reviewed some of the advantages and disadvantages. We strongly recommended that you review your personal situation and the goals of your company before you make any decisions. But don't forget that decisions made are not permanent; you can often make changes later down the road.

For-Profit versus Nonprofit Corporations

The focus of this book is on for-profit corporations, but some of you might be wondering about a nonprofit corporation. Often, the process for creating a nonprofit corporation is similar to that of a for-profit, but it may require a few extra forms. Below, we briefly cover the topic of a nonprofit corporation. Hopefully it will clarify some of the reasons why you may want to consider forming a nonprofit corporation.

What Qualifies as a Nonprofit Corporation?

Under Federal Tax Code Section 501(c)(3), a nonprofit corporation may be formed to operate for some religious, charitable, educational, literary, or scientific purpose. Individual states usually also include this same list as valid purposes to form a nonprofit corporation.

How Does It Differ from a For-Profit Corporation?

Under Federal Tax Code Section 501(c)(3), a tax-exempt corporation cannot pay dividends, *and* upon dissolution, it must distribute its remaining assets to another nonprofit group. This means that one major difference between a for-profit and a nonprofit corporation is that the latter can neither issue shares nor pay dividends, while the for-profit corporation is authorized by the state to issue stock to its shareholders in exchange for capital investments, which often take the form of money and/or equipment.

Advantages of a Nonprofit Corporation

Tax Exemptions. Federal Tax Code Section 501(c)(3) states that a nonprofit corporation is eligible for certain federal and state tax exemptions. These vary from state to state, and as a result, if you are considering forming a nonprofit corporation, we strongly advise that you consult with a tax accountant. With proper planning and filing, the corporation should be exempt from certain state and federal taxes.

TRAP

Although the nonprofit corporation should be tax exempt for certain taxes, an informational return and annual reports may still be required by the state and federal governments.

Funding Possibilities. Many companies and individuals seek out tax deductions or exemptions by donating money to nonprofit organizations. Some individuals seek out tax exemptions that exist for property transferred at death to such a nonprofit organization. Many organizations are even required by law to donate a certain percentage of their funds to such organizations to avoid endangering their own tax-exempt status.

Other Advantages. Many of the advantages of a for-profit corporation still apply to a nonprofit corporation, such as Employee Benefits, Continuance, and Limited Liability. But nonprofit corporations also have additional advantages, such as receiving lower postal rates on bulk mail, possibly discounted advertising rates, lower membership rates from many national chains. Also, employees may qualify for job training and other programs subsidized by the federal government.

Disadvantages of a Nonprofit Corporation

Increased Paperwork. As with for-profit corporations, increased paperwork is still an issue. Articles of Incorporation must be prepared and filed, minutes must be maintained, etc. As discussed before, there are agencies available to help with the filings and paperwork, but additional effort is required above and beyond that which is required with nonincorporated entities.

More Complicated Taxes.   In addition to these paperwork requirements, tax exemption filings (IRS Form 1023) must be sent to federal and state agencies within 15 months of the date of inception to qualify for tax-exempt status. This tax-exempt status will be retroactive to the date that your Articles of Incorporation were filed.

Other Disadvantages.   There are other disadvantages or limitations that result from forming a nonprofit corporation. As mentioned before, a nonprofit corporation is not permitted to distribute profits or dividends to its members. Also, corporate assets must only be distributed to another tax-exempt organization upon dissolution. Such issues complicate how the corporation functions, and attention must be given to ensure that all requirements are being met to maintain the tax-exempt status.

2

Choosing Which Business Entity Is Best for You

One of the first and most important decisions you face when starting or restructuring a business is choosing the type of business structure that will work best for you. There is no simple answer to the question, "Which business structure should I choose?" The type of business structure affects many other aspects of your business, such as taxes, liability, and ease of management, so it's important to consider carefully before making your decision.

The six most common business entities are:

- Sole proprietorship
- General partnership
- Limited partnership
- Limited liability company
- C corporation
- S corporation

In this chapter we will discuss these six entities in detail, giving the advantages and disadvantages of each. At the end of the chapter, Table 2-1 compares the various entities and lists their similarities and differences.

TIP

Take the time at the beginning to properly research and decide which entity is right for you. It is easier to choose the right entity at the beginning than to change to a different entity later.

Sole Proprietorship

A sole proprietorship is simply a single person doing business. Just by starting to sell goods or services, a person is automatically a sole proprietorship. There are no forms to fill out or state organization to register with. Some sole proprietors want to register a business name with their state to secure a name for their business. This is called "Doing Business As," or DBA. Registering a DBA is a simple process of filling out a single form and filing it with your state. Because of its simplicity, this is the most popular way to start a single person business.

TRAP

Many business owners start their businesses as a sole proprietorship at first to cut costs. Often they don't consider the disadvantages (see below) until it's too late. The cost to set up another entity type is often far less than the costs of self-employment tax or potential litigation.

Advantages of a Sole Proprietorship

The main advantage of a sole proprietorship is how it is formed. Without any legal forms or filing with the state, you are up and running simply by doing business. Another advantage is that it is easy to operate. There are no requirements for meetings or keeping minutes. Further, the income from the business is not reported separately from the business owner for federal income tax purposes. The income and expenses from the business are reported on the individual's Form 1040 on Schedule C. A sole proprietorship does not have to file a separate tax return.

Disadvantages of a Sole Proprietorship

The main disadvantage of a sole proprietorship is unlimited liability. This means that everything the business owner owns is at risk if the business loses a lawsuit. For example, Jim's Pizza Parlor (a sole proprietorship) was sued because an employee caused a car wreck that hurt Fred. Afterward, Fred decided to sue Jim. Fred won the case. He could then take all of the business assets (cash, equipment) and also go after Jim's house, car, boat, and personal savings.

A lesser disadvantage than unlimited liability, but one that should be noted, is that it's often difficult for a sole proprietorship to obtain a loan for the business without collateral. And finally, a sole proprietorship is limited to only one business owner.

Special Tax Considerations

All of the net income from the business is subject to self-employment tax, which is 15.3 percent in addition to income tax. Many business owners find out too late about self-employment tax.

General Partnership

A general partnership, more commonly referred to merely as a "partnership," is a relationship between two or more people who own and share the profits of a business. A partnership can be started with a verbal agreement. No official paperwork has to be filed. However, it is wise to at least create a partnership agreement detailing how profits will be distributed, how losses will be shared, and the policy to sell a partner's portion of the partnership.

Advantages of a Partnership

Like a sole proprietorship, a partnership is easily formed. It does not require any filing with the state. The partners merely have to agree to do business together to form the partnership. A partnership never pays any tax. The income is passed through to the partners to be reported on their individual tax return.

Disadvantages of a Partnership

Like sole proprietorships, general partnerships are subject to unlimited liability. But the liability is even greater in a partnership because each partner is personally liable for the business and is also held personally liable for the contracts or agreements made on behalf of the partnership by the other partners. A creditor can go after any one partner for the entire debt of the business without consideration of the partner's ownership percentage. Another disadvantage of a partnership is that if one of the partners dies, the partnership is automatically dissolved or ceases to exist.

Special Tax Consideration

As mentioned above, a partnership will never pay any tax; however, an information tax return, Form 1065, has to be filed. All of the net income from the business is subject to self-employment tax. Again, self-employment tax is 15.3 percent in addition to income tax.

Limited Partnership

A limited partnership is a partnership with two types of partners: general partners and limited partners. General partners manage the business and have the same unlimited liability as a partner in a general partnership. Limited partners contribute capital to the partnership and do not manage the business operations. Limited partners are only held liable up to the amount of the capital that was contributed. For instance, if a limited partner contributed $1,000, then a creditor could only take the limited partner's $1,000. The creditor could not go after the limited partner's personal assets to satisfy the debt.

Advantages of a Limited Partnership

The main advantage of a limited partnership is that the limited partners have limited personal liability. The personal assets of the limited partners are not at risk. A limited partnership also has the advantage of more easily raising capital because potential limited partners do not have to worry that their personal assets will be in jeopardy.

Disadvantages of a Limited Partnership

A main disadvantage of limited partnerships is that the general partners still have unlimited liability, just like partners in a general partnership. Another disadvantage is its complexity. Forms have to be filed with the state to form limited partnership. Also, limited partners have no say in the management of their investment, or they risk losing the limited liability protection.

Special Tax Consideration

A partnership will never pay any tax, as we said before; however, an information tax return, Form 1065, has to be filed. All of the net income from the business is subject to self-employment tax of 15.3 percent, in addition to income tax.

Limited Liability Company

Limited liability companies, or LLCs, are a fairly new type of business structure. Wyoming was the first state to introduce the limited liability company, in 1977. The owners of an LLC are called "members," and the LLC is run by managers. LLCs are not corporations, but offer many of the same advantages. Many small business owners and entrepreneurs like LLCs because they use the "pass-through" taxation of a sole proprietorship or partnership, and have the limited liability protection of a corporation.

As with a general partnership, having a partnership agreement is wise: to create an operating agreement detailing how profits will be distributed, how losses will be shared, and how the LLC is to be managed; to set forth the duties and responsibilities of the members; and to set out the policy to sell a member's ownership.

Advantages of a Limited Liability Company

The creditors of a limited liability company cannot go after the personal assets of the members. LLCs do not have to follow the rigorous requirements of following bylaws, holding shareholder and directors meetings, and keeping minutes and records of those meetings, like a corporation. Foreign investors prefer LLCs because they do not have the restrictions of an S corporation (discussed below).

Disadvantages of a Limited Liability Company

Because limited liability companies have not been around as long as the other business entities, there is not as much court history and rulings involving LLCs. Also, forms have to be filed with the state to form a limited liability company.

Special Tax Considerations

A limited liability company can be taxed as a corporation or a partnership for federal income tax purposes. If the LLC elects to be taxed as a corporation, it would file Form 1120 or Form 1120s. If the LLC elects to be taxed as a partnership, it would file Form 1065.

C Corporations

A C corporation, or regular corporation, is a legal entity separate from its owners. It is owned by shareholders who elect a Board of Directors that oversees the business by hiring corporate officers to manage the day-to-day operations. Almost every large business in the United States is a C corporation.

Advantages of a C Corporation

The main advantage of a C corporation is the limited liability protection for its shareholders. The shareholders are not held personally liable for the debts of the corporation—only their investment is at risk. A C corporation has a "perpetual existence," meaning it can keep going as long as the shareholders want. It does not terminate at the death of a shareholder. Further, a C corporation can have a fiscal tax year other than a calendar tax year.

Disadvantages of a C Corporation

As we touched on in the introductory chapter, corporations have rigorous requirements: following bylaws, holding shareholder and directors meetings, and keeping minutes and records of those meetings. These requirements need to be followed in order to protect the limited liability protection. Personal money cannot be commingled with corporate funds. When a general corporation makes a profit, it pays a federal corporate income tax on the profit. Also, if the business declares a dividend, the stockholders must report the dividend as personal income, and they end up paying more taxes. This double taxation is a disadvantage to the C corporation.

Special Tax Considerations

Loans given to the shareholders or other related parties will be treated as dividends if the loans are below the market interest rate. Loans should not be used as a way to avoid the double taxation.

TIP

Money paid to a shareholder needs to be an expense to the corporation in order to avoid the double taxation. For instance, the shareholder can lease office equipment to the corporation and receive a lease payment.

S Corporations

A subchapter S corporation is a general corporation that has elected a special tax status with the IRS once the corporation is formed. S corporations are best for small business owners who prefer to be taxed as if they were still sole proprietors or partners. S corporations get around the double taxation—once at the corporate level, and again at the personal level—because all income or loss is reported only once on the personal tax returns of the stockholders. For a lot of small businesses, the S corporation offers them the best of both worlds by combining the tax advantages of a sole proprietorship or partnership with the limited liability and enduring life of a corporate structure.

For an S corporation status, your corporation must follow these guidelines:

1. Stockholders (all of them) must be citizens or permanent residents of the United States.

2. Seventy-five is the maximum number of stockholders an S corporation may have.

3. If an S corporation is held by an "electing small business trust," then all beneficiaries of the trust must be individuals, estates, or charitable organizations. Interests in the trust cannot be purchased.

4. Only one class of stock may be issued for an S corporation.

5. Only or up to 25 percent of the gross corporate income may be derived from passive income.

6. Some general business corporations are not able to receive S corporation status. These are:

   - A bank that is a financial institution
   - Insurance companies taxed under Subchapter L
   - DISC (Domestic International Sales Corporation)
   - Different affiliated groups of corporations

TIP

File Form 2553 within 75 days of incorporating. Failure to file Form 2553 on time will delay S corporation status until the following year.

Advantages of an S Corporation

The main advantage of an S corporation is that it eliminates the double taxation of a C corporation. The S corporation is considered a pass-through entity, like a partnership, and taxed at the individual shareholder level.

Therefore, the S corporation has all of the advantages of a C corporation without the downside.

Disadvantages of an S Corporation

As with a C corporation, an S corporation has rigorous requirements: following bylaws, holding shareholder and directors meetings, and keeping minutes and records of those meetings. These requirements need to be followed in order to keep the limited liability protection. Further, personal money cannot be commingled with corporate funds.

Special Tax Considerations

In general, an S corporation is not taxed for federal income tax purposes. The income of the S corporation is passed through to the shareholders and taxed on their individual tax returns. However, there are certain instances when an S corporation may have to pay taxes. If the S corporation had tax on excess passive investment income, certain capital gains, or built-in gains, it would have to pay the tax. The S corporation would also have to pay the taxes from recomputing a prior year's investment credit or recapturing LIFO inventory.

Another tax consideration of an S corporation is the fact that the shareholders are not subject to self-employment tax. As long as the shareholders take a reasonable wage, then the distribution of profits is not subject to this tax.

TRAP

If the shareholders of the S corporation do not take a reasonable wage, the IRS can go back and reclassify the distribution of profits as a wage, at its discretion.

Comparison of Business Entities
LLCs versus S Corporations
What Are the Similarities?

1. Both are separate legal entities that are created by a state filing.

2. They offer the same limited liability protection; the owners are typically not personally responsible for the debts and liabilities of the business.

3. Both are pass-through tax entities, which means that the income or loss generated by the business is reflected on the personal income tax return of the owners.

What Are the Differences?

1. The ownership of an S corporation is restricted; however, a limited liability company does not possess these same limitations.

   a. An LLC can have an unlimited number of members (owners), while an S corporation is restricted to no more than 75 shareholders.

   b. Non-U.S. residents can be members of an LLC, while an S corporation may not have non-U.S. residents as shareholders.

   c. S corporations cannot be owned by C corporations, other S corporations, many trusts, LLCs, or partnerships. Limited liability companies are not subject to these restrictions.

2. LLCs are allowed to have subsidiaries without restriction. S corporations are not allowed to own 80 percent or more of another corporation's shares.

3. Formalities:

   a. An S corporation requires formalities: Annual meetings of shareholders and directors are required each year, and meeting minutes are required to be kept with the corporation's records.

   b. LLCs are not required to hold such meetings; however, it is a good idea to document major decisions of the company.

4. An S corporation's existence is perpetual. Conversely, an LLC typically has a limited life span. Most states require that an LLC list a dissolution date in its articles of organization, and certain events—such as the death or withdrawal of a member—can cause the LLC to dissolve.

5. The stock of an S corporation is freely transferable, while the interest (ownership) of LLC is not—typically the approval of the other members must be received.

6. An S corporation may have advantages with self-employment taxes in comparison with an LLC. For more information on this issue, consult with your tax advisor.

C Corporations versus S Corporations

What Are the Similarities?

1. An S corporation is simply a C corporation (also known as a regular corporation) that files IRS Form 2553 to elect a special tax status with the IRS. The Articles of Incorporation that are filed with the state are the same whether a corporation is an S corporation or C corporation.

2. They are both separate legal entities that are created by a state filing.

3. Both offer the same limited liability protection, the owners are typically not personally responsible for the debts and liabilities of the business.

4. Both entities are required to follow the same formalities. They must hold annual meetings of shareholders and directors, and meeting minutes must be kept with the corporate records.

What Are the Differences?

1. Taxation:
   a. The S corporation is a pass-through tax entity, which means that the income or loss generated by the business is reflected on the personal income tax return of the owner(s).
   b. A C corporation is a separately taxable entity. The profits and losses are taxed directly to the corporation. This can lead to double taxation on dividends that are paid out of corporate profits to the owners.

2. The ownership of an S corporation is restricted; however, the C corporation does not possess these same limitations.
   a. The C corporation can have an unlimited number of shareholders, while an S corporation is restricted to no more than 75 shareholders.
   b. Non-U.S. residents can be owners of a C corporation, while an S corporation may not have non-U.S. residents as shareholders.
   c. S corporations cannot be owned by C corporations, other S corporations, many trusts, LLCs, or partnerships. C corporations are not subject to these restrictions.

3. The S corporation must make a timely election of S corporation status. The election, which is made by filing IRS Form 2553, must be made by March 15 in order for the election to take effect for that year. If the election is made after March 15 but within 75 days of the incorporation date, the election will be effective for the next calendar year. If the S corporation is not a calendar year taxpayer, the election must be made within 75 days of the beginning of the corporation's tax year.

LLCs versus C Corporations

What Are the Similarities?

1. Both are separate legal entities that are created by a state filing.

2. Both offer the same limited liability protection; the owners are typically not personally responsible for the debts and liabilities of the business.

3. Both entities have few ownership restrictions. The owners are not required to be U.S. residents, and the number of owners is without limitation. Further, the owners are not required to be individuals, as with an S corporation.

4. The ownership (stock with corporation or membership interest with LLC) can be divided into numerous classes.

What Are the Differences?

1. Taxation:

   a. The LLC is a pass-through tax entity, which means that the income or loss generated by the business is reflected on the personal income tax return of the owners.

   b. A C corporation is a separately taxable entity. The profits and loses are taxed directly to the corporation. This can lead to double taxation on dividends that are paid out of corporate profits to the owners.

2. Formalities:

   a. A C corporation requires that certain formalities be followed. The corporation must hold annual meetings of shareholders and directors, and meeting minutes must be kept with the corporation's records.

   b. LLCs are not required to hold such meetings; however, it is a good idea to document major decisions of the company and hold regular meetings of members.

3. Transferability of Interest: Transferring stock in a corporation is generally easier than the transfer of ownership with an LLC. Typically, a shareholder of a corporation is not required to get approval from the other shareholders before selling stock. For an LLC, the usual rule is that the owners must obtain approval from the other owners before ownership can be sold.

Table 2-1. Entity Comparison

	Sole Proprietorship	General Partnership	Limited Partnership	Limited Liability Company	C Corporation	S Corporation
Starting requirements	None	None	File with state	File with state	File with state	File with state
Owner	One individual	Two partners	General and limited partners	Members	Shareholders	Shareholders
Maximum number of owners	One	Many	Many	Unlimited	75	Many
Minimum number of owners	One	Two	Two	One	One	One (except for Massachusetts)
Manager	Owner	Partners	General partner	Manager	Directors	Directors
How taxed	Individual level	Individual level	Individual level	Individual level	Corporate level	Individual level
Liability	Unlimited	Unlimited	General partner is unlimited; Limited partner is limited	Limited	Limited	Limited

3

Incorporating

Now that you understand what a corporation is and its advantages and disadvantages, and we've gone into the different business entities that you can form, let's get started. But first, a disclaimer: This book is not intended to provide legal advice. Our intent is to help walk you through the necessary steps in order to form a corporation. We will, however, point out some of the areas where things can get complicated, and guide you through those difficult spots. In fact, it *is* possible to incorporate yourself with little or no outside help!

Checklist for Incorporating

Below we provide a checklist for forming a simple corporation. By keeping your organizational structure simple and following the instructions in this chapter, you will be able to form a corporation on your own.

What about a Limited Liability Company, or L.L.C.?

If you want to form an LLC, the process is *very* similar to that of forming a corporation. This chapter will still be of value in terms of the filing process, but the templates we discuss will differ slightly. In addition to a few differences in the templates, some of the forms have different names (e.g., the articles are usually referred to as "Articles of Organization," and instead of bylaws you will need an "Operating Agreement").

- ☐ Choose a corporate name.
- ☐ Choose a business structure/type of corporation.
- ☐ Choose the state in which you will incorporate.
- ☐ Prepare and file key documents for incorporating.
- ☐ Determine stock composition (if necessary, meet with securities lawyer regarding stock sales).
- ☐ Choose corporate directors.
- ☐ Choose a Registered Agent.
- ☐ Prepare your Articles of Incorporation.
- ☐ Prepare other key documents.
- ☐ File the key documents.
- ☐ Request Federal Employer Identification Number (IRS Form SS-4).
- ☐ If necessary, prepare Shareholders Agreement.
- ☐ Hold organizational meeting.
- ☐ Open a bank account.
- ☐ If an S corporation is formed, file Form 2553.
- ☐ Organize corporate records.
- ☐ Operate your corporation.

Choose a Corporate Name

To begin the process you must select a name under which you will conduct business. You'll need to thoroughly check to make sure the name you wish to use is not being used by another business. Some businesses have wasted thousands of dollars in logos, advertising preparations, and printed materials only to discover that their chosen name is already being used by another company. There are many locations on the Internet through which you can perform name searches to see if your name is available, such as www.KnowX.com. Also, your Secretary of State's office may be able to assist with this matter—you can contact them via letters, phone, or the Internet.

Some businesses fail to properly register their names but may still have rights to the name. You should check general business listings to ensure that the name is not being used. Business directories, phone books, online "yellow pages," and other listings of businesses may serve as a valuable resource as you check for informal uses of your prospective company name.

The name of a business may not be registered as a trademark, but the name on goods or services may be registered and provide for exclusive rights to use that name. To ensure that you will not be violating a registered trademark, you should search the records of the U.S. Patent and Trademark Office as well. Their Web site can be found at www.uspto.gov. Their site includes a link to search through current and pending trademarks, as well as fee information, online form submittals, and more.

States require that certain words be included in your corporate name. These words vary from state to state and may depend on the entity type that you choose. For the specific name requirements of your state, refer to the office of the Secretary of State. More information about these requirements is also provided in Appendix A. The most widely accepted words that must be included are:

- Company
- Co.
- Corporation
- Corp.
- Incorporated
- Inc.

This may seem a trivial step in the process, but it does require careful attention. If you do not choose your corporate name carefully the first time, you may be required to change it later. This might require amending your Articles of Incorporation, redesigning logos, changing your domain name, changing your listings in telephone and other directories, purchasing new business cards and stationery, and so on. It is better to get your name right the first time—hopefully you'll be using that name for a long time.

Common Questions

Why does your company name have to include certain words? This informs persons dealing with the business that they are dealing with a corporation. This protects shareholders from liability.

Do I need a logo right away? Although a logo will add professionalism to your company image, enhance your value, increase recognition, and make your business stand out, it may not be the right time for a logo. If you plan to send out correspondence and hand out business cards, then it may be time to start the process. Many companies do not have a lot of revenue up front or may not have a clear view of who their main customer base will be, so they may want to wait before getting a logo.

TIP

If you feel the time is right for a logo, there are hundreds of companies online with great rates. Pull up your favorite search engine and look for keywords like *logo design, custom logos,* or *logo designers.* Shop around. Look for a company that has an online portfolio full of logos that are similar to what you want. Sites like www.logoworks.com or www.lushlogo.com will provide you with a wide variety of packages depending on your price range.

What if I need help coming up with a name? There are many design companies that specialize in corporate identities and corporate branding. They have creative resources and for the right price will assist you in coming up with a unique name. This can be a costly process, since you involve others. Don't be afraid to ask friends and family for ideas and to be creative with word combinations.

Choose a Business Type

At this point, our assumption is that you have reviewed Chapter 2 and decided upon the type of business structure you would like to form. The focus of this book is on forming an S corporation (S corp) or a C corporation (C corp), but the information below may also assist you in forming an LLC. If you remember, there are some slight differences between the S corp and the C corp. Mainly, an S corporation elects to be taxed under Subchapter S of the Internal Revenue Code.

Choose a State in Which to Incorporate

There is no legal requirement stating that you must incorporate in the state in which you live and work. Due to the fact that laws governing corporations vary from state to state, a typical question before incorporating is, "In which state should I incorporate?" The most common answer is that you should incorporate in the state in which you will conduct the majority of your business. If your intention is to only do business in a single state, then it's recommended that you incorporate in that state.

However, there may be good reasons to incorporate in a state other than the one in which you live. You may wish to incorporate in a state due to its flexible corporation laws, lack of corporate income tax, tax benefits, and so on. Some states purposely enact corporation laws that will attract businesses to incorporate in their states, even though the corporations will do business elsewhere. Arizona, Delaware, Maine, New Jersey, Nevada, and a few others were among the first states to enact such laws. Delaware is clearly the most successful when it comes to attracting outside companies. Nearly one-half of all New York Stock Exchange corporations are incorporated in Delaware, even though their business is conducted elsewhere.

Domestic versus Foreign Corporation

A domestic corporation is a business that is formed in the state in which it will be conducting most of its business. Anytime you conduct most of your business outside your incorporating state, you must be filed as a foreign corporation. A foreign corporation must qualify to do business in the other state, and will have to pay additional fees and costs. Additional filing requirements and paperwork are also required of foreign corporations. However, if your corporation conducts business in more than one state, the additional costs and paperwork may be well worth the hassle.

Delaware Corporation

Delaware, as we noted, is the state most often selected in which to incorporate. Delaware courts have over 200 years of legal precedent as makers of corporation law and the state has one of the most advanced and flexible corporation statutes in the United States. The Delaware Court of Chancery has a longstanding reputation and is principally a business law court. Other states have enacted similar laws to Delaware's and created similar specialty courts, but they have not yet achieved the same reputation.

There are several benefits to incorporating in Delaware. They include:

- Low incorporation fees
- No requirement for disclosure of names or addresses for the initial Board of Directors
- All corporate offices may be held by a single individual
- No state corporation income tax for corporations operating outside of Delaware
- No requirement to have a business office in Delaware (but the corporation must have a Registered Agent in the state)

TIP

If your company will conduct business in more than one state or if you are a large, publicly held corporation, you may benefit from incorporating in Delaware for the reasons listed above.

TRAP

If you are a small, privately held corporation that will only conduct business outside of the state of Delaware, then the benefits of a Delaware corporation may not be worth the extra costs and paperwork.

Nevada Corporation

Nevada is another state enacting corporate-friendly laws in order to attract more businesses to incorporate there. Their courts do not have the long-standing history of Delaware, but are making an attempt to provide many benefits to their corporations. These include:

- Stockholders are allowed to withhold their names from becoming part of public records
- No state corporate tax on profits
- No state annual franchise tax
- All corporate offices may be held by a single individual

Secretary of State

No matter where you incorporate, there will be a state agency through which you will file and pay your fees. For most states, the office of the Secretary of State is your contact point. But be aware: Some states do not refer to this agency as the office of the Secretary of State. It may be called the Department of State, the Division of Corporations, Department of Commerce, and so on. For simplicity, we'll refer to these agencies as the "Secretary of State" in this book.

The Secretary of State is the official responsible for handling each state's business filings. Each state's Secretary of State has a Web site on which they maintain current filing and fee information. See Appendix A for a listing for each state, along with helpful Web sites.

Key Documents for Incorporating

In order to create a corporation, a document must be filed with the state agency that keeps corporate records. As noted above, this agency is generally called the Secretary of State. In most states, the document required to be filed is called the Articles of Incorporation; however, some states call the document the Certificate of Incorporation, the Charter of Incorporation, and so on. For simplicity, in this book we will refer to this document as the Articles of Incorporation.

It is unnecessary to create long, detailed articles that describe numerous powers and functions of the corporation. To justify their fees, some attorneys prepare such long Articles of Incorporation, detailing corporate powers that are already defined in state laws and do not need to be repeated. Short articles allow for more flexibility and are just as legal as long ones.

TIP

Many of the Web sites provided by the Secretary of State will allow online filings that may help you avoid the cost of paying an accountant or a lawyer to form your corporation. Some of these sites also include step-by-step help.

TIP

There are several incorporation services companies that will assist you in preparing and filing your documents. There are also several online companies that sell software and will provide step-by-step instructions on what to do to prepare the documents yourself. Pull up your favorite search engine and look for keywords such as *corporation services, incorporation services,* or *incorporate your business.* Helpful sites include: www.americanbusiness solutions.com, www.bizfilings.com, and www.mycorporation.com.

Sample Articles of Incorporation can be found in Appendix B. State requirements change over time, and requirements vary from state to state, but these templates should serve as an example of what will be required of you.

Determine Stock Composition

Before you can prepare your articles, there are several important decisions that must be made. First, you must determine the stock composition of your corporation. All company stock can be owned by a single individual. If this is the case, most of this section will not apply to your situation, but may serve as educational information for a later time. Issuing stock to additional individuals will provide for an opportunity to raise capital for your corporation but is not always required.

TIP

If you authorize more stock than what will be initially issued, the unissued stock can be issued later in order to raise more capital for your corporation. This additional stock may be issued to new investors, new business members, or current stockholders who are contributing increased amounts of capital.

There are several options available when it comes to the structure and composition of a corporation's stock. Keeping your stock structure simple (only a single class of stock) will provide for an inexpensive model. Keeping your initial number of shares to a lower number will help you qualify for the minimum annual state filing fee. After your corporation begins to grow, or when it requires raising additional capital, then an amendment to your Articles of Incorporation can be filed with the state at any time.

TIP

There are several different classes of stock, such as common and preferred, voting and nonvoting. If you are considering issuing different classes of stock, it is recommended that you consult with an attorney or accountant. If you would like to learn more about different types of stock you can search on the Web for *different types of corporate stock* or search for *types of stock* at either www.investopedia.com or www.investorguide.com.

TRAP

Issuing different classes of stock is not necessary, but may be required by your situation. If different classes are issued, then the Articles of Incorporation must provide a statement defining the differences of those classes. This statement should include relative rights of each class as well as any preferences or limitations.

Security Laws. These are laws that have been enacted in order to protect outside investors who are putting money into your business. A *security* is stock in a company, as well as debt. The issuance of securities is subject to federal and state securities laws. Any investment that is determined to involve a security is subject to strict rules. If the rules are not followed, criminal penalties and civil damages may result.

When one person, a husband and wife, or a few partners run the business and all shareholders are active in the business, there may be federal exemptions from security laws. These simple organizations are the focus of this book. Due to the complicated nature of securities laws and the strictness with which you must follow them, if you are planning on selling stock to outside investors, you should consult with an attorney.

Where to Go for More Information. While it is recommended that you keep your stock composition simple as you begin your new corporation, perhaps you need to raise outside capital and would like to find out more information on your own. A great place to begin would be the Web site for the U.S. Securities and Exchange Commission. Their home page can be found at www.sec.gov, and it provides basic information for you to research. There are links from their home page to Laws and Regulations as well as links to describe what their purposes are.

Choose Corporate Directors

Another key step before filing your Articles of Incorporation is to determine who your corporate officers will be. In small corporations, the officers are usually the same people as the Board of Directors. This keeps your corporate structure simple and allows you to quickly be on your way. But in case you would like to designate different individuals than your officers, let's briefly discuss the roles of the Board of Directors.

While day-to-day business practices are carried out by the officers and employees of the corporation, the Board of Directors may supervise their work or define directives under which operations are performed. The Board of Directors act as the management body of a corporation, and thus establish corporate policies and approve major expenses, decisions, contracts, etc. The Board of Directors may also elect the corporate officers.

Choose a Registered Agent

Finally, you must choose a Registered Agent. If you are incorporating in the state in which you live, this can be a simple decision. It is most often the person who is filing the paperwork. Formally, as stated in Chapter 1, this is the person who will receive all of the tax and official correspondence. The main purpose is to provide, on public records, an address of a live person to whom potential claims and legal documents may be delivered.

Prepare Your Articles of Incorporation

Now that you have made your decisions about stock and corporate officers, it's finally time to start generating the documents required in order to form your corporation. The articles contain basic information about the corporation, its structure, and its purpose. This is the primary legal document of a corporation, is required by state law, and serves as the constitution of your corporation. After approving your articles, the state issues a Certificate of Incorporation. This certificate and your articles together become the "Charter of Incorporation."

What is required in your Articles of Incorporation varies from state to state. You will need to familiarize yourself with the requirements of the state in which you will incorporate, or you will need to find an individual who is experienced in that state to help you. In Appendix B you'll find a further discussion of and a template for Articles of Incorporation. And, again, Appendix B contains templates acceptable in each state. Also, templates are often provided online by the Secretary of State.

TIP

Make sure that your Articles of Incorporation are completely filled out. If you attempt to deviate from the templates provided in Appendix B or the templates supplied by your Secretary of State, you will run the risk of having them sent back to you with a request for changes. We have known of articles being rejected in some states because the supplied template was not followed exactly or had sections out of order.

In general, state law only requires a minimal amount of detail to be outlined in the articles. It is recommended that only required information be provided in the articles, since any changes to your articles will necessitate a complicated amendment process. Such additional information and detail should be added to your bylaws, as opposed to the articles themselves. For the most part, there is a small list of common requirements across each state. These include the following:

Corporate Address. The street address of the principal office where business will be conducted and the mailing address must be provided.

Corporate Stock. The amount of shared stock the corporation is authorized to issue. This is usually a nicely rounded number like 1,000, 10,000, or 100,000. There are different classes of stock that may also be issued, and if differing classes are issued, then the Articles of Incorporation must contain the designation of the classes and a statement of the relative rights of each class. Descriptions of some of these classes are defined in the "Determine Stock Composition" section of this chapter.

Duration. Some states do not require the duration to be specified unless it is other than perpetual. Even if the duration is perpetual, some states require this to be explicitly stated.

Effective or Start Date. A date of inception of the corporation may be required by some states. If such a date is required, state laws vary as to the delay before or after the filing in which the articles become effective.

Incorporator Name and Address. The name and address of the person filing the paperwork with the state agency will be required. This person is not necessarily a shareholder or officer, but may still file the paperwork on behalf of the corporation.

Registered Agent Name and Address. In most cases, the address submitted must be a street address and not a P.O. box. This individual may be part of the corporation, or he or she can be another individual (such as an attorney) who is responsible for receiving the legal papers for the corporation. The address of this agent may or may not be the same as the corporate address.

Signatures. The signature of the incorporator and the date signed are required. Usually, the Registered Agent must also sign a statement accepting his or her duties and responsibilities. Signatures may be required in the presence of a notary as well.

Prepare Other Key Documents

The Articles of Incorporation is not the only document that is required to be filed by state law. Each corporation must have bylaws and also maintain a set of minutes of its meetings. Typically, the bylaws are written at the first meeting, which is often referred to as the "organizational meeting." At this meeting, officers and Board of Director members are elected, bylaws and the articles are created and amended, and any other organizational decisions are made. Minutes from this first meeting should be kept to record the proceedings.

Bylaws.   These act as the rules that govern a corporation's organization and operation. State law requires that bylaws exist for each corporation. Templates for such bylaws can be found on the Internet, and you can find a sample template in Appendix E.

Minutes.   Another formal requirement of corporations is that minutes be kept of meetings that are held with shareholders and the Board of Directors. Usually only one meeting per year is required of these groups, but additional meetings may be necessary if major decisions are required or changes in officers or board members have occurred.

Licenses and Permits

There are several different types of licenses or permits that may be required of your corporation, depending on the type of business you are to conduct. We will review some of the most common types. If you have any questions or concerns about your particular business and whether you need a license or permit, some sources of additional information include local city government offices, city or state Chambers of Commerce, similar companies in your area, or trade associations.

Business License.   It is likely that you'll have to obtain a business license from the city in which your corporation has its principal place of business. Two purposes of a local business license are (1) collection of local taxes and (2) public safety. A business license is a form of registration with your city's tax collector for the collection of local taxes. The county or city clerk will have more information about this license and the amount of taxes that you will incur. Local taxes are based on a range of criterion, like business type, number of employees, net profit, total payroll, and so on.

Zoning Permits.   The location of your business may need to be approved by your city government. The City Planning Department is usually responsible for local zoning permits and regulations. Zoning laws are local ordinances that may restrict or regulate certain types of business from being conducted at particular property locations.

State and Federal Licenses and Permits. Certain types of businesses require additional licenses or permits from state or federal agencies. These additional licenses or permits focus on the type of work done by a business and the qualifications your corporation has to do that work. Types of businesses that may have a high likelihood of causing harm to the public due to mismanagement of your business may require additional licenses or permits, e.g., car repair, health care, etc. Examples of federal agencies that govern certain types of businesses include:

- The Bureau of Alcohol, Tobacco, and Firearms governs the making or selling of firearms and the manufacturing of alcohol or tobacco products. More information can be found at www.atf.gov.

- The Securities and Exchange Commission governs providing investment or counseling advice. More information can be found at www.sec.gov.

File Key Documents

The Articles of Incorporation must be filed with the Secretary of State, and fees must be paid at this time. Methods of submission vary from state to state but include mail, fax, and online submittals. Each state varies in its methods of acceptance, but information on submittals and related fees should be available from each state office.

Federal Employer Identification Number

The purpose of IRS Form SS-4, "Application for Employer Identification Number," is to apply for an employer identification number (EIN), also known as a Federal Tax Identification Number. This is a nine-digit number (e.g., 12-3456789) used by employers, sole proprietors, corporations, partnerships, estates, trusts, nonprofit organizations, and other entities for tax filings and reporting purposes. The Form SS-4 (along with instructions on how to fill it out) is provided in Appendix C.

TIP

Form SS-4 can be filled out and submitted online on the Internal Revenue Service Web site. You can find the link by going to www.irs.gov and typing *SS4* in the search box. PDF versions of this form can also be downloaded from this site and filled in at a later time.

Shareholders Agreement

If there is more than one shareholder for your corporation, then you should consider writing a Shareholders Agreement. This agreement should define what happens if a disagreement between shareholders exists. This agreement can be complicated and will likely require the assistance of an attorney. A sample Shareholders Agreement has been included in Appendix E (Article II of the Bylaws).

Organizational Meeting

The first meeting of the incorporators and Board of Directors usually marks the birth of a corporation. The first set of minutes recorded for a corporation should be from this meeting, often referred to as the organizational meeting. At this meeting the following agenda items are often covered:

- Review and acceptance of the Articles of Incorporation
- Election of directors
- Election of officers
- Adoption/amendments to bylaws
- Approvals/issuance of stock
- Approvals for major expenses
- Adoption of resolutions (such as S corporation status)
- Choosing a banking institution
- Recording of those present

Open a Bank Account

Every corporation will need a bank account. Funds paid to and from your corporation should not be transferred through your personal bank account. Attempting to keep your business and personal transactions separate while in the same account is not only complicated, it may lead to legal issues later. Therefore, it's vital that your corporation have its own account.

Chapter 6 goes into more detail on how to set up your bank account. The key at this point in the process is to shop around for the right business account. If you only have personal accounts, you may be shocked by the rates and fees that banks charge corporations. If you are not in a rush, take the time to shop around and find out what rates, fees, and benefits each bank and credit union in your area will offer you.

File Form 2553 for an S Corporation

Upon filing your Articles of Incorporation at the state level, your corporation will begin its existence as a general, for-profit corporation (a C corporation). As discussed earlier, a C corporation is required to pay income tax on taxable income similar to an individual. However, the corporation may elect S corporation status by submitting IRS Form 2553 to the Internal Revenue Service. In some states a state filing is required as well.

S corporation status allows the company to be taxed like a partnership or sole proprietorship rather than as a separate entity. Individual tax returns of the shareholders will report the income or loss generated by an S corporation since income is passed through.

A copy of IRS Form 2553 and a copy of the instructions for this form, provided by the IRS, can be found in Appendix D. An electronic copy of the form may be obtained at www.irs.gov by typing *2553* into the search box.

Organize Corporate Records

It is recommended that all corporation records including minutes be kept together. These documents can be kept in a formal corporate binder or in a simple three-ring binder. This collection should include: the letter from the Secretary of State approving the filing of the Articles of Incorporation, a copy of the Articles of Incorporation, a copy of the bylaws, minutes from the organizational meeting, minutes from subsequent meetings, stock certificates, stock ledger, tax forms, and so on.

You're Ready to Operate Your Corporation

Congratulations! Now that you have your paperwork filed, you are ready to begin. As a separate legal entity, your corporation must now follow certain formalities in order to maintain its status. The following chapters will help you understand how to follow these corporate formalities and how to respond to your new responsibilities.

4

Running Your Corporation

Role of Directors and Officers

Now that we have covered the details that allow you to incorporate yourself, it's time to discuss how to run your new corporation. Most likely you're forming a corporation in which you will serve as officer, director, and shareholder. If this is your situation, it's easier to accomplish your work because you won't have to worry about getting other people together for meetings or concern yourself with whether everyone will agree on a decision to be made. And in that case, this section may not apply to you. But you should be familiar with each corporate role anyway, in case your company grows later.

TRAP

Many small businesses find it easy to ignore some important administrative tasks, such as maintaining corporate records, because decision making is a simplified process with no need to call together large groups of individuals or to debate decisions.

TRAP

Officers and directors risk personal liability issues when they cause financial harm to the corporation, commit a crime, or act on their own behalf and to the detriment of the corporation.

Officers

Corporations are required by law to have at least two officers: a president and a secretary. These can be held by the same person. The officers of a corporation run and manage the corporation's day-to-day activities. They are also employees, elected by and subject to the control of the Board of Directors. The other employees of a corporation are subject to the control of the officers.

Executive officers have the authority to legally bind the corporation, but are generally not personally liable for any (lawful) acts while acting in behalf of the corporation. The roles, duties, and obligations of the officers should be outlined in your bylaws.

President or CEO. The president, or chief executive officer, acts as the corporation's official agent. He or she signs all legal documents, such as contracts and loans, on behalf of the corporation. The president has ultimate responsibility for the day-to-day activities of the corporation, but may delegate these responsibilities to other officers, or employees, of the corporation.

Secretary. The secretary is responsible for keeping minutes of the board and shareholder meetings. This individual may be required to also provide certification for financial institutions or to "attest" the president's signature.

Other Officers. Some corporations choose to elect additional officers into roles such as vice president, treasurer, chief financial officer, chief operations officer, etc. The duties and responsibilities of each of these additional roles vary from corporation to corporation and should be contained in your bylaws.

Directors

The Board of Directors elects the officers of a corporation and makes all of the important management decisions. The directors are elected by the shareholders. The board sets the policy and direction of the corporation and is ultimately responsible for the actions of the corporation.

The Board of Directors is composed of individuals referred to, of course, as "directors." Each director must be a real person and not a business entity. Most states also require that directors be at least 18 years of age. Directors are not required to be shareholders, nor required to live in the state where the company is incorporated. The number of directors required to form a corporation is dependent upon the state in which you will file, information you can find in Appendix A.

The initial Board of Directors is either defined in your Articles of Incorporation or appointed by the individual forming your corporation. After this initial appointment or election of directors, the directors are elected annually by the shareholders. Also, all subsequent elections or appointments should be addressed in your corporation's bylaws.

Role of Bylaws and Corporate Minutes

Now that you have filed the necessary documents to form your corporation, there are other documents you need to create and maintain to keep your corporation running properly. We describe these documents below; templates are also provided in Appendixes E, F, and G.

Bylaws

Shortly after a corporation is formed, bylaws are usually adopted. The bylaws should establish many of the procedural standards and rules governing the management of a corporation, such as the date and location of annual stockholders and directors meetings, quorum requirements for voting, voting standards and procedures, and officers' duties. The bylaws are not public records and usually there is no requirement that they be filed with any government agencies.

The bylaws should identify officer positions and define their general duties. They also should include an indemnification clause in order to protect the officers. In this clause, the corporation would agree to indemnify—i.e., pay—the expenses of officers, directors, agents, and employees who are sued while performing corporate duties.

TIP

Insurance policies are available to protect against potential liability to indemnify officers and directors. The common names for this kind of insurance are: Officer and Director (O&D) and Errors and Omission (E&O) insurance. While your corporation is new and only has a small number of stockholders, this insurance may not be needed, but your bylaws should still include the appropriate indemnification provisions.

Bylaws are typically adopted at the first meeting of the Board of Directors immediately after the corporation is formed. The laws governing who may

Although bylaws are only required for corporations, similar documents are required by a limited liability company (LLC) and a limited liability partnership (LLP). The limited liability company must have an Operating Agreement that contains most of the same content as the bylaws for a corporation. The limited liability partnership requires a Partnership Agreement that would serve this function.

adopt the corporation's initial bylaws differ for each state. In most states only the Board of Directors may adopt the initial bylaws. Some other states have given the incorporators, or sometimes even the shareholders, this authority.

As mentioned before, we have provided a sample bylaws template in Appendix E. There is also state-specific information in Appendix A concerning which group is authorized to adopt the initial bylaws. The contents of the bylaws may vary from corporation to corporation, but they typically will include the following:

- Address of the principal office of your corporation
- How many directors, along with their tenure and qualifications
- Procedures for election, resignation, and removal of directors
- The time and place for meetings of officers, directors, and shareholders
- Quorum required for voting
- Title and compensation of the corporate officers
- Define what committees are formed and what their powers are
- The fiscal year of the corporation
- How bylaws are amended and who can amend them
- Who will review and inspect the corporate books, and when
- Rules governing the approval of contracts, loans, and stock certificates
- Rules governing who can sign checks and how large payments will be approved

TIP

You may want to create your bylaws from scratch, but there are also many computer programs or online programs that can be of assistance in creating your bylaws.

What if you don't have any bylaws? Then some form of "business corporation act" from each state governs the lawful operation of business entities. If your bylaws do not cover basic requirements for operation, then by default the provisions in this act will. Your bylaws will then include variances from the state's business corporation act and will also include additional items that were not covered.

TRAP

Although some form of business corporation act from your state will cover the needs for items that are lacking in your bylaws, this is not an excuse to avoid creating bylaws for your corporation. General guidelines established by such an act may not cover all of the specifics you will need for your particular corporation.

Corporate Minutes

As a corporation, you are required to hold shareholders and directors meetings. Minutes should be maintained at each of these meetings. Neglecting to document major corporate decisions may cause your business to run into legal trouble in trying to establish your corporate status with a court. In such a case, you may be held personally liable for your corporation's debts.

The key with corporate minutes is to make sure you are documenting the decision-making process of your corporation. There is no need to document small, routine decisions made by your corporation, but you should prepare written minutes or consent resolutions for decisions or events that require formal approval by the Board of Directors or shareholders. Examples of decisions that may require documentation include the purchase of real property, the approval of a long-term lease, authorization of a significant loan amount or line of credit, and the issuance of stock.

If you remember to document important corporate decisions, you will protect your limited liability status. This documentation can either be kept through formal written minutes or through less formal consent resolutions. However you choose to do it, this documentation will protect you later if key decisions are questioned by courts or the IRS.

Corporate minutes should be prepared by the secretary of the corporation and then signed by the Board of Directors or shareholders. These minutes should always include who was present and indicate that there was a quorum. Voting results should be documented, including all abstaining and dissenting votes, for the protection of the individuals abstaining or dissenting.

How to Run Your Corporation

Now that you are a corporation, you must remember to always refer to the corporation as a corporation. You must always use the complete corporate name, including designations such as Incorporated, Inc., Corporation, or Corp. on everything.

As for day-to-day activities, you have created your corporation in order to perform a certain service, to produce items for sale, or for some other means through which to bring in income. It is not within the scope of this book to tell you how to conduct business in your particular area of industry, but we will focus on some of the other formalities you need to follow.

Bank Accounts and Funds

You will find that there are not many differences between running a corporation and running any other type of business. One of the most important points to remember is not to commingle funds of the corporation and individual shareholders. Any transfers of funds, whether taken out or put into the corporation, should be documented. In Chapter 6 we go into more detail on how to set up your bank account.

Maintain Good Records

You will now be responsible for maintaining good corporate records. These records should be kept together and organized so they can be easily retrieved when needed. Some types of corporate records you will now need to keep are:

- Accounting, bookkeeping, and financial records
- Bank records
- Business licenses and permits
- Contracts signed
- Correspondence from your company to other entities
- Employee records
- Intellectual property records
- Stock records
- Tax records

Signing Documents

You must sign all documents as a corporation; in other words, corporate officers must always sign corporate documents in their corporate capacity. This includes having the officers' titles clearly written next to their names each time they sign a document. This will help avoid personal liability issues and protect against third parties that might claim that an officer was transacting business on his or her own behalf and not on behalf of the corporation.

Here's an example of how corporate documents need to be signed:

Sincerely,

Your Corporate Name, Incorporated

By: _____

Your Name

Your Title

Annual Reports

In most states, the Secretary of State will send each corporation a simple one-page form that constitutes an annual report. This annual report is required by most states, and some states require a biannual report. The form mailed to you by the Secretary of State may already be filled out and only require your review and signature before it is returned. The form will also include a due date and possibly a required fee.

TIP

Many states allow you to submit your annual report online through the Web site for your Secretary of State. Find the URL for the Web site of your state in Appendix A and check it for a link for online submittals.

This annual report usually contains information such as the Federal Tax Identification Number, names and addresses of the directors and officers, name and address of the Registered Agent, and the address of the registered office. If the report is not returned, the state may mail you additional forms requesting notice to determine whether your corporation has been dissolved.

TIP

Many states allow a corporation to change information, such as the Registered Agent, at the time of returning this annual report without an additional fee. This may help you reduce needless fees when you need to make changes.

Other Formalities

Now that you are a corporation, there are a few other formalities you must observe. You must remember your annual state filings, such as corporate reports, franchise taxes, and corporate taxes (both federal and state). You must also remember to keep a record of shareholders, including their names and addresses, and the number, class, and series of shares they own. If there are shareholders other than yourself, you must also furnish each of them with a financial statement, including an end-of-the-year balance sheet and yearly income and cash flow statements, unless this is exempted by a shareholder resolution.

Hold Corporate Meetings

Another corporate formality is to hold regularly scheduled meetings of the Board of Directors and shareholders. Although being required to hold annual meetings sounds formal, it does not have to be. These meetings may in fact be formal and held at your registered office, principal place of business, or even a restaurant. They may also be informal and held in your home. The important thing is that they are held and that minutes are kept, even if you are a one-person corporation. These regular meetings and minutes are evidence to a court that your corporation is legitimate, and the record of these meetings will protect you if the issue ever comes up in court.

Directors Meetings

The bylaws for your corporation should define how often the Board of Directors will meet. The Board of Directors is typically required to have at least an annual meeting. During the annual meeting, the board reviews certain actions of the corporation for approval. Here are some examples of corporate actions that may require the board's approval:

- Amend the Articles of Incorporation or bylaws
- Adopt corporate policies

- Adopt or amend employee benefit plans
- Elect officers of the corporation
- Approve major expenses, loans, contracts, or other corporate commitments

The minutes from these meetings should include all decisions that are made. A single act by the board to approve or adopt a change is referred to as a *resolution.* These may often include changes to your Articles of Incorporation or bylaws. Such resolutions are considered official acts of the Board of Directors and must be documented in your minutes and kept with your corporate records.

A formal meeting is not required for resolutions to be made by the Board of Directors. You may wish to take action through the use of a written consent resolution, which allows for greater flexibility. Consent resolutions are very useful for corporations with a small Board of Directors. They should include a clear description of the decision being made and the signature of most of the Board of Directors. This form should then be included with your corporate minutes.

TRAP

Many one-person corporations forget to document major decisions being made since they do not require the approval of others. Don't fall into this trap. In order to protect your liability and your corporate status, it is wise to document all major decisions.

Shareholders Meetings

Typically, shareholders are required to have at least an annual meeting. The main reason for this meeting is to elect the directors of the corporation. Shareholders must receive written notification of this meeting, and your state may require a minimum notice time (usually 10 to 60 days) before the meeting.

In addition to an annual meeting, your corporate bylaws may require shareholders to meet more often in order to approve certain corporate actions. If a special meeting is called, only the matters stated in the notice of the meeting may be covered. A special meeting may be called to receive shareholder approval for items such as amending the Articles of Incorporation, amending the corporate bylaws, dissolving of the corporation, and merging the corporation with another.

Special Issues for
One-Person Corporations

In order to retain your corporate existence and receive the benefits of the limited liability and added tax savings, you must remember to observe the corporate formalities listed in this chapter. Even a one-person corporation must observe these formalities, and thus must act in different roles, depending on the occasion. The single person must still be responsible for being the sole shareholder, director, and officer of the corporation.

No matter how many individuals are in your corporation, you must observe certain corporate formalities. The formalities listed in this chapter may seem simple but are easy to overlook. As you will learn in later chapters, they will assist you if your corporate status is ever questioned by a court of law.

5

Learning Basic Accounting and Finance

Accounting is the language of business. To succeed in the business world, you have to become proficient in its language. Accounting data is summarized in reports called "financial statements." To operate his or her business effectively, the owner needs to know what is in the financial statements. To understand accounting, we need to (1) understand what the financial statements are saying and (2) how to analyze the accounting data through ratio analysis.

Financial Statements

There are three basic reports that show the financial condition of the business: the balance sheet, the income statement, and the statement of cash flows. Each of these reports reveals a different financial aspect.

Balance Sheet

The balance sheet tells the financial condition of the business at a point in time. It comprises assets, liabilities, and owner's equity. The balance sheet always stays in balance, with total assets equaling total liabilities and total owner's equity.

Assets.   These are defined as economic resources that are owned or controlled by an entity. They include cash, accounts receivable, inventory, notes receivable, equipment, land, and buildings. Assets are also classified as either current or noncurrent. Current assets (short-term assets) are those that can be converted to cash within a year. Examples of current assets are cash, accounts receivable, and inventory. Noncurrent assets (long-term assets) are converted into cash longer than a year. Examples are equipment, land, and buildings (fixed assets).

Liabilities.   These are obligations of a business to pay cash or transfer other assets. Liabilities include accounts payable, payroll taxes, and notes payable. They are also classified as current and noncurrent. Current liabilities (short-term liabilities) are the liabilities that will be paid off within a year, and noncurrent liabilities (long-term liabilities) are those that take more than a year to pay off.

Owner's Equity.   This is the ownership interest in the assets of an entity. Owner's equity includes capital stock and retained earnings.

Figure 5-1 is a sample balance sheet, and as such, it shows the abovementioned assets, liabilities, and owner's (or stockholders') equity.

Income Statement

The income statement tells the financial results of the business for a period of time. It shows the income earned (revenue) and the expenses incurred. Revenues are increases in a business's assets from the sale of goods or services. Expenses are the costs incurred in the normal course of business to generate revenue. The net income or loss is the difference between the revenue generated and the expenses incurred.

Figure 5-2 shows a sample income statement.

TRAP

An income statement can be misleading. Just because the income statement has net income does not mean that the business is doing well. If the business has net income but its customers are not paying for the goods or services the business provided, then the business will struggle with cash. All of the financial statements need to be considered to grasp the whole picture of the business's financial condition.

XYZ Enterprises, Inc.
Balance Sheet
December 31, 20XX

Assets:

Current Assets		
Cash		$ 9,535
Accounts Receivable		4,354
Employee Advances		200
Inventory		86,932
Total Current Assets		101,021
Fixed Assets		
Vehicles		15,500
Equipment		47,200
Accumulated Depreciation		(8,641)
Total Fixed Assets		54,059
Total Assets		155,080
Liabilities and Stockholders' Equity:		
Current Liabilities		
Accounts Payable		18,216
Current Portion of Notes Payable		5,213
Line of Credit		14,259
Total Current Liabilities		37,688
Long-Term Liabilities		
Note Payable: Bank of USA		65,114
Total Liabilities		102,802
Stockholders' Equity		
Capital Stock		10,000
Retained Earnings		42,278
Total Stockholders' Equity		52,278
Total Liabilities and Stockholders' Equity		$155,080

Figure 5-1. Sample balance sheet.

Enterprises, Inc.
Statement of Income and Retained Earnings
Year Ended December 31, 20XX

Income	$197,010
Cost of Goods Sold	85,026
Gross Profit	111,984
Expenses:	
Accounting	2,160
Bank Charges	591
Depreciation	8,641
Dues and Subscriptions	140
Insurance	4,694
Licenses and Permits	120
Office	4,739
Postage and Delivery	68
Printing and Reproductions	63
Repairs and Maintenance	2,458
Salaries and Wages	33,196
Taxes	3,295
Telephone	1,516
Tools	73
Total	61,754
Income from Operations	50,230
Other Income/(Expense)	
Interest Expense	(7,952)
Net Income	42,278
Beginning Retained Earnings	0
Dividends	0
Ending Retained Earnings	$ 42,278

Figure 5-2. Sample income statement.

Statement of Cash Flows

The statement of cash flows tells the cash inflows and outflows of the business for a period of time. This statement is usually divided into three sections: operating, investing, and financing. The operating section shows the cash flow from normal operations of the business. The investing section shows the cash flow from purchasing or selling equipment. The financing section shows the cash flow from receiving or repaying loans, and receiving or repaying money from owners.

Figure 5-3 is a sample statement of cash flows.

TIP

Notice how all of the financial statements work together. The income statement and the balance sheet each show the amount of retained earnings. The income statement and the statement of cash flows each show the net income of the business. The balance sheet and the statement of cash flows each show the amount of ending cash. If these amounts do not match, then the financial statements are incorrect.

Ratio Analysis

Ratios can help the business owner understand the financial statements and the current financial position of the business. They can also help the owner understand the trends and direction in which the company is going. Ratios are grouped into the following categories: short-term solvency or liquidity ratios, long-term solvency or financial leverage ratios, asset management or turnover ratios, profitability ratios, and market value ratios.

TIP

Ratio analysis is useful in comparing two different companies. It is a way of comparing apples to apples.

Short-Term Solvency

Short-term solvency ratios or liquidity ratios are concerned with the business's ability to pay its short-term liabilities (current liabilities) with its short-term assets (current assets).

XYZ Enterprises, Inc.
Statement of Cash Flows
Year Ended December 31, 20XX

Cash Flows from Operating Activities
Net Loss $ 42,278
Adjustments to reconcile net income to net cash provided
  by operating activities:
  Depreciation   8,641
  Increase in Accounts Receivable   (4,354)
  Increase in Employee Advances   (200)
  Increase in Inventory   (86,932)
  Increase in Accounts Payable   18,216

        Net Cash USED by Operating Activities   (22,351)

Cash Flows from Investing Activities
  Purchase of Equipment   (62,700)

        Net Cash USED by Investing Activities   (62,700)

Cash Flows from Financing Activities
  Increase in Line of Credit   14,259
  Increase in Note Payable   70,327
  Owner Contributions   10,000

        Net Cash PROVIDED by Financing Activities   94,586

Net Increase in Cash   9,535

Cash at Beginning of Period   0

Cash at End of Period $ 9,535

Figure 5-3. Sample statement of cash flows.

$$\text{Current ratio} = \frac{\text{Current assets}}{\text{Current liabilities}}$$

$$\text{Quick ratio or Acid-Test ratio} = \frac{\text{Current assets} - \text{Inventory}}{\text{Current liabilities}}$$

$$\text{Cash ratio} = \frac{\text{Cash}}{\text{Current liabilities}}$$

$$\text{Net working capital to total assets} = \frac{\text{Net working capital}}{\text{Total assets}}$$

$$\text{Interval measure} = \frac{\text{Current assets}}{\text{Average daily operating costs}}$$

Long-Term Solvency

Long-term solvency ratios focus on the business's ability to stay in business longer than a year.

$$\text{Total debt ratio} = \frac{\text{Total assets} - \text{Total equity}}{\text{Total assets}}$$

$$\text{Debt to Equity ratio} = \frac{\text{Total debt}}{\text{Total equity}}$$

$$\text{Equity multiplier} = \frac{\text{Total assets}}{\text{Total equity}}$$

$$\text{Long-term debt ratio} = \frac{\text{Long-term debt}}{\text{Long-term debt} + \text{Total equity}}$$

$$\text{Long-term debt} + \text{Total equity} = \frac{\text{EBIT*}}{\text{Interest}}$$

$$\text{Cash coverage ratio} = \frac{\text{EBIT} + \text{Depreciation}}{\text{Interest}}$$

*Earnings Before Interest and Taxes

TRAP

Be sure you calculate the ratios the same way every time; otherwise your results will be tainted.

Asset Management

Asset management ratios show how the business effectively uses its assets to produce sales.

$$\text{Inventory turnover} = \frac{\text{Cost of goods sold}}{\text{Inventory}}$$

$$\text{Days' sales in inventory} = \frac{365}{\text{Inventory turnover ratio}}$$

$$\text{Receivables turnover} = \frac{\text{Revenue}}{\text{Accounts receivable}}$$

$$\text{Days' sales in receivables} = \frac{365}{\text{Receivables turnover ratio}}$$

$$\text{Net working capital turnover} = \frac{\text{Revenue}}{\text{Net working capital*}}$$

$$\text{Fixed asset turnover} = \frac{\text{Revenue}}{\text{Net fixed assets†}}$$

$$\text{Total asset turnover} = \frac{\text{Revenue}}{\text{Total assets}}$$

*Net working capital is current assets minus current liabilities
†Net fixed assets are total fixed assets minus accumulated depreciation

Profitability Ratio

Profitability ratios measure how effectively a business manages its operations.

$$\text{Profit margin} = \frac{\text{Net income}}{\text{Revenue}}$$

$$\text{Return on assets} = \frac{\text{Net income}}{\text{Total assets}}$$

$$\text{Return on equity} = \frac{\text{Net income}}{\text{Total equity}}$$

Accounting data is summarized in financial statements. The balance sheet, income statement, and statement of cash flows tell the financial condition of the business. Understanding what the financial statements are reporting and how to analyze the information with ratio analysis is critical to knowing the direction of the business. Understanding the accounting data will help you be successful. Learn to speak the language of business!

6

Managing Your Business

Understanding the financials of your business is essential to making critical business decisions. Having accurate financial information will help make those decisions easier. Choosing the right accounting system, the right checking account, and the amount of involvement from your accountant will ensure that you have the accurate information you need to be successful.

Accounting Systems

There are two types of accounting systems to keep track of your financial information: the single entry system and the double entry system.

Single Entry. This system is very simple to use, and in fact should only be used by very small businesses. It is based off the income statement. Only the entries to the income statement are recorded in a single entry system.

Double Entry. This system uses checks and balances to ensure that your books are accurate, and is recommended for exactly this reason. It gets its name because every transaction affects at least two accounts. The double entry system records income and expenses like a single entry system but also records assets, liabilities, and owner's equity. In a double entry system, debits always equal credits. Most accounting software programs use a double entry system.

Basics of the Double Entry System

A double entry accounting system captures the financial information from your day-to-day transactions and organizes it into useful reports. The accounting system starts with individual transactions. Each transaction is recorded in chronological order in a journal. Commonly these journals are called the sales journal, cash receipts journal, and cash disbursement journal.

After the transactions are recorded in the journals, the information is summarized in ledgers. The ledgers summarize the information according to accounts. Each account, whether it is an asset, liability, owner's equity, income, or expense account, has its own ledger. Every transaction that affects that particular account is summarized in its ledger.

The balance of each ledger account is then transferred to the financial statements. The assets, liabilities, and owner's equity accounts are reported on the balance sheet. The income and expense accounts are reported on the income statement.

TIP

Most accounting software programs handle all these steps automatically. You simply enter the transaction into the program and it posts the information to the journals and ledger and creates the financial statements.

Why Keep Records?

Good records increase the likelihood of success for your business. They can help you understand aspects of your business, like which products are selling the best, which cost your business the most, and what products are most profitable. Without accurate financial information it is hard to know exactly how your business is doing.

Reviewing the financial information should be a part of every business decision. Should we buy a new piece of manufacturing equipment now, or should we wait? Should we introduce a new product line? Consult your records. Further, keeping good records is not only a wise business decision, it is required by the Internal Revenue Service. For expenses to be deductible, the IRS requires good supporting documentation.

TRAP

The IRS will disregard any expense that is not adequately documented. As the business owner, the burden of proof is on you to prove that the expense is truly deductible.

Types of Supporting Documentation

Each transaction will have its own supporting documentation. These include receipts, canceled checks, or bills that support your expenditures. To be considered adequate, the supporting documents must show the amount, date, place, and essential character of the expense. The supporting documents will vary depending upon the type of transaction.

Assets are economic resources that are owned or controlled by the business. The supporting documents show the date, amount, and description of the asset. Here are some examples of supporting documents for assets:

- Canceled check
- Receipt
- Invoice
- Credit card receipt
- Account statement

Liabilities are obligations of a business to pay cash or transfer other assets. The supporting documents show the date, amount, and description of the asset. Here are some examples of supporting documents for liabilities:

- Credit card statement
- Loan documentation
- Vendor invoice

Gross sales are the income generated from the sales of goods and services. The supporting documents show the date, amount, and source of the income. These would include:

- Cash register tape
- Bank deposit slip
- Invoice
- Credit card receipt

Purchases are when you buy items to resell to your customer. The document should show the date, amount, and to whom the purchase was paid. Supporting documents include:

- Canceled check
- Cash register tape
- Credit card receipt
- Invoice

Expenses are the ordinary costs of running and maintaining your business. The supporting documentation for expenses show the date, amount, and to whom the expense was paid. Examples of supporting documentation for expenses are:

- Canceled check
- Cash register tape
- Account statement
- Credit card receipt
- Invoice

Table 6-1 gives a brief picture of various expenses and what's required in the way of documentation for each.

How Long to Keep Records

It's often asked: "How long should we keep our records and supporting documents?" According to the Internal Revenue Service, you should keep your records as long as they are needed for the administration of any provision of the Internal Revenue Code. The basic rule of thumb is you should keep your records three years from the date you file the tax return. If you file the tax return before the due date, then you should keep your records three years from the due date of the tax return.

Table 6-2 lists various kinds of records and the amount of time they should be retained.

TIP

When it comes to records, it's better to keep them too long than not long enough.

Table 6-1. What Needs to Be Documented

Expense	Amount	When	Where	Purpose	Relationship
Travel	Amount of each expense for travel, lodging, meals	Dates of trip and number of business days	Destination	Business purpose of trip	N/A
Entertainment	Amount of each expense	Date of entertainment	Location of entertainment	Business purpose of entertainment	Name and title of person entertained
Gifts	Amount of gift	Date of gift		Business purpose of gift and description of gift	Name and title of person to whom the gift was given
Transportation	Amount of expense	Date of expense	Destination	Business purpose of transportation	N/A

Table 6-2.   Guidelines for Record Retention

Records	Retention Time
Bank Deposit Slips	Three years
Bank Statements	Six years
Canceled Checks	Three years
Contracts and Leases	Six years from the end date
Corporate Stock Records	Permanent
Daily Sales Records	Three years
Depreciation Schedules	Three years after life of the asset
Employee Records	Three years after termination date
Employee Time Cards	Three years
Entertainment Records	Three years
Expense Reports	Three years
Financial Statements	Permanent
General Ledger and Journals	Permanent
Inventory Records	Three years
Invoices	Three years
Meeting Minutes	Permanent
Real Estate Records	Permanent
Tax Returns	Permanent
Tax and Legal Correspondence	Permanent

A Business Checkbook

A key aspect of keeping good records is having a business checking account. This will help in tracking income and expenses. A business checking account will also help you to avoid commingling personal money with business money. Let's discuss your business checking account needs and the steps to signing up for an account.

Business Checking Account Needs

There are many considerations when choosing a business checking account. But before you can shop around for an account that's right for you, you need to understand your business's checking account needs.

Think about how your business is structured (sole proprietorship, partnership, limited partnership, limited liability company, corporation, or S corporation). Then estimate the number of deposits you will make each week or month, the number of checks you'll write each week or month, and the average amount that you will keep in the account, as well as the minimum amount that you'll have in the account. Finally, decide if you want access to an ATM or online banking. With these estimates in mind you can refine your search and find a bank that meets all your business needs.

TIP

Find a bank that is conveniently located and easily accessible. Banking should not take too much time out of your already busy schedule.

TRAP

Take your time choosing the right business checking account for your business. The wrong checking account can cost you in high bank service charges. Chances are, you will have the checking account for a long time.

What to Bring When Opening an Account

Take the appropriate documentation to the bank, showing how your business is structured (sole proprietorship, partnership, limited partnership, limited liability company, corporation, or S corporation). You should also bring your Federal Employer Identification Number and two forms of identification for each person authorized to sign checks.

Getting Help from an Accountant

You will probably use an accountant to at least some degree with your business. There is a wide range of help you can receive from him or her. Accounting services vary, from hiring your own full-time accountant to meeting with an outside accountant once a year to prepare your tax return. The amount you use your accountant will depend on the size of your business and the extent of your accounting knowledge.

TIP

When it comes to accounting, do as much as you feel comfortable doing yourself. The more work you do yourself, the less you'll have to pay in accounting fees.

Business owners need to make critical decisions every day. Understanding the finances of their business is essential to making those decisions. Choosing the right accounting system, the right checking account, and the amount of involvement from your accountant will ensure that you have the accurate information you need.

7

Filing Taxes

Benjamin Franklin stated that in this world nothing is certain but death and taxes. A lot of newly formed businesses do not plan effectively for taxes, and as a result find that there is not enough cash to pay the taxes, or they miss the deadlines when the taxes are due. The key to avoiding problems with the IRS is to understand the information necessary to prepare taxes, know professionals who can assist with the preparation, know what forms to file, and file the forms on the proper dates.

Accounting Year

Businesses may use different time periods or tax years to calculate their taxable income. A tax year is a 12-month period in which the business keeps records of its income and expenses for the year. The tax year is determined when Form SS-4: Application for Employer Identification Number (Appendix C) is filed with the Internal Revenue Service. The tax year must be used from that point on, unless the IRS gives approval to change your tax year. To apply for a change in your tax year you will need Form 1128: Application to Adopt, Change, or Retain a Tax Year.

TIP

Consider very carefully what your tax year is going to be. It is more difficult to change after the business has already started operating.

Calendar Year. A calendar year goes from January 1 to December 31. Individuals are automatically on a calendar year. Some businesses are required to report their income on a calendar year basis.

Fiscal Year. A fiscal year is any 12-month period other than January to December. For example, your fiscal year could be from February 1 to January 31, or July 1 to June 30, or September 1 to August 31. There are several reasons for electing a fiscal year other than a calendar year. One of the most common reasons is to match your business cycle. For instance, a retail store selling boating accessories perhaps could elect a fiscal year ending after the busy summer season on August 31.

Accounting Method

An accounting method is a set of rules followed to determine the net income or loss for the business. These rules set the guidelines the business owner must follow in determining when to recognize the income and expenses for the business. The business owner must decide which accounting method the business is going to use when it files its first tax return. After the method is determined, it should be used consistently year after year. The business cannot switch its accounting method from year to year to help its tax situation. It is relatively difficult to switch accounting methods and involves special permission from the IRS.

The two most common accounting methods of determining the financial results of the business are the cash method and the accrual method, both of which are described below.

Cash Method

The cash method of reporting income and expenses is used by all individuals and a lot of small businesses. It is simple to use. Income is recognized when cash (any form of payment cash, checks, and credit cards) is received. If Company XYZ performs a service or sells an item to another business in December 2004 but does not receive payment for that service or item until January 2005, then Company XYZ would not report that income until 2005.

Expenses are recognized when cash is paid out. If Company XYZ receives a telephone bill in December 2004 but does not pay the bill until January 2005, then the expense should be reported on Company XYZ's 2005 tax return. Some things need to be considered when using the cash method: First, there are special rules to account for inventory, and second, some businesses are not allowed to use the cash method.

TIP

With the cash method, you are only being taxed on money you have received. You have received the cash, so you have the means of paying the taxes.

Accrual Method

The accrual method of reporting income and expenses is more accurate because it matches the income earned with the expenses incurred for the same period of time. Income is recognized once the work has been substantially completed and an exchange has taken place for those goods or services. If Company XYZ performs a service or sells an item to another business in December 2004 but does not receive payment for that service or item until January 2005, Company XYZ would still report that as income earned in 2004.

Expenses are recognized in the same fashion when they are incurred, not when cash is paid out. If Company XYZ receives a telephone bill in December 2004 but does not pay the bill until January 2005, the expense should be reported on Company XYZ's 2004 tax return. The accrual method is a more accurate depiction of the business's financial condition because it follows what is called the "matching principle." This basically means that the expenses are accounted for in the same period as the income that those expenses produced. When considering which accounting method to follow, it will be helpful to get advice from a tax professional. The IRS has information regarding accounting methods in IRS Publication 538 "Accounting Periods and Methods."

Tax Professionals

There are many things to consider when choosing a tax professional. The experts in tax preparation are Certified Public Accountants, tax attorneys, and Enrolled Agents for the IRS. The education or experience of the tax professional should be checked out to ensure that the professional understands your specific business needs. Ask for a list of references of current clients, as well as former clients, whom you can contact. This will enable you to make sure the tax professional is right for you.

TIP

Contact the tax professional in September, October, or November. This will give you enough time to discuss your situation with him or her. The tax professional will also have more free time during these months than during the tax season.

Another thing to consider is the services that the tax professional offers. The tax professional might offer payroll services, for example, or business consultation that you could use. It is easier to deal with one vendor than several. It is recommended that you receive a detailed quote of the services the tax professional will perform. This will prevent misunderstandings after the work is completed.

TRAP

Understand how you are being billed before the tax professional starts the project. If you're billed hourly, you could receive a bill for the full hour you spent in his or her office even though the first 15 minutes was spent catching up on personal matters.

Forms to File

To understand taxes, we need to first understand how income is defined by the IRS. There are two main categories of income defined by the IRS tax code. The first is *active income,* which includes wages, salaries, commissions, bonuses, and profit from a business when the owner materially participates. The second type is *passive income,* which includes interest income, dividends, annuities, royalties, and rents. The type of income that is produced by the business influences the taxes that need to be paid.

There are three main types of taxes that businesses are responsible to pay:

- Income tax
- Self-employment tax
- Employment tax

Following is an explanation of each of these.

Income Tax

Income tax is paid either by the owner of the business or the business itself, depending upon how the business is formed (sole proprietorship, general partnership, limited liability company, S corporation, and corporation). The sole proprietorship does not pay any income tax; the business owner pays the income tax. All income and expenses are reported on the business owner's 1040 tax return using Schedule C or Schedule C-EZ. The profit is included with all the business owner's other income to come up with his or

Table 7-1. Individual Tax Brackets 2004

	10% up to	15% up to	25% up to	28% up to	33% up to	35% up to
Married, filing jointly or qualifying widower	14,300	58,100	117,250	178,650	319,100	319,100
Head of household	10,200	38,900	100,500	162,700	319,100	319,100
Married, filing separately	7,150	29,050	58,625	89,325	159,550	159,550
Single	7,150	29,050	70,350	146,750	319,100	319,100

her total income. If the business has incurred a loss, then the loss is deducted from the business owner's other income. The individual is then taxed on the income that he or she has earned.

Table 7-1 breaks down the payments, in various categories, for the different federal tax brackets.

All partnerships, including general partnerships and LLCs, are not subject to income tax. The partnership has to file what is called an "information tax return." However, there are never any taxes due with this return. The information tax return (Form 1065) is required to show the IRS the profit/loss of the business and who will report that profit/loss on their individual tax returns (the owners). The owners of the partnership will receive a Schedule K-1 from the partnership tax return that shows their portion of the partnership profit/loss. This reported profit/loss will be included on the individual's 1040 tax return using Schedule E and subject to the individual income tax listed above.

S corporations are taxed similar to partnerships, in that they are not subject to income tax but only have to file an information tax return. The shareholders of the S corporation will receive a Schedule K-1 from the S corporation tax return (Form 1120S) showing the portion of the profit/loss the shareholder is responsible for. The profit/loss reported on Schedule K-1 will be included on the individual's 1040 tax return using Schedule E and subject to the individual income tax listed above.

Corporations *are* subject to income tax. The corporation files Form 1120 with the IRS. This form includes the gross income for the corporation as well as the deductions the corporation has in business expenses. The net income of the corporation is taxed at the corporation's tax bracket. Table 7-2 goes into some of the details.

Table 7-2.   Corporation Tax Brackets 2004

Over	but not over	Tax is	plus	of the amount over
—	50,000		15%	
50,000	75,000	7,500	25%	50,000
75,000	100,000	13,750	34%	75,000
100,000	335,000	22,250	39%	100,000
335,000	10,000,000	113,900	34%	335,000
10,000,000	15,000,000	3,400,000	35%	10,000,000
15,000,000	18,333,333	5,150,000	38%	15,000,000
18,333,333			35%	

Self-Employment Tax

The second tax businesses are responsible to pay is self-employment tax. This is the Social Security and Medicare tax for business owners.

As an employee, the employer takes Social Security (at 6.20 percent) and Medicare taxes (at 1.45 percent) out of your paycheck. The employer also matches these amounts, bringing the total amount that is paid for Social Security and Medicare taxes to 15.3 percent. A self-employed individual pays both the employer and the employee portion of the Social Security and Medicare taxes, or 15.3 percent, on business net income that is active income. Sole proprietors and partners in a partnership are subject to self-employment tax if the business is involved in active income. Shareholders in an S corporation are not subject to self-employment tax even if the S corporation is involved in active income. Passive income is not subject to self-employment tax.

TIP

Self-employment tax is paid into the Social Security and Medicare programs. These programs could be building up a type of retirement for the self-employed individual. If the taxpayer is trying to reduce the amount of self-employment tax he or she is paying then he or she should plan another type of retirement.

Employment Tax

The third tax businesses are responsible to pay is employment tax. Businesses are subject to employment tax if they have employees. These taxes include Social Security, Medicare, federal income tax withholding, and federal unemployment tax. As was mentioned previously, half of Social Security and Medicare taxes is paid from the employee's paycheck, and half is paid by the employer. Federal income tax withholding is deducted from the employee's paycheck and paid by the employer. Federal unemployment tax is a tax paid solely by the employer.

TRAP

A word of caution with regard to payroll taxes: The government is relentless if payments are not made in a timely manner. The penalties and interest can add up quickly. Consider using a payroll service. The cost is relatively low, and you will find it well worth the money spent.

Tables 7-3 and 7-4 on the following spread summarize the tax forms that need to be filed, and the calendar year when certain types of taxes and forms are due.

Table 7-3.   Summary of Tax Forms to File

Entity Type	Type of Tax		Forms to File
Sole Proprietorship	Income tax		1040 Schedule C
	Self-employment tax		1040 Schedule SE
	Employment tax	Social Security, Medicare, and federal withholding	941
		Federal unemployment tax	940
		Depositing employment taxes	8109
Partnership or LLC	Income tax		1065
	Employment tax	Social Security, Medicare, and federal withholding	941
		Federal unemployment tax	940
		Depositing employment taxes	8109
S corporation	Income tax		1120S
	Employment tax	Social Security, Medicare, and federal withholding	941
		Federal unemployment tax	940
		Depositing employment taxes	8109
Corporation	Income tax		1120
	Employment tax	Social Security, Medicare, and federal withholding	941
		Federal unemployment tax	940
		Depositing employment taxes	8109

Table 7-4.   Calendar Year Taxes and Forms

Date		Type of Tax	Forms
January	15	Pay payroll taxes for December	8109
	15	Individuals pay 4th quarter estimated tax	1040-ES
	31	Provide copies of W-2 to employees	W-2
	31	File 940	940
	31	File 941	941
	31	Provide Form 1099 to individual contractors	1099
February	15	Pay payroll taxes for January	8109
	28	File Form 1099	1099
	28	File Form W-3 with copy A of W-2	W-3, W-2
March	15	Pay payroll taxes for February	8109
	15	Calendar year corporations file taxes	1120, 1120S
April	15	Pay payroll taxes for March	8109
	15	Individuals file taxes	1040
	15	Individuals pay 1st quarter estimated tax	1040-ES
	15	Partnerships file taxes	1065
	30	File Form 941, 1st quarter	941
May	15	Pay payroll taxes for April	8109
June	15	Pay payroll taxes for May	8109
	15	Individuals pay 2nd quarter estimated tax	1040-ES
July	15	Pay payroll taxes for June	8109
	31	File Form 941, 2nd quarter	941
August	15	Pay payroll taxes for July	8109
September	15	Pay payroll taxes for August	8109
	15	Individuals pay 3rd quarter estimated tax	1040-ES
October	15	Pay payroll taxes for September	8109
	31	File Form 941, 3rd quarter	941
November	15	Pay payroll taxes for October	8109
December	15	Pay payroll taxes for November	8109

8

Minimizing Taxes

Mark Twain said: "I shall never use profanity except in discussing house, rent, and taxes. Indeed, upon second thought, I will not even use it then, for it is un-Christian, inelegant, and degrading—though to speak truly I do not see how house, rent, and taxes are going to be discussed worth a cent without it." Although everybody dislikes paying taxes, there is no legal way around it.

TIP

The key to minimizing your taxes is deducting all the business expenses that are legally possible.

What Is Deductible?

To be considered a business expense and deductible under the IRS tax code, an expense needs to be ordinary and necessary. The definition of ordinary in this context is that the expense is common to the industry of your business. Necessary is defined as an expense that is helpful and appropriate for your business. The total cost of a business expense can be deducted as long as the expense meets the criteria of being ordinary and necessary.

Advertising

As long as the cost is for making the public aware of your business and is directly related to your business, advertising is deductible. Advertising expenses should have the potential of gaining new business in the future.

Automobile

The two methods of deducting automobile expenses are actual expense and standard mileage rate. You must decide which method you are going to use in the first year the vehicle is used for the business.

Actual expense method is just that—using the actual automobile expenses. These include:

- Gas
- Oil
- Insurance
- Tolls
- Depreciation
- Parking fees
- Tires
- Repairs
- Registration fees

If the automobile is used for business and personal use, the percentage used for business can be deducted as a business expense.

The standard mileage method takes the number of business miles driven multiplied by the standard mileage rate. The rate changes from year to year. For the 2004 tax year the standard mileage rate was $0.375, or 37.5 cents, per mile.

Bad Debts

Bad debts are debts that are owed to your business but are now worthless. The debt has to be business related to be deductible as business expense. You consider a debt worthless when there is no chance that the amount owed will be paid back. Most of the bad debts result from customers not paying the accounts they owe you. These accounts receivable are written off as bad debt if they were previously counted in gross income. Another type of bad debt is a loan to clients, suppliers, distributors, or employees that becomes worthless. If at a later time you recover the debt after you wrote it off, then the amount you recover needs to be included as income.

TRAP

Businesses using the cash method cannot deduct bad debt because the income is not recorded until the cash is paid.

Dues and Subscriptions

Dues for membership in organizations are deductible if the organization is related to your business and there is a specific business purpose for joining the organization. For instance, if you were to join the Chamber of Commerce in your area to get your name out and meet potential new clients, that would be deductible. Subscriptions to magazines or trade journals are deductible as long as the reason for buying the magazines is related to your business.

Education

Training of yourself and employees if it is ordinary, necessary, and related to your business is deductible. The cost to attend a trade seminar or trade show is deductible if it is directly related to your business. Continuing Professional Education (CPE) classes or seminars are deductible if you can demonstrate that the education maintains or improves skills required in your business or is required for licensing.

Entertainment

Expenses to entertain clients, customers, and employees may be deductible depending on the circumstances. Entertainment is any activity that provides entertainment, amusement, or recreation. There are two tests to determine the deductibility of entertainment expenses, in addition to being ordinary and necessary. The first test is whether the entertainment's main purpose was to conduct business, that you conducted business during the entertainment, or that you had the expectation of gaining business as a result of the entertainment. The second test is whether the entertainment is associated with your business and occurs directly before or after a business discussion.

Gifts

Gifts given to customers, employees, or vendors can be deducted as a business expense. You can deduct a gift up to $25 per person per year. A gift made to a member of a customer's family is considered a gift made to that customer. Incidental costs of the gift such as engraving, packaging, and shipping are not included in the $25 limit. Items you regularly distribute to clients that cost less than four dollars and have your name printed on them are not considered gifts. Other items that are not considered gifts are signs, display racks, or promotional material to be used by the person receiving them.

Insurance

Insurance costs can be deducted as long as the insurance is, again, for the ordinary course of business and is necessary. For the cash method of accounting, insurance is deducted in the year the premiums were paid. Using the accrual method, insurance is deducted in the year the premiums accrued.

Deductible Insurance. There are many types of insurance premiums that are deductible. Premiums paid for the employees' group health insurance is deductible. In a partnership, premiums paid for the partners' health insurance is deductible as guaranteed payments to the partners. In an S corporation, premiums paid for the health insurance of a shareholder who owns more than 2 percent of the corporation can be deducted but the premiums have to be included on the shareholders W-2 form, subject to federal income tax withholding. Other insurance premiums that are deductible include the following.

- Liability insurance
- Malpractice insurance
- Worker's compensation
- Insurance for fire, storm, theft, accident, or similar losses
- Insurance that covers bad debt
- Errors and omissions insurance
- Overhead insurance
- Business interruption insurance

Nondeductible Insurance. There are some insurance premiums that are not deductible. The premiums are not deductible for a life insurance policy that lists you as the beneficiary and covers a person who has a financial interest in your business. The premiums on an insurance policy to secure a loan are not deductible. Self-insurance reserve funds are not deductible.

Interest Expense

Depending on how the proceeds of the loan are used determines the deductibility of the interest. Interest on business loans that were disbursed for personal use is not deductible. For the interest to be deductible as a business expense, the following conditions must be met:

- The proceeds of the loan are used for the ordinary course of business.
- You and the lender expect the loan to be paid back.

- There is a creditor/debtor relationship between you and the lender.
- You are legally liable for the loan.

TIP

Business credit cards should be used strictly for business expenses. Commingling personal expenses and business expenses can get complicated. Commingling business and personal funds is one of the main reasons courts can go after personal assets.

How you deduct interest as an expense depends on which accounting method you are using. Using the cash method, only the interest that is actually paid is deducted that year. Under the accrual method, the interest that has accrued can be deducted.

Legal and Professional

Payments to accountants and attorneys are deductible if they are ordinary, necessary, and related to your business. If the bill for legal and professional fees contains items of a personal nature, such as a will, those items should be subtracted from the bill and paid from personal funds.

Office

The expenses to conduct business, such as paper, Post-it notes, pens, pencils, toner cartridges, and paper clips are only a small list of the items that can be deducted as office expenses. For these items to be deductible, they need to be related to your business and not for personal use.

Rent Expense

Rent is an expense to use property that you do not own. To be considered a business expense, the property that is rented must be used in the ordinary course of business.

Conditional Sale. If at the end of the rental agreement there is any equity or ownership, then the rent cannot be deducted. The facts and circumstances at the start of the agreement help determine whether it is a lease or a conditional sale. Here is a list of circumstances where an agreement would be considered a conditional sale instead of a lease:

- You have the option to buy the property at a nominal price compared to the market value of the property at the end of the agreement.
- You have the option to buy the property at a nominal price compared to the amount you paid during the agreement.
- You pay more than reasonable rent.
- You get title of the property at the end of the agreement.
- Part of the payment is considered interest and part is considered principal or equity.
- The rent you pay to use the property is a high portion of the amount you would have paid to purchase the property.

Related Parties.   When rent is to a related party, it has to be reasonable to be a business deduction. To be considered reasonable, the rent should mimic rents paid by other businesses in similar properties. The portion of rent that is determined as unreasonable cannot be deducted as business expense.

Other Deductions Included with Rent.   Any costs incurred to cancel a lease or rental agreement early is deducted as rent expense by the business. Taxes paid for property that is rented is additional rent expense. Any cost incurred to acquire a lease can be deducted as a business expense; however, that cost needs to be spread out over the term of the lease. For example, if it cost an additional $1,000 to acquire a lease with a term of five years, $200 would be expensed each year of the lease.

Repairs

Often there are costs related to maintaining property for your business. Normal maintenance of property to keep it up and running is deductible. If the maintenance or repair does not increase the useful life or value of the property, it is deductible. If the maintenance or repair does increase the useful life or value of the property, the cost should be capitalized and spread over the remaining useful life. Repair costs can include the cost of labor and supplies.

TRAP

If you did the work yourself, then you can only deduct the cost of the supplies involved. You cannot deduct the cost of your labor.

Salaries and Wages

The salaries and wages that you pay your employees for the work they perform are deductible. Also deductible as employee compensation are commissions, bonuses, fringe benefits, and vacation allowances. The payment for the work they perform may be in the form of cash, property, or services. To be deductible as business expenses, the salaries and wages must meet the criteria of being ordinary and necessary to your business. In addition to that requirement, the salaries and wages must be reasonable and must be for work performed.

Reasonable Compensation. There are many factors in trying to determine reasonable compensation. These factors vary by industry. Here is a list of some of the factors to help you determine reasonable compensation:

- Work performed by the employee
- Pay history for all employees
- Compensation policy for all employees
- The cost of living in the city where they are employed
- Time required to perform the work
- Complexities of your business
- Ability and accomplishments of the employee
- Compensation compared to gross and net profit of the business
- Compensation compared to distributions to owners
- Responsibilities of the employee
- Amount of work performed

Compensation for Work Performed. Compensation has to be for work actually performed by the employee. If a business owner decides to hire his or her child as an employee to do cleaning in the office, the child needs to actually work at the place of business.

TRAP

A business owner cannot pay his or her child for doing chores around the house and then deduct the payment as a business expense.

Taxes

Taxes are deducted when they are paid, regardless of which accounting method is being used. If a tax refund is issued for a prior year, that amount should be included in income for this year. If a tax refund is issued for the current year, that amount should be included in and offset by tax expense for this year.

Income Taxes.   No individual, partnership, or corporation can deduct federal income tax as a business deduction. State and local income taxes can be deducted by a partnership or a corporation if the tax was charged to the business.

Employment Taxes.   If your business has employees, then you deduct various taxes, such as Social Security, Medicare, federal withholding, and state withholding from your employees' paychecks. These taxes are deductible as a business expense but should be classified as gross wages. The employer's portion of Social Security and Medicare, along with federal unemployment and state unemployment, are also deductible as a business expense.

Other Taxes.   There are several other taxes that can be deducted if they are incurred by the business. The following is a list of some of those taxes:

- Excise tax
- Franchise tax
- Fuel tax
- Occupational tax
- Personal property tax
- Real estate tax
- Sales tax

Telephone and Utilities

Gas, electricity, telephone, water, and sewer that are related to your business are deductible as business expenses. Only a portion of the utilities can be deducted if you maintain a home office. For example, your home office is 10 feet by 15 feet, or 150 square feet, and the total square footage of your home is 1,500 square feet, then you can deduct 10 percent of your home utility payments.

Travel

Travel is defined as being away from the general area of your home for a period of time longer than an ordinary day's work, when you need to sleep or rest to accomplish the work. Here is a list of expenses that are deductible:

- Transportation
- Fares for taxis, commuter bus, shuttles, and airport limousine
- Baggage and shipping
- Rental car
- Lodging and meals
- Dry cleaning and laundry
- Telephone
- Tips

Travel expenses are deductible depending on the purpose of the trip. If the trip is primarily for a business purpose, you can deduct the business portion of the travel expense. If the trip is primarily for personal purposes, the cost of the trip is not deductible. Any expenses related to the business while on personal travel are deductible.

To determine the amount of your trip that is deductible when a portion of the trip is for personal purposes, you have to determine the number of days that are business days versus personal days. Business days include transportation days (days traveling to and from the location), days your presence is required (if you are required to be at a specific event or place for business reasons), days spent on business (the main activity during the working hours is related to your business, which includes days you would have worked but were not able to due to circumstances beyond your control), and weekends and holidays (if they fall in between business days).

TIP

Take full advantage of business travel by including some personal purpose along with it. Just make sure that you stay within the guidelines listed above.

9
Liability

Preventing the Corporate Veil from Being Pierced

As mentioned in Chapter 3, one of the biggest advantages to incorporating is that of limited liability for the employees, directors, shareholders, etc. This liability is usually thought of as protecting your personal assets from the creditors of the corporation. Under some circumstances, there will be business entities and/or individuals who will attempt to pierce the corporate shield and seek the personal assets of the owners or shareholders once the assets of the corporation are exhausted.

The legal term for attempting to set aside the corporation for purposes of litigation in an effort to attain personal assets is to "pierce the corporate veil." This typically occurs when the corporation is believed to have inadequate assets to cover its liabilities. The entity taking legal action alleges that the corporation is actually a fraud, or that the corporation only exists to advance the private interests of the shareholders.

It is not possible to tell you everything you must do in order to avoid personal liability, but we will provide you with enough information to help you establish a solid foundation to protect yourself. Every court may choose to apply varying factors to varying degrees when determining whether to "pierce your corporate veil," so it's difficult to define a list of items and guarantee your protection.

A court may pierce through the veil of liability if the corporation does not follow corporate formalities, as outlined in Chapter 4, or if it is shown to be a sham with the intent to defraud. Although laws governing corporations differ from state to state, there are some common factors that a court will consider when determining the legitimacy of your corporation:

- Was the corporation properly formed? Were directors appointed? Stock issued?
- Are annual meetings being held, including minutes and records of decisions made?
- Are annual reports being filed with the state?
- Does the corporation observe bylaws?
- Are financial records and accounts maintained?
- Are the shareholders using the corporation to advance personal purposes?

Reasons the Veil May Be Pierced

There are many reasons a corporate veil may be pierced:

- Criminal acts of the officers, shareholders, or directors of a corporation will always cause the corporate veil to be pierced.
- Federal and state tax laws also may impose personal liability on individuals who are responsible for filing sales and income tax returns for the corporation.
- Shareholders disregard the fact that their corporation is legally a separate entity, and the corporation acts as an alter ego for the shareholders' personal dealings.
- Corporate formalities are not observed; annual meetings are not held, minutes are not kept, there is an absence of corporate records, etc.
- Major shareholders are siphoning money from the corporation for their personal use.
- Officers elected by the shareholders are not actively involved with the corporation.
- Personal and corporate funds are commingled. Funds are not kept in separate accounts, nor are financial records separated.
- Payments are taken for services or products without the intent to deliver.

Protection of Corporate Minutes

Although we have already discussed meetings, and the minutes of those meetings, we cannot stress their importance enough. Corporate minutes are the first line of defense against parties making claims in an attempt to pierce the corporate veil. These minutes help protect you against claims from the IRS, creditors, and others who are protesting your corporate status. The lack of annual minutes weakens your corporate status, and may weaken your claim to limited liability. This may be even more difficult to remember for small corporations that involve only one or two people, but they are still just as important.

Alternatives to Lawsuits

Before you consider going to court, listen and talk through the issues with the other person in the dispute. Most people are able to settle potential suits long before they go to court. There are many other low-cost alternatives, including arbitration, mediation, and small claims court.

Mediation

Small businesses are just as likely as large businesses to have a conflict with employees, customers, vendors, and other businesses. Often, small businesses do not have the time and money to resolve small conflicts, nor do they have the legal departments and public relations groups of a large corporation. If you are unable to negotiate a settlement with another party on your own, then mediation may be a solution. Most noncriminal cases can be mediated, including disputes that involve contracts, leases, business ownership, and employment.

Typically, the costs for mediation are less than the costs of going to court. For one thing, the cost of hiring a mediator is shared between both parties, as opposed to each party paying for their own lawyer. A mediator also does not spend hours preparing for the case, as a lawyer would.

Although the process of mediation is simple to follow, it is still more structured than many imagine. We have outlined some possible mediation steps you can follow, but these may have to be adjusted by the mediator you agree to use.

Agreement to Mediate.   Both parties need to understand the mediation process and to make an informed decision to mediate. Both parties will need to agree upon a mediator, educate themselves about the process, and schedule the time for the mediation.

TIP

How do you locate a mediator? There are often community mediation centers that offer a low-cost mediation service. Look up *mediation* or *conflict resolution* in your local phone book. Sometimes your local Chamber of Commerce or the Better Business Bureau also has a mediation program that is tailored to small businesses.

A Mediator Begins the Process. After all parties have arrived at the mediation, the mediator will introduce everyone and provide an overview of the goals and rules of the mediation.

Present Viewpoints. Each party will be given a chance to present their viewpoint of the issues, and each party will listen to the other to identify issues of interest and concern. While the other party is describing the issues from their own viewpoint, no one else in the room is allowed to interrupt. Each party may also present general ideas about how to resolve the issues.

Define Problems through Joint Discussion. The mediator may give both parties time to participate in a joint discussion and to discuss each other's viewpoints. Both parties should agree upon a statement defining the problem.

Private Sessions with the Mediator. The mediator may choose to spend time with each party in a private meeting to discuss the strengths and weaknesses of their position. The mediator may also discuss possible ideas for settlement and meet with both parties several times if he or she feels it is needed.

Negotiate Possible Solutions. Parties are brought back together and possible solutions are discussed openly between both sides. Possible solutions to the problem are jointly evaluated along with alternative solutions.

Bring the Mediation to a Close. If an agreement has been reached, the mediator will write a formal document and review it with both parties. Both parties will sign the agreement, and the mediator may suggest that they take it to a lawyer to review. If both parties choose, they may write up a legally binding agreement. If no agreement is reached, both parties may choose to revisit mediation at a later time, go to arbitration, or go to court.

Arbitration

Arbitration is another legal alternative to going to court. Like mediation, arbitration can cost a fraction of the time and money. One difference between mediation and arbitration is that the mediator has no authority to establish a legally binding agreement between the two parties. In mediation, the third party assists the two parties in resolving their disagreement and in defining a solution. Arbitration is a more formal process, one that enables a neutral third party to act similar to a judge and to issue a final decision that is legally binding.

One practice when using arbitration is for each party to choose an arbitrator and for the two arbitrators to select a third. These arbitrators then form a panel, and together they act in a similar fashion to a judge, reviewing all the evidence and presentations of both parties. The panel listens to the facts and then renders a judgment. The arbitration is conducted similar to a trial, and may not be as conducive to reaching a reasonable business compromise to a business dispute.

Parties may appeal the arbitrator's decision to a court, but often the courts will not change the arbitrator's decisions. The court may only focus on whether the arbitrator was guilty of malfeasance, or whether the arbitrator exceeded his or her authority, or decide whether the decision conflicts with positive laws. In fact, some jurisdictions have established a limited grace period during which the decision may be appealed, after which there can be no appeal.

TIP

To learn more about arbitration or to locate an arbitrator, you can visit www.adr.org, which is the official Web site for the American Arbitration Association. They have more than 8,000 arbitrators and mediators worldwide.

Small Claims Court

The small claims court is an informal court where parties can sue for money without a lawyer. There are limits to the total amount of money for which you can sue, and this limit varies from state to state. Table 9-1 defines the limits set by each state at the time this book was written. To check for updates to these limits, you can perform a quick search through your favorite search engine. Typing in something like *small claims court maximum for [your state name]* will help you quickly find the limits.

Small claims court is a court of law, but you are not required to bring a lawyer to represent your case. The intent is a "do it yourself" court where the parties handle their own cases. Any individual who is over 18 years of age can bring a dispute to small claims court, but a corporation cannot. If you're being sued by an individual, we offer this as an alternative to going to court, but it requires you to talk the claimant into taking the case to small claims court.

How to Find a Good Lawyer

If the above strategies to stay out of the courtroom fail, you will need to find a lawyer. One of the easiest ways to find a lawyer whom you can trust is to

Table 9-1. Small Claims Court Limitations

State	Maximum Dollar Amount	State	Maximum Dollar Amount
Alabama	$3,000	Montana	$3,000
Alaska	$7,500	Nebraska	$2,400
Arizona	$2,500	Nevada	$5,000
Arkansas	$5,000	New Hampshire	$5,000
California	$5,000	New Jersey	$3,000
Colorado	$7,500	New Mexico	$10,000
Connecticut	$3,500	New York	$3,000
Delaware	$15,000	North Carolina	$4,000
District of Columbia	$5,000	North Dakota	$5,000
Florida	$5,000	Ohio	$3,000
Georgia	$15,000	Oklahoma	$4,500
Hawaii	$3,500	Oregon	$5,000
Idaho	$4,000	Pennsylvania	$10,000
Illinois	$5,000	Rhode Island	$1,500
Indiana	$3,000	South Carolina	$7,500
Iowa	$5,000	South Dakota	$8,000
Kansas	$4,000	Tennessee	$10,000
Kentucky	$1,500	Texas	$5,000
Louisiana	$3,000	Utah	$7,500
Maine	$4,500	Vermont	$3,500
Maryland	$5,000	Virginia	$2,000
Massachusetts	$2,000	Washington	$4,000
Michigan	$3,000	West Virginia	$5,000
Minnesota	$7,500	Wisconsin	$5,000
Mississippi	$2,500	Wyoming	$7,000
Missouri	$3,000		

speak with friends and other people whom you trust and see if they can recommend a good lawyer. It is likely that someone you know has used a lawyer in the past or is friends with a trustworthy lawyer.

If you can't find a lawyer through a friend or business associate, you can start by looking in your local phone book under *law* or *lawyer*. Another good place to begin looking is to search online by typing in words like *how to find a good lawyer.*

It doesn't take much time to find a long list of lawyers in your area, but how do you know which one to call? Here are some tips to consider when evaluating that list:

- Ask a prospective lawyer how much things will cost and who will do the work. Try to understand their fee structures. Lawyers will charge you by the hour, so it's a good idea to monitor them closely and to make sure you are not being overcharged.

- Find a lawyer who is familiar with your specific circumstance. You'll need to hire a specialist in your area. Review their biographies and Web sites to determine if they have expertise in the area of business law that you need.

- Hire a lawyer with whom you get along and you can spend time. You will need to work closely with this lawyer to be effective. Look for a list of clients they have represented in the past, and contact those clients to hear their opinions.

- Search the Internet for the name of the lawyer you are considering. Are there any articles or information online that give you a level of comfort?

- Contact your state bar association to find out if the lawyer is in good standing.

10
Raising Capital

In starting any new business one of the main questions or concerns is: How are we going to fund this venture? This can be the most difficult part of starting a new business. One of the main reasons is that most national banks will not grant a loan to a business that has not existed for more than two years. There's a good reason for this: A majority of small businesses fail in the first year of existence. Banks are looking for security for their investments. They do not want to fund a business without security.

In this chapter we will outline the many ways to fund your small to medium business. We will break it down into two categories, based on how many years your business has existed. The first category is for businesses that have existed from zero to two years. The second category is for businesses that have existed for more than two years.

Businesses that are in existence for two years or less may have a harder time receiving certain types of funding because of the risk factor. Many traditional lending institutions will not lend your business money until it has been around at least two years. So what are your options in funding your small business?

There are a variety of resources to draw from when you look for funding to start your business:

- State and federal money
- Loans
- Venture capital
- Creative ideas

State and Federal Money

Loans

Money lent by a federal or state agency for a specific period of time and with a reasonable expectation of repayment. These loans may or may not require a payment of interest.

SBA Loans

There are several different loan programs available through the Small Business Association (SBA), which is an agency of the federal government. The sole purpose of this agency is to help small business owners. In order to receive the loan, you must meet all the SBA's loan requirements. Here are some basic loan programs offered by the SBA:

Basic 7(a) Loan Guaranty. This is the main loan program offered by the SBA. It functions like this: You get a loan from a commercial lender, and then a certain percentage of that loan is guaranteed by the SBA. This money can be used for a lot of your business needs, from working capital to machinery to land and building purchases.

Certified Development Company. The CDC program is specifically used for the purpose of purchasing real estate, machinery, or equipment for expansion or modernization. This is called the 504 Loan Program. Usually, this loan is secured from a commercial lender, and then a CDC can provide a second junior lien.

Microloan. The 7(m) Loan Program is a small business loan up to $35,000 for small businesses and not-for-profit child-care centers to provide working capital. These loans are not guaranteed by the SBA. Not all states have the microloan available.

For more information on all the programs available through the SBA go to www.sba.gov.

TIP

Before you go to see if you qualify for one of the SBA programs, make sure that you have identified your business needs. You will want a detailed business plan.

Loan Guarantees

Programs in which the federal or state agencies agree to pay back all or part of a loan to a private lender if the borrower defaults.

Grants

- Money given by federal or state agencies for a fixed period of time and which does not have to be repaid. There are thousands of grants available for small businesses.

- Each grant will have specific qualifications that need to be met in order for the grant to be awarded. Some grants will require you to spend the money in certain ways, and others will allow you to spend the money any way you want. Some of the best places to look for grants are www.firstgov.org.

TRAP

There are many programs that are soliciting and will tell you they have direct access to available grants. They want to charge a fee for you to gain access to their e-book and online directory. Avoid them. They give information that you can find for free at www.firstgov.org.

Direct Payments

Funds provided by federal or state agencies to individuals, private firms, and institutions. The use of direct payments may be "specified" to perform a particular service or for "unrestricted" use.

Government Contracts

If you can get a government contract, your business will be very happy. The great thing about government contracts are that they are, in fact, contracts. You are now working with the federal government. They are great repeat customers and they pay on time.

Funding through Loans

As you know, a loan is based on a very old concept: Someone gives you money, and you promise to pay it back, usually with interest over a certain amount of time. Since you must pay back the lender whether your business is a fabulous success or a miserable failure, the entire risk of the business is placed on you.

Of course, nothing in business, or in life for that matter, is without risk. Nevertheless, a commercial lender will be unwilling to lend you money if it looks like there's not much chance the money will be repaid. To help keep the risk low, a lender is likely to ask for "security" for the loan. For example, the lending institution may ask you to put your house up as collateral on the loan. They may be willing to accept other assets that you or your business might have. They do this in case you forfeit on the loan, since they could then repossess the asset and sell it to recoup their investment in your business.

Your sources for loans include banks, credit unions, family, friends, and private investors.

The lender will almost always want you to sign a written promissory note—a paper that basically says, "I promise to pay you $XX plus interest of X percent," and then describes how and when payments are to be made. You will always want to have some sort of agreement between you and the lender. A bank or other commercial lender will use a form with a bit more wording than this, but the basic idea is always the same.

The private investor will have a different document than a bank. Generally speaking, he or she will charge a lot more interest and have a lot more penalties if you fail to pay. If you're borrowing from family or friends, always insist on a written agreement, even if they say a handshake is okay. The main reason for this is to certify that, regardless of whether the business succeeds or fails, the loan will still be repaid. I have seen many families and friendships ruined over this. As the old saying goes, "Fences between houses make for good neighbors." If you have everything in writing, you, your business, and the lender will be protected. You would never want the lender claiming they own 50 percent of your business when you thought they were only lending you $5,000 at 10 percent over two years.

When you sign the promissory note, make sure you get a copy of it for your records. And once you pay it off, be sure to get the original promissory note back, along with a document stating that you have paid it off in full.

If the interest rate on the loan doesn't exceed the maximum rate allowed by your state's usury law, you and the lender are free to work out the terms of repayment.

Typically, a state's usury law will allow a lender to charge a higher rate when lending money for business purposes than for personal reasons. In fact, in several states there's no limit at all on the interest rate that can be charged on business loans, as long as the business borrower agrees to the rate in writing. In a few states, the higher limit, or the absence of any limit, applies only when the business borrower is organized as a corporation. In other states the higher rates permitted for business borrowers are legal even if the borrower is a sole proprietorship, partnership, or limited liability company.

Assuming there are no usury law problems, you and the lender can agree on any number of repayment plans. Let's say you borrow $20,000 with interest at the rate of 10 percent a year.

Here are just a few of the repayment possibilities:

Lump Sum Repayments. You agree, for example, to pay principal and interest in one lump sum at the end of one year. Under this plan, 12 months later you'd pay the lender $20,000 in "principal"—the borrowed amount—plus $2,000 in interest.

Periodic Interest and Lump Sum Repayment of Principal. You agree, for example, to pay interest only for two years and then interest and principal at the end of the third year. With this type of loan plan—often called a "balloon" loan because of the big payment at the end—you'd pay $2,000 in interest at the end of the first and second years, then $20,000 in principal and $2,000 in interest at the end of the third year.

Periodic Payments of Principal and Interest. You agree, for example, to repay $5,000 of the principal each year for four years, plus interest at the end of each year. Under this plan, your payments would look like this:

End of Year One:	$5,000 principal + $2,000 interest
End of Year Two:	$5,000 principal + $1,500 interest
End of Year Three:	$5,000 principal + $1,000 interest
End of Year Four:	$5,000 principal + $500 interest

Amortized Payments. You agree, for example, to make equal monthly payments so that principal and interest are fully paid in five years. Under this plan, you'd consult an amortization table in a book, on computer software, or on the Internet to figure out how much must be paid each month for five years to fully pay off a $10,000 loan plus the 10 percent interest. The table would say you'd have to pay $212.48 a month. Each of your payments would consist of both principal and interest. At the beginning of the repayment period, the interest portion of each payment would be large; at the end, it would be small.

Amortized Payments with a Balloon. You agree, for example, to make equal monthly payments based on a five-year amortization schedule, but to pay off the remaining principal at the end of the third year. Under this plan, you'd pay $212.48 each month for three years. At the end of the third year, after making the normal monthly payment, there'd still be $4,604.42 in unpaid principal, so along with your normal payment of $212.48, you'd make a balloon payment to cover the remaining principal.

Lenders, with the possible exception of friends or relatives, will probably require you to provide some valuable property—called security or collateral, as we said—which they can seize and sell to collect their money if you can't keep up with the loan repayment plan. For example, the lender may seek a second mortgage or deed of trust on your house, or may ask for a security interest or lien on your mutual funds or the equipment, inventory, and accounts receivable of your business. Again, the reason for this is that if you don't make your payments, the lender can sell the pledged assets (the security) to pay off the loan.

It's important to realize that a lender isn't limited to using the pledged assets to satisfy the loan. If you don't make good on your repayment commitment, a lender has the right to sue you. Typically, a lender will seize pledged assets first and then sue you if the funds realized from those assets are insufficient to pay off the loan. But that's not a legal requirement. A lender may decide to sue you before using up the pledged assets. If the lender wins the lawsuit and gets a judgment against you, assets you haven't specifically pledged as security are at risk, as is a portion of your future earnings.

In short, before you borrow money—under either a secured or unsecured promissory note—think about what will happen if you run into financial problems.

If you lack sufficient assets to pledge as security for a loan, a lender may try other methods to attempt to guarantee that the loan will be repaid. One is to ask you to get someone who is richer than you to cosign or guarantee the loan. That means the lender will have two people rather than one to collect from if you don't make your payments. When asking friends or relatives to cosign or guarantee a promissory note, be sure they understand that they're risking their personal assets if you don't repay it.

If you're married, the lender may insist that your spouse cosign the promissory note. Be aware that if your spouse signs, not only are your personal assets at risk, but also those assets that the two of you jointly own—a house or a bank account, for example. What's more, if your spouse has a job, his or her earnings will be subject to garnishment if the lender sues and gets a judgment against the two of you.

When you get a loan to start a new business, or a loan to expand it, you will reap the benefits by maintaining full ownership and control as a reward for the hard work you put into the business.

That's the upside; the downside to this type of funding is that you'll be responsible for the loan whether your business succeeds or fails. You may end up paying that loan back for years after your business has failed. You must decide if being the sole owner and having control of the company is worth the risk.

Funding through Venture Capital

Venture capital is a great way to start or grow your business. Generally, the individual or entity investing in your business will want a piece of your company.

Sometimes these individuals are called "equity investors," "angel investors," or "venture capitalists." These individuals or entities will become co-owners and share in the fortunes and misfortunes of your business. Like you, they can make or lose a bundle. If your business does badly, you're usually under no obligation to pay back the money. However, some equity investors would like to have their cake and eat it too—they want you to guarantee some return on their investment even if the business does poorly. Unless you're desperate for the cash, avoid an investor who wants a guarantee. It's simply too risky a proposition for someone starting or running a small business.

Because venture capitalists own the business, they may be exposed to personal liability for all business debts unless your business is a corporation, limited partnership, or limited liability company. If you recruit a venture capitalist for what has been your sole proprietorship, your business will now be treated as a general partnership. This means your equity investors will be considered general partners, whether or not they take part in running the business. And as far as people outside of the business are concerned—people who are owed money or who have a judgment against the business—general partners are all personally liable for the debts of the partnership.

Venture capitalists often want to limit their losses to what they put into the business. An investor who puts in $10,000 may be prepared to lose the $10,000 but no more. In short, the investor doesn't want to put the rest of his or her assets at risk. The investor will want to avoid being—or being treated as—a general partner.

Fortunately, there are three common ways to organize your business so you can offer an investor protection from losses beyond the money being invested: corporation, limited liability company, and limited partnership.

Encourage investors to determine their own degree of risk. An investor in a business organized as a corporation, limited partnership, or limited liability company usually stands to lose no more than his or her investment. However, state laws must be followed carefully to achieve this result. To avoid having investors accuse you of giving misleading assurances, recommend that they check with their own financial and legal advisors to evaluate if their investment exposes them to the possibility of incurring additional losses.

Someone who invests in your business may be willing to face the loss of the entire investment and not insist that you guarantee repayment. But to offset the risk of losing the invested money, the investor may want to receive substantial benefits if the business is successful. For example, an investor may insist on a generous percentage of the business profits, and to help assure that there are such profits, may seek to put a cap on your salary. The terms are always negotiable—there's no formula for figuring out what's fair to both you and the investor.

The law treats corporate shares and limited partnership interests as securities. Issuing these securities to investors is regulated by federal and state law. In some cases, an investor's interest in a limited liability company may also come under these laws.

This means that before selling an investor an interest in your business, you'll need to learn more about the requirements of the securities laws. Fortunately, there are generous exemptions that normally allow a small business to provide a limited number of investors with an interest in the business without complicated paperwork. Chances are good that your business will be able to qualify for these exemptions. In the rare cases in which the exemptions won't work for your small business and you have to meet the complex requirements of the securities laws—such as distributing an approval prospectus to potential investors—it's probably too much trouble to do the deal unless a great deal of money is involved.

Creative Alternatives

We have discussed government funding, loans, and venture capital. Now it is time to discuss some other possibilities that can help you fund your new or existing business. There are several creative ways to find capital for your business, and some may have less risk than others.

Credit Cards

Credit cards can be an easy way to start or grow your existing business. They are very accessible. There is no asset tied to the credit. It is a personal loan with only a personal guarantee that you will pay back the debt. Credit card companies have a variety of offers from zero percent interest for your first year to cash you get back from your purchases. You will receive checks from the credit card company that you use.

The main pitfall of using credit cards to expand your business is the fact that credit card companies have high interest rates. After the initial offer period is over, you may be paying anywhere from 10 to 29 percent. You need to be cautious when using credit cards to grow you business because if the business fails, you will be paying the high interest for a long time.

Home Equity Loan

If you own a home, this may be a good way to finance your business. If you have equity in your home, you may want to refinance your home and use some of that equity. Interest rates for home loans have been at or near all-time lows for years. The nice thing about a home equity loan is that you will have a lower interest rate amortized at 15 to 30 years, keeping your payments manageable. Generally speaking, you will pay $7 to $9 per month for each $1,000 you borrow from your home.

TRAP

When using your home equity or credit cards to fund your business, remember that you are personally liable for that debt. You will want to make sure that you're capable and willing to make the monthly payments.

Equipment Leasing

Equipment leasing is a great way to expand your business if equipment is holding you back from growth. Is there certain equipment that will allow you to do something that your competitors can't do? Will it speed up production time, allowing you to fulfill more orders? Equipment leasing requires a third party to purchase the equipment for you. They hold the asset, then turn around and lease the equipment back to you. Your lease payments are now tax deductible, and you can grow your business without using a lot of your cash reserves.

Purchase Order Funding

Purchase order funding has been around for years. Many big companies use it to fill big orders. This allows you to fill orders for larger companies that may require a substantial amount of money.

For example, let's say that I get an order from ABC Retail Outlet. They want to buy 100,000 candles from Candle Makers Inc. for the price of $2 per candle. Candle Makers Inc. may not have the funds to fill this order because it costs them $1 to make each candle. They do not want to miss this opportunity, but they need $100,000 to fill the order. There are companies that will buy the purchase order from Candle Makers Inc. They will fund up to 50 percent of the purchase order today, and then after the order has been filled and delivered, will fund the remaining amount minus their commission, which is generally 3 to 5 percent of the total purchase order amount. Many companies that do purchase order funding will want to factor the receivables, which are another way you can increase cash flow into your business, helping you succeed.

Account Receivable Funding

Account receivable funding is a good way to increase your cash flow, especially if you are having a tough time collecting your account receivables or if you'd like to extend credit terms to your existing or future clients. Companies will pay you 60 to 70 percent of your receivable up front. Then the company will collect the receivables for you with the terms that you have set with your client. Once they receive the amount paid to you, they will keep 3 to 5 percent as their commission. The remaining amount will go to you.

TIP

Equipment leasing, factoring, and purchase order funding are great ways to keep more money in your business accounts for working capital. Make sure that you work with well-established funding sources.

Summary

As you look at funding your existing or new business, you must ask yourself several questions. If the business fails, do I have to pay off the funding? How will the funding be secured? Am I willing to have partners in my business? If so, how many? Am I willing to lose control of my business? How you answer these questions will help you determine which funding avenue is best for your business.

11
Managing Employees

Planning for Employees

As your business starts to grow, you may need to hire some employees. Employees can be a blessing or a curse. It just depends on how you hire, train, and manage them. The following steps will help you ready your company for new employees.

Have a Mission Statement

The first thing you need to do when hiring new employees is define what your company stands for. A company mission statement is a great way for you to decide what your company stands for and what it is going to live by. Here are some sample mission statements:

Motorola: The company exists "to honorably serve the community by providing products and services of superior quality at a fair price."

Wal-Mart: "We exist to provide value to our customers—to make their lives better via lower prices and greater selection; all else is secondary."

And here are some questions to help you build your own business mission statement:

What is the history of the business or group?

What is the structure and organization of the business or group?

What is your core business?

What do you do?

What do you think you could do?

Who are your clients?

What do they expect?

Are there timelines?

As you brainstorm and respond to these questions, draft out a possible mission statement. Present it to the whole group for reaction. Don't be surprised if your initial statement is longer than you would like. We suggest that you let your draft sit for a week or so as you ponder changes. Remember that eventually you will live by the mission statement: It will inspire new employees with what the group desires to achieve by way of service and product; and it will inspire and capture the imagination of your clients.

Make Sure You're Incorporated

The second thing you need to do before hiring new employees is to make sure you're set up as a corporation. If you are a sole proprietor, remember, you're liable for the business—and that includes what your employees do. After all, they are representing you and your company. This is why we stress having a company mission statement before hiring employees. They need to know what they represent. You want that risk removed from you and placed on the corporation's back. This is one of the best reasons to have a corporation.

Define the Position to Be Filled

The third thing to do before hiring a new employee is to define his or her role. You might want to ask yourself some of the questions below before hiring anyone. Remember, the more extensively you have defined the role or responsibilities, the easier it will be for you to manage your new employee.

What will this new employee's main responsibility be?

What skills must this employee have?

What are the hours that this employee must work?

What work experience or related experience must this employee have?

How can I hold the employee accountable?

Is there a way that I can gauge the employee's productivity?

How critical is the employee to the success of the company?

TRAP

Many new business owners make the mistake of treating new and existing employees as if they are more important than the company itself. Your employees are important, but remember that your business is more important. If the company is your main concern, it will be around a long time.

Decide on Employee Training

Training is the fourth thing that should be considered. How will you train your new employee? If you are a small business, this may be difficult because you might be the one who needs to do the training. You will still have to accomplish your daily tasks, of course, while spending the time training. If you are a larger company, other employees on your current staff might be able to do the training.

Set up a specific process that you use to train all new employees, even if you're hiring them for different jobs. The consistency will only benefit you and them. It's also advisable to have a new-hire packet in which you can gather all the local and state papers that may be required of your company. Items like W4, emergency contact form, noncompete agreement, benefits info, nondisclosure agreement also know as NDA, and any other agreement or form that you may want your employees to adhere to. You must decide how your training will take place. Does it need to be more hands on? Can they read a manual? Can they watch you or someone perform the task? Training your new employee will be a critical aspect of your business. The better you train and the better they understand their new job, the more likely it is that long-term success will occur.

What if you need to hire new employees quickly? Can you train them fast enough, and will they be able to provide the same quality support that your clients have come to expect in the past? It's good to have a plan in place in case of growth spurts.

For example, we currently run a business helping small business succeed online. It generally takes us one month to train one of our support employees. There are three ways we've been able to handle quick spurts of growth in our company. The first is by having our managers or another department handle the work overflow until our new employees are trained. The second is to outsource some of our support work until we can handle it internally. The third is to find individuals who are willing to be trained on their own by promising them they will be hired to fill an existing opening. People are willing to be trained on their own because of the benefits and the atmosphere that we have at the office. (Later, we will discuss a great way to hire and keep your employees.)

Having the right plan will save you time in the long run. In time management they say that 15 minutes of good planning will save you anywhere from two to three hours daily. The same applies to the training of new employees.

TIP

The better your training system, the more time you'll save. With a training system in place, you will be able to hire and train more efficiently.

Where Can I Look for Employees?

There are many avenues that you may take to hire employees. As you advertise, keep in mind that you want the best individual at the best possible price. For example, one secretary can be worth triple what another is worth, due to the speed at which he or she works. We know one secretary who had to be replaced by three new employees because that was the only way to complete all the tasks that she'd been accomplishing! Race, religion, and gender do not matter—you need to find the best person for the job. Below, we'll go into the cost and benefits of the various avenues you can take to finding employees.

TIP

Set a budget of what you are willing to spend to acquire a new employee. Using all of the methods below can be costly.

Family Members

This can be an inexpensive way to hire new employees. You should have no advertising cost. The main concern is whether the individual is qualified to do the work. And consider this: If they do a lousy job and you fire them, will it cause family problems? Of course, some families have had great success working together. You have to decide if that's a risk you want to take. But keep in mind that if all the promotions or hiring you do goes to family members, it may reflect negatively on your company.

Classified Ads

This is the most common way to advertise a new position, and it is still the number one way that individuals find new jobs. When placing an ad, you'll want to consider the circulation, the length of time it will run, and your target audience. It's also a good idea to check the paper to see what other companies are advertising. Ask yourself, while composing an ad: What differentiates my job opening from those of similar businesses? What can I say that makes my job offer better? Finally, look at the words and abbreviations other advertisers use. Remember, you will be paying per character or line, and advertising in the local paper can be costly in certain regions of the country.

TIP

Have your job description ready for the person who takes the calls that come in. Most people who read the ad and call will want a brief description of the job and what it entails. They'll want to know if it's worth their time to fax their résumé. At the same time, you want to make sure the person is qualified for the position.

Job Placement Companies

These companies are often called "headhunters." Their job is to help companies find the right candidate for their job openings. In the past, their main business was hiring executive type positions. They have now moved toward all types of positions, from secretaries to managers, executives to personal assistants. Job placement companies will handle almost all of the work of hiring for you, including advertising your available position(s), screening all the résumés, and conducting the interviews. They will then suggest two or three candidates, and will even assist you in the next phase of interviews and in making the final decision.

Using this type of service can save you time and help you find the best available candidate for your needs. However, it comes with a price tag. Generally, the fees of job placement companies vary from 20 to 30 percent of the hired person's first year salary. For example, if you were looking for a personal assistant and were planning to pay $30,000 for a first-year salary, then the job placement company would receive a commission of $6,000 to $9,000. This may seem high, but if you are only filling one position, you might pay that amount to just run the ad in the local paper. You have to weigh all the benefits of this service. The nice thing is that you do not pay until someone is hired for that position.

Temporary Agencies

These companies will allow you to use their employees on a temporary basis. This type of employment has been used typically in the past for manufacturing industries, where companies have had a hard time maintaining a consistent flow of business. They may have a thousand orders to fill one week and then a hundred orders the next. Companies in this situation have turned to temporary agencies to help meet their employee needs. In recent years these agencies have moved into the professional industries, providing secretaries, bookkeepers, managers, etc. The temporary agency will take care of paying the employee, covering his or her benefits, and paying the associated tax and unemployment insurance necessary for each employee. Temp agencies can be a great way to tap into a large employee base.

Recently, some of these temporary agencies have begun to function like job placement companies. They will allow you to use their pool of employees on a temporary basis. If you like the employee, you have an opportunity to hire him or her full-time. If you decide to do that, you pay the temp agency a small fee, just as you would a job placement company. If you don't like the employee you have been using, you can always ask for a different person. This is a great way to try before you buy. If you find the right employee at the right time, it can be beneficial for your business.

College Campus: Internships

A lot of Fortune 500 companies use college students to help with their labor needs. Internships are a fantastic way for you to meet the needs of your growing company. Many college students require an internship or work experience in their related field and are avidly seeking these positions.

We have found many great employees who are looking for work experience in their related major. Often, they are willing to work for a lot less than the going rate, because they're looking for employment that will build their résumés. One of the downsides to this will be a high turnover of employees, since they are working for you only while going to school. But you may find a student who enjoys working for you and is willing to continue even after graduation.

Internships can be offered with or without pay. Since an internship is considered part of a student's education, it is not necessary to pay an intern. If you opt to pay, you would generally offer half of the going rate. For example, if your normal full-time employee makes $10 an hour, then you would offer the internship at $5 an hour. Our public schools use internships all the time. Student teachers usually student-teach for half the year with no pay.

Many public schools will allow a student to do an internship for a full year with half the pay of a regular starting teacher.

You do not have to be a well-established company to take advantage of this system. For instance, one company that started a new division found that a local university needed companies to offer internships to its students in a specific major. We met with one of the department heads, filled out the paperwork, and were assigned a student who would be working for us for the semester, roughly 20 hours a week, for free. Remember, you need to meet the right requirements. Just like applying for a grant, you must fit the need. Sometimes you may need to modify your opening if you want to get free help.

Internet Job Boards

Internet job classifieds are popping up all over the Web. They are becoming an ever cheaper way to advertise your new job openings, and they allow you to reach thousands of tech-savvy applicants. These job boards offer various services, and you need to decide which is best for you. You can use job boards to search all of the résumés that have been posted by job seekers, or you can place an ad for a period of time.

Other Hiring Considerations

Now that you're ready to expand your business, have considered the responsibilities that your new employee will have, and know where to look for applicants, you must determine what type of employee you are looking to hire. Are you looking for a short-term or long-term employee? How much are you willing to pay your new employee?

There are many ways you can compete with companies that are paying a higher wage. What you need to do is outline what separates you from your competition. What benefits are you going to offer your employees? We've found that if we offer a good benefits package and have a good family atmosphere, we can hire employees for less than competitors can. To estimate your cost for each new employee, take the hourly pay rate and then multiply it by 1.3. This is a good rough estimate as to what your new employee will cost you. For example, if you are paying someone $10 an hour, $10 $\times$ 1.3 = $13 an hour.

There are many reasons to offer benefits to your employees. You'll find that you can keep employees longer and they will be willing to work for less money. One person we know was working for a company for a base salary plus commission. They were making next to nothing but were willing to stay with the company because of benefits, and because the company had many work parties.

When you're offering benefits, make sure that you have employees who are committed to your company. Many employees will be willing to wait for certain benefits. For example, you might offer health insurance to employees only after they've been employed for 90 days. You also need to consider how much you're willing to cover. If you cover 50 percent of the employee's health insurance, for instance, and their premium is $400, then you will pay $200 more for their benefits. If you take $200 and break it out over 40 hours a week, you are only paying the employee $1.50 more an hour.

Hiring employees is a crucial aspect of growing your business, and it should be done with careful consideration. Your employees can help you take your business to the next level. Thoughtful planning is a necessary step in making the hiring process enjoyable and successful.

12
Offering Benefits to Your Employees

There are many things that keep a company together. Employees play a huge part in your business success, so as an employer you shouldn't be solely focused on the clients, but also on your relationship with your employees. In this chapter we will discuss how the relationship between employee and employer can be improved. Keeping your employees happy can be quite a task.

There are two main reasons for offering benefits: the first is to offer benefits to your employees, and the second is to offer benefits to yourself as the owner. We will go into the options available to you and your employees. Our focus mainly will be on offering benefits to your employees as a way to recruit and maintain a good workforce.

Benefits play a large part in keeping employees satisfied and also elicit the interest of those who are seeking a position with your company. Many companies offer such fringe benefits as health insurance, paid vacation, sick leave, and, depending upon the company, dental, optical, prepaid legal assistance, and life insurance. Obviously, employees desire these benefits, and providing them will spark employees to give their best back to you. Probably the most important benefit is health insurance, so we'll look at that first.

Health Insurance

Health insurance is on everyone's mind these days. With the cost of insurance on the rise, families are looking for ways to cover themselves. Offering health insurance doesn't have to cost you much, and will help attract employees to

113

your business. You can pay some or all of the employee's premium. If you decide to provide health insurance, you will need to determine the waiting period before employees are eligible to start receiving their coverage.

If you've been reading newspapers, you know that the cost of health insurance is on the rise. To lower your cost for health insurance you can increase your deductible and go with a gap plan that will cover your deductible. The available options in the health insurance industry are constantly changing, so you should deal with an experienced insurance agency when setting up your health insurance plan.

TIP

Structure your plan so that the percentage you pay of your employee's health insurance premium increases as the employee's time with your company increases.

In order to qualify for a group policy, you need to have at least one employee. There are many benefits to a group policy. You will get better coverage, and keep in mind that maternity coverage is usually only offered in group policies.

401(k) Retirement Plans

Another benefit that needs to be discussed is a 401(k) retirement plan. This is a voluntary retirement plan offered to employees of a company that allows up to a certain percentage of their pretax pay to be set aside and invested within the retirement plan. The funds and the growth are not taxed until the funds are withdrawn. The percentage of pretax pay varies from company to company and can increase with each year of employment. As the employer, you can also contribute funds to the employee's plan if you wish, by matching your employee's contributions.

Keep in mind that as the business owner, it is your responsibility to manage the fund. Further, you will need to decide if you want the main benefit of the 401(k) to go to you or your employees.

TRAP

There are restrictions as to when and how one can withdraw 401(k) funds without penalties. Some plans will not allow you to pull your money out until you reach the fine age of 59½. If you decide that you need the money before you reach that age, there will be a 10 percent tax added on.

TIP

Decide early on what your future retirement plans are. If you're planning to retire before you are 59½, you will need to make sure that you have other income avenues available.

SBO-401(k)

SBO stands for "Small-Business Owner," though this specific type of 401(k) also goes by a few other names, such as the Uni-K plan or self-employed 401(k). An SBO-401(k) plan is very specific about who qualifies. You may qualify if you own a business, and the owner is the only person eligible for this type of account. If you have employees who are eligible as well, you cannot qualify for this type of plan. However, if your employees are your family, this will not hinder your eligibility.

There are two parts to this type of retirement plan. First is the salary deferral. This will allow you to put up to 100 percent of your income into the account (however, this cannot exceed $12,000 for the year). Second is the profit-sharing contribution. This will allow the business to add 25 percent of your compensation, but the amount cannot exceed $40,000 for the year. If you are above a certain age, this can fluctuate.

There are a few benefits to this type of account, such as the possibility of making loans from the account, no discrimination testing, and deducting contributions. This plan is very popular with small businesses.

SIMPLE 401(k)

Another type of 401(k) account is the SIMPLE 401(k). It is available to those same employers who are eligible to adopt a traditional 401(k) plan; this includes sole proprietors, partnerships, and corporations. However, while there is no restriction on the number of employees for the traditional 401(k) plan, only employers who adhere to the 100-employee limit can adopt a SIMPLE 401(k) plan. Under the 100-employee limitation rule, a SIMPLE may be established by an employer who has no more than 100 employees who received at least $5,000 in compensation for the previous year.

Employees are also eligible for this type of retirement plan. All employees have to do to qualify is to fulfill one year of employment and be over the age of 21. All employees who are eligible for the account must be sent an annual deferral notice for each year the plan is maintained by the employer. This plan will benefit your employees.

TIP

Many studies show that as your employees gain financial stability, they are able to perform their jobs better.

IRA Retirement Plans

There are other retirement plans that also can be beneficial to you as the business owner and to your employees, such as IRA retirement plans. There are five different types of IRA:

IRA

You can contribute up to $2,000 per year into an IRA (individual retirement account). The amount of this contribution that is deductible on your income tax return depends on your Adjusted Gross Income (AGI) and whether your employees are under an employer-sponsored qualified retirement plan. Thus, depending on your filing status (single, joint, etc.) and your AGI, your contributions may range from fully deductible to totally nondeductible. So be aware: Even though you are eligible to contribute to your IRA, you may be in a position where none of these contributions are in fact deductible.

Education IRA

You can put away up to $500 per year into an education IRA. The money grows tax-free and has preferential tax treatment upon distribution to the beneficiary who uses it for authorized education expenses. These plans are not common because they are very restrictive when it comes to who can make contributions to them, the amount of total contributions allowable each year, and the limitations on what education expenses qualify. Your financial planner should be able to assist you in evaluating what savings plan will prepare you for higher education costs, as well as in reviewing many of the tax-sheltered savings plans now sponsored by the various states, even for nonstate residents.

SEP IRA

The SEP IRA, or the Simplified Employee Pension IRA, is established and funded by you, the employer. It allows you to put up to 15 percent of your compensation into a special IRA account. Sole proprietors may establish these plans for their own benefit. They are sometimes used instead of

Keogh (profit-sharing or money-purchase plans) retirement plans because they have fewer administrative and tax filing requirements.

SIMPLE IRA

This is a new creation, but one that is rapidly becoming more popular. It's another employer-sponsored and employer-administered retirement plan. Its attractive features include not only the ability for the employer to establish and fund a retirement plan for his or her own benefit and that of the employees, but it also permits employees to contribute up to 100 percent— but no more than $6,500—per year, into an IRA. Separate rules relating to required employer contributions and premature distributions apply.

Roth IRA

Contributions are NOT deductible when the funds are contributed, but the Roth IRA earnings accumulate tax free and remain tax free upon distribution. To be eligible to contribute, your Adjusted Gross Income must be under $95,000 for singles and under $150,000 for married couples, as of December 2000. You cannot withdraw your funds within the first five years after the establishment of the Roth without a penalty. Since this five-year testing period can successfully be addressed by proper tax planning, the establishment and at least partial funding of a Roth IRA account should be addressed by the financial advisor of every taxpayer who qualifies to open such a plan. All of these plans can be beneficial to you as the employer, and in certain cases to the employee, depending upon which plan you decide to use for retirement investment.

TRAP

Do not tie up all your retirement funds so that they are available only when you turn 59½. You may want to retire earlier or be able to pull some of your money out sooner.

Fringe Benefits

Fringe benefits are basically payments to employees that are not salary-based, meaning payments that do not show up on their paychecks. Many companies offer these types of benefits to give incentive to their employees to work harder and do a better job for the company. Health insurance is probably the most important benefit to offer employees, but as an option with the health insurance, employers may offer optical, dental, and life insurance coverage.

There are a variety of other options when looking into offering these benefits. Many businesses will offer their employees fringe benefits such as paid vacations and sick leave; others offer a vehicle for the employee and paid mileage. There are simple things that a company can do, such as offer lunch and hidden bonuses. Employers who offer these benefits do so with the purpose of keeping their employees and lowering employee turnover. It also inspires those looking for work to consider your business. It is a win-win situation for both the employee and employer.

Exit Strategy

As a business owner, a big part of your retirement plan should be an exit strategy from your business. When building your business, you want to make sure that you are creating a salable business; that is, you don't want to spend years building a business that you cannot sell. Your procedures, accounts, clients, inventory, suppliers, trained employees, and assets make your business salable. You may sell it to family, an existing employee, a competitor, or a stranger. This can be a good part of your retirement.

TIP

As you grow your business, keep in mind that you are trying to create a salable business. If you do this from day one, it will make your business more valuable.

All of these options are great for providing a better work environment for you and your employees and future retirement for you as the owner. By providing these options you can make money and give investing options to those who are under you. These options can boost morale and keep the focus of your employees on improving the company. Since the laws governing these plans are often changing, you may want to seek the advice of a financial advisor.

13

Labor and Employment Law

There are six Federal Equal Employment Opportunity (EEO) laws enforced by the federal government that you need to be aware of as an employer. They cover a wide span of activities and discriminatory behaviors.

TIP

We have talked a lot in the previous chapters about hiring quality employees. You want the best employee to work for you. Do not discriminate on any level!

Title VII of the Civil Rights Act of 1964.   Often referred to simply as the "Civil Rights Act," this law prohibits employment discrimination based on race, color, religion, sex, or national origin.

Equal Pay Act of 1963 (EPA).   Protects men and women who perform substantially equal work in the same establishment from sex-based wage discrimination.

Age Discrimination in Employment Act of 1967.   The ADEA protects individuals who are 40 years of age or older against discrimination.

Title I and Title V of the Americans with Disabilities Act of 1990 (ADA).
Prohibit employment discrimination against qualified individuals with disabilities in the private sector and in state and local governments.

Sections 501 and 505 of the Rehabilitation Act of 1973.   Prohibit discrimination against qualified individuals with disabilities who work in the federal government.

Civil Rights Act of 1991.   Among other things, this law provides monetary damages in cases of intentional employment discrimination.

Note that for Title VII, ADEA, and ADA, it is illegal to discriminate under any of the following conditions:

- Hiring and firing
- Compensation
- Classification of employees
- Transfers, promotions, layoffs
- Job postings
- Recruitment
- Use of company facilities
- Training programs
- Fringe benefits
- Pay, including retirement plans, or disability leave

We go into more detail about each of the federal EEO laws below. For more information you can visit www.eeoc.gov or www.eeoc.gov/facts/qanda.html.

Title VII

Title VII protects against intentional discrimination and practices that can be considered discriminatory. Examples of this would be discriminating against someone because of birthplace, ancestry, culture, or language. Also, an employer must accommodate an employee's religious beliefs, except in cases when accommodating the employee causes the employer to suffer undue hardship.

Another major aspect of Title VII is sex discrimination. There are two main categories: The first precludes discriminating against someone because of his or her sex, and the second deals with sexual harassment. In fact, sexual harassment can cover anything from direct requests for sexual favors to same-sex harassment that causes someone to feel that the workplace is a hostile environment.

Sexual Harassment

One of the most common problems in a work environment is sexual harassment. This is classified as unwanted sexual advances (whether expressed physically or verbally), as well as jokes or inappropriate actions in a work setting. Any of these advances, actions, or jokes can be considered sexual harassment if it causes an individual to feel intimidated or threatened in their work environment.

Here are some important notes on sexual harassment:

- The individual being harassed can be a man or a woman, and it does not have to be a person of the opposite sex to be considered sexual harassment.

- Any employee can commit sexual harassment; it is not just a boss-to-employee occurrence.

- Sexual harassment is not limited to the person the advances are directed at; anyone offended by sexual comments or actions in the workplace can be considered a victim of sexual harassment.

- The sexual advances must be unwanted.

TRAP

Do not believe that this cannot occur in your business. Make sure that you have a great policy in place. Prevention is the best way to avoid any type of sexual harassment. Always be aware of situations that might foster sexual harassment.

Ways to Prevent Sexual Harassment.? There are a number of steps that you can take to reduce the risk of sexual harassment occurring in your workplace. Although you may not be able to follow all of the steps listed below, you should follow as many of them as you can.

- *Adopt a Clear Sexual Harassment Policy.* In your employee handbook, you should have an entire policy devoted to sexual harassment. It should define sexual harassment, state in no uncertain terms that you will not tolerate sexual harassment, state that you will discipline or fire any wrongdoers, set out a clear procedure for filing sexual harassment complaints, state that you will investigate fully any complaint that you receive, and state that you will not tolerate retaliation against anyone who complains about sexual harassment. For tips on creating an employee handbook, use your favorite search engine and search for *employee handbooks.*

- *Train Employees.* At least once a year, conduct training sessions for employees. These sessions should teach employees what sexual harassment is, explain that employees have a right to a workplace free of sexual harassment, review your complaint procedure and encourage employees to use it.

- *Train Supervisors and Managers.* At least once a year, conduct training sessions for supervisors and managers that are separate from the employee sessions. The sessions should educate the managers and supervisors about sexual harassment and explain how to deal with employee complaints. For helpful advice on how to handle employee complaints, try using your favorite search engine to search for *guidelines for handling discrimination* or similar terms.

- *Monitor Your Workplace.* Get out among your employees periodically. Talk to them about the work environment. Ask for their input. Look around the workplace itself. Do you see any offensive posters or notes? Talk to your supervisors and managers about what is going on. Keep the lines of communication open.

- *Take All Complaints Seriously.* If someone complains about sexual harassment, act immediately to investigate the complaint. If the complaint turns out to be valid, your response should be swift and effective.

Equal Pay in Employment Act

The Equal Pay in Employment Act forbids discrimination on the basis of sex when paying wages or benefits in situations where men and women perform the same work and hold the same responsibilities for an employer.

General Rules

- Employers may not reduce the wages of either sex to equalize pay between men and women.

- A violation of the EPA may occur where a different wage was or is paid to a person who worked or works in the same job before or after an employee of the opposite sex.

- A violation may also occur in cases where a labor union causes the employer to violate the law.

Age Discrimination in Employment Act

The ADEA, while broadly banning age discrimination, also specifically:

- Prohibits statements or specifications of age preference and limitations in job notices or advertisements. An age limit may only be specified in the rare circumstance where age has been proven to be a bona fide occupational qualification (BFOQ).

- Prohibits discrimination on the basis of age by apprenticeship programs, including joint labor-management apprenticeship programs.

- Prohibits denial of benefits to older employees. An employer may reduce benefits based on age only if the cost of providing the reduced benefits to older workers is the same as the cost of providing benefits to younger workers.

Title I and Title V of the Americans with Disabilities Act

The ADA forbids discrimination because of disability in all employment practices. Here are some important definitions that you might find helpful when considering illegal discrimination:

Individual with a Disability. Someone who has a physical or mental impairment that limits at least one or more general functions, such as walking, breathing, seeing, etc. Also, an individual with medical records of a previous impairment.

Qualified Individual with Disability. Someone who can perform all tasks that are required by a job even with a disability.

Reasonable Accommodation. An employer is required to make reasonable accommodations to allow for employees who have disabilities. These include modifications of work schedules, trainings, and work materials in order to give the same job opportunities to the disabled and people without disabilities.

Undue Hardship. An employer must accommodate individuals unless it would cause the employer to suffer significantly financially or in other areas of general operations.

Prohibited Inquiries and Examinations. During an interview, an employer cannot ask about the extent to which a person is disabled, but can ask about the potential employee's ability to perform job functions. A medical exam is only allowed if all other employees are subject to the same exam.

Sections 501 and 505 of the Rehabilitation Act of 1973

This act is specific to individuals with disabilities who work for the federal government, and so is unlikely to affect your corporation.

Civil Rights Act of 1991

This act allows for the payment of punitive damages in cases of intentional discrimination.

Other Important Laws and Acts
Fair Labor Standards Act

The FLSA sets minimum wage, overtime pay, record-keeping, and child labor standards for employment. Unless exempt, employees covered by the Equal Employment Opportunity (EEO) laws must be paid at least the minimum wage and not less than one and one-half times their regular rates of pay for overtime hours worked. For more information on the FLSA and how to determine if you and your employees are covered, visit www.dol.gov/esa/regs/compliance/whd/whdfs21.html.

Every covered employer must keep certain records for each nonexempt worker. The act requires no particular form for the records, but does require that the records include certain identifying information about the employee, and data about the hours worked and the wages earned. The law requires this information to be accurate. The following is a listing of the basic records an employer must maintain for each employee:

1. Employee's full name and Social Security number
2. Address, including zip code
3. Birth date, if younger than 19
4. Sex and occupation
5. Time and day of week when employee's workweek begins
6. Hours worked each day
7. Total hours worked each workweek
8. Basis on which employee's wages are paid (e.g., $6 an hour, $220 a week, piecework)
9. Regular hourly pay rate
10. Total daily or weekly straight-time earnings

11. Total overtime earnings for the workweek

12. All additions to or deductions from the employee's wages

13. Total wages paid each pay period

14. Date of payment and the pay period covered by the payment

For more information visit www.dol.gov/esa/regs/compliance/whd/whdfs21.html.

TIP

Record keeping is an essential part of any business, whether you are keeping track of employees or keeping the books. If you have a weakness in this area, find someone you can hire to be your record keeper.

Child Labor Laws

Child labor laws are part of the Fair Labor Standards Act, but there are several specifics we will look at here. An employer can work a 14- to 15-year-old only three hours a day after school hours, and a total of only 18 hours a week. Here are some exceptions that apply to individuals under the age of 14. They can hold jobs such as delivering newspapers; performing in radio, television, movie, or theatrical productions; and working for parents in their solely owned nonfarm business (except in manufacturing or in hazardous jobs). For a 16- to 17-year-old, there are no federal laws on the number of hours that can be worked on weekdays or total hours for the week.

There are 17 prohibited jobs for youth under the age of 18:

1. Manufacturing or storing explosives

2. Driving a motor vehicle and being an outside helper on a motor vehicle

3. Coal mining

4. Logging and sawmilling

5. Power-driven woodworking machines

6. Exposure to radioactive substances and to ionizing radiations

7. Power-driven hoisting equipment

8. Power-driven, metal-forming, punching and shearing machines

9. Mining, other than coal mining

10. Meat packing or processing (including power-driven meat slicing machines)

11. Power-driven bakery machines

12. Power-driven paper products machines

13. Manufacturing brick, tile, and related products

14. Power-driven circular saws, band saws, and guillotine shears

15. Wrecking, demolition, and ship-breaking operations

16. Roofing operations

17. Excavation operations

For more information on child labor laws, visit www.stopchildlabor.org/USchildlabor/fact1.htm.

The Occupational Safety and Health Act

The Occupational Safety and Health Act, also know as OSHA, was created to protect workers and their families from unsafe working or living conditions. OSHA has set different laws and regulations for different lines of work. Guidelines are set in different industries in order to protect worker safety. You can visit www.osha.gov for more information.

Summary

Now that we've given you an overview of the labor laws that affect you as an employer, it is important to keep these laws in mind as you hire employees and operate your corporation. To keep out of legal trouble, have a good hiring process and document everything you do. As we've said in previous chapters, it's important to have good records for all aspects of your corporation. Start a file for every employee, and include documentation such as:

- A copy of the necessary hiring ID
- A signed document verifying that the employee has read the employee handbook
- Any other documents that you may require employees to sign, such as a nondisclosure or noncompete agreement
- A record of any disciplinary action or advancement
- By keeping complete files and proper documentation, you will be well protected.

State Specific Information

Alabama

Corporate Name Endings

The name of the corporation shall contain the word "Corporation," "Incorporated," or an abbreviation. If the corporation is a banking corporation, the words "Bank," "Banking," or "Bankers" may be used. The name may not contain language stating or implying that the corporation is organized for a purpose other than that permitted by the Articles of Incorporation. The name cannot be the same as or deceptively similar to the corporate name of a domestic corporation or a foreign qualified corporation.

Corporation Requirements

Director Information

- Minimum number: One or more.
- Residence requirements: None.

- Age requirements: Directors must be a natural person[*] at least 19 years of age.
- Directors are not required to be listed in the Articles of Incorporation.

Officer Information. Officers are not required to be listed in the Articles of Incorporation.

Stock Information. An increase in shares or par value does not affect initial filing fees.

Corporate Records. The Articles of Incorporation and the minutes of shareholders' meetings and records of all actions taken by shareholders without a meeting for the past three years must be kept at the

---

[*] In jurisprudence, a "natural person" is a human being perceptible through the senses and subject to physical laws, as opposed to an "artificial person," i.e., an organization that the law treats for some purposes as if it were a person distinct from its members or owners.

corporation's principal office. Further, a list of names and business addresses of current directors and officers and the most recent annual report or public record information must be kept at its principal office.

Taxes and Fees

Annual Statements. Annual statements are required as part of Form PSA. See "Taxes" section below. The fee is $10 annually.

Taxes. Businesses must generally file Alabama Form PSA, Alabama Business Privilege Tax Return, Corporate Shares Tax Return, and Annual Return, within 2½ months after the beginning of their tax year. For corporations filing on a calendar year basis, the return must be filed by March 15 of the current year.

Income Tax Rate. The rate is 6.5 percent of net income.

Business Privilege Tax. The minimum privilege tax imposed is $100 and the maximum is generally $15,000. The tax is based on both the taxable income of the corporation and the net worth of the corporation. The tax rate is determined by the taxable income of the corporation. If the taxable income is between $0 and $1, the tax rate is $0.25 per $1,000 of net worth. If taxable income is more than $1 but less than $200,000, the tax rate is $1 per $1,000 of net worth. If taxable income is more than $200,000 but less than $500,000, the tax rate is $1.25 per $1,000 of net worth of the corporation. If taxable income is more than $500,000 but less than $2,500,000, the tax rate is $1.50 per $1,000 of net worth of the

corporation, and if the taxable income is more than $2,500,000, the tax rate is $1.75 per $1,000 of net worth of the corporation.

S Corporation

S corporation status is recognized by the State of Alabama. A separate state election from the federal election is not required.

License Requirements

Alabama requires most businesses to obtain a license and pay a fee if operating in the state. Please check with the state to make sure your business is complying with the license requirements for your particular profession.

For more information on taxes, visit www.ador.state.al.us

For additional or updated information, visit www.sos.state.al.us

Mailing Address

Secretary of State
Corporation Division
State Office Building, Room 536
P.O. Box 5616
Montgomery, AL 36130-5616
Tel: (334) 242-5324
Fax: (334) 240-3138

Alaska
Corporate Name Endings

The name must contain the word "Corporation," "Company," "Incorporated," "Limited," or an abbreviation thereof. The name must not contain words implying a different purpose from those purposes in the Articles of Incorporation. Corporate names must not contain the word "City," "Borough," or "Village." The name must not be the same as or deceptively similar to a name already in use, or a registered or reserved name.

Corporation Requirements

Director Information

- Minimum number: One or more.

- Residence requirements: No provision.

- Age requirements: Directors must be a natural person[*] at least 19 years of age.

- Directors are not required to be listed in the Articles of Incorporation.

Officer Information. Officers are not required to be listed in the Articles of Incorporation.

Stock Information. An increase in shares or par value does not affect initial filing fees.

Corporate Records. A list of shareholders, books and records of account, and the minutes of shareholders' and directors' meetings must be kept at the registered office or principal place of business.

Taxes and Fees

Annual Statements. All corporations must file a biennial report. The cost of the report

---

[*] In jurisprudence, a "natural person" is a human being perceptible through the senses and subject to physical laws, as opposed to an "artificial person," i.e., an organization that the law treats for some purposes as if it were a person distinct from its members or owners.

is $100 for domestic corporations and $200 for foreign corporations. The report must be filed by January 2 of the filing year, and every two years thereafter. It is delinquent if not filed before February 1.

Income Tax Rate. Rates range from 1 to 9.4 percent of taxable income.

S Corporation

S corporation status is recognized by the State of Alaska. Further, Alaska does not have a personal income tax; thus, shareholders will not be taxed on corporate earnings. A separate state election from the federal election is not required.

License Requirements

Alaska requires most businesses to obtain a license and pay a fee if operating in the state. Please check with the state to make sure your business is complying with the license requirements for your particular profession. Business licenses typically cost $50 and must be filed every two years.

For more information on taxes, visit www.revenue.state.ak.us

For additional or updated information, visit www.commerce.state.ak.us/occ

Mailing Address

Department of Commerce
Attention: Corporations Section
P.O. Box 110808
Juneau, AK 99811-0808
Tel: (907) 465-2530
Fax: (907) 465-3257

Arizona

Corporate Name Endings

The name must contain the word "Association," "Corporation," "Company," "Incorporated," "Limited," or an abbreviation thereof. The name shall not contain language stating or implying that the corporation is organized for an unlawful purpose. The name shall be distinguishable from the name of domestic, nonprofit, or foreign corporations authorized to transact business; the reserved or registered name of a corporation; the fictitious name of a foreign corporation; the name of a limited liability company or foreign limited liability company; the partnership name of a limited liability partnership, registered limited liability partnership, or registered foreign limited liability partnership.

Corporation Requirements

Director Information

- Minimum number: One or more.

- Residence requirements: No provision.

- Age requirements: None.

- Directors are required to be listed in the Articles of Incorporation.

Officer Information. Officers are not required to be listed in the Articles of Incorporation.

Stock Information. An increase in shares or par value does not affect initial filing fees.

Corporate Records. The following items must be kept with the corporation records: the Articles of Incorporation and all amendments; the current bylaws; minutes of share-holders' meetings; records of shareholders' actions taken without a meeting; written communications to shareholders within the past three years; a list of names and business addresses of current directors and officers; the most recent annual report; and any agreements among shareholders.

Taxes and Fees

Annual Statements. An annual report and certificate of disclosure must be filed each year. The filing fee is $45. The statement must be filed with the Corporation Commission by the due date (typically three months after the original formation date of the corporation in Arizona).

Income Tax Rate. The income tax rate is 7.968 percent of net income or $50, whichever is greater. The minimum tax is $50.

S Corporation

S corporation status is recognized by the State of Arizona. A separate state election is not required.

License Requirements

Certain types of businesses in the state are required to obtain a license and pay a fee. The following is partial list.

- Agricultural marketing cooperatives
- Auto dealers
- Barbers
- Citrus brokers or merchants
- Contractors
- Cosmetologists
- Employment agencies

- Fruit and vegetable dealers and shippers
- Insurance personnel
- Real estate brokers and salespeople
- Securities dealers

Please check with the state to make sure your business is complying with the license requirements for your particular profession.

For more information on taxes, visit www.revenue.state.az.us

For additional or updated information, visit www.azsos.gov

Mailing Address

Secretary of State
1700 West Washington Street,
7th Floor
Phoenix, AZ 85007-2888
Tel: (602) 542-4285 or (800) 458-5842

Arkansas
Corporate Name Endings

The name must contain the word "Corporation," "Incorporated," "Company," "Limited," or an abbreviation thereof. The name may not contain language stating or implying the corporation is organized for other purposes, and must be distinguishable from names in use by certain other enumerated entities.

Corporation Requirements
Director Information

- Minimum number: Not less than three, unless there are only one or two shareholders of record; then the number of directors may be less than three but not less than the number of shareholders.
- Residence requirements: No provision.
- Age requirements: None.
- Directors are not required to be listed in the Articles of Incorporation.

Officer Information. Officers are not required to be listed in the Articles of Incorporation.

Stock Information. An increase in shares or par value does not affect initial filing fees.

Corporate Records. The Articles of Incorporation, bylaws, and all amendments must be kept at the principal place of business or transfer agent's office within the state. Additionally, resolutions by the board of directors; minutes of all shareholders' meetings; all written communications to shareholders during the last three years; a list of names and business addresses of current directors and officers; and the most recent annual franchise tax report must be maintained. Further, the shareholder lists must be kept at a principal place of business or transfer agent's office within the state.

Taxes and Fees
Annual Statements

- The annual statement, called the Franchise Tax Report, is due by June 1.
- The franchise tax rate is 0.27 percent of the company's capital stock multiplied by the ratio of the corporation's property in Arkansas to its total property. The minimum tax is $50. Corporations without authorized capital stock

pay $100. Shares with no par value are assessed at $25 each.

Income Tax Rate. Income tax is due on net income attributable to business in Arkansas. Tax rates range from 1 to 6.5 percent.

S Corporation

S corporation status is recognized by the State of Arkansas. A separate state election is required.

License Requirements

Certain types of businesses in the state are required to obtain a license and pay a fee. The following is partial list.

- Accountants
- Barbers
- Child-care facilities
- Contractors
- Cosmetologists
- Electricians
- Food service establishments
- Insurance: agents, brokers, solicitors, and adjusters
- Nursing homes
- Real estate brokers and salespeople
- Surveyors
- Travel bureaus or services

Please check with the state to make sure your business is complying with the license requirements for your particular profession.

For more information on taxes, visit www.arkansas.gov/dfa/

For additional or updated information, visit www.sosweb.state.ar.us

Mailing Address

Secretary of State
Corporation Division
State Capitol, Room 256
Little Rock, AR 72201
Tel: (501) 682-1010

California
Corporate Name Endings

The name must not be likely to mislead the public, be the same as, or resemble so closely as to lead to deception, the name of a domestic or qualified foreign corporation, a name under reservation, or the registered or assumed name of a foreign corporation. The name would need Superintendent of Bank's approval if it contained the words "Bank," "Trust," or "Trustee."

Corporate Requirements
Director Information

- Minimum number: Not less than three, unless there are only one or two shareholders of record; then the number of directors may be less than three but not less than the number of shareholders.
- Residence requirements: No provision.
- Age requirements: None.
- Directors are not required to be listed in the Articles of Incorporation.

Officer Information. Officers are not required to be listed in the Articles of Incorporation.

Stock Information. An increase in shares or par value does not affect initial filing fees.

Corporate Records. An original or a copy of bylaws must be kept at the principal executive office or principal business office in the State of California. The minutes of directors' and shareholders' meetings must be kept at the principal office.

Taxes and Fees
Annual Statements

- Domestic corporations must file with the Secretary of State within 90 days after filing the Articles of Incorporation. A statement of domestic stock corporation must be filed annually by the end of the calendar month during which the original Articles of Incorporation were filed. The cost is $20.

- Foreign corporations must file a biennial statement by foreign corporation. The cost is $20.

Income Tax Rate

- California imposes a franchise tax on both California corporations (domestic) and non-California corporations (foreign) for the privilege of doing business in the state. The franchise tax is actually a tax of net income; the rate is 8.84 percent of net income for corporations. S corporations still must pay the franchise tax; the rate is 1.5 percent of net income.

- California imposes a minimum franchise tax of $800. So, even if your corporation does not have net income, it still must pay this minimum tax. The minimum tax does not have to be paid during the corporation's first year; however, taxes based on income must be paid during this first year.

S Corporation

S corporation status is recognized by the State of California; however, the corporation is still required to pay franchise tax at a rate of 1.5 percent of net income. A separate state election is required.

License Requirements

California may require that you obtain a business license and pay a licensing fee based on your business type or profession. Please check with the state to make sure your business is complying with the license requirements for your particular profession.

For more information on taxes, visit www.ftb.ca.gov or www.taxes.ca.gov

For additional or updated information, visit www.ss.ca.gov

Mailing Address

Secretary of State
1500 11th Street
Sacramento, CA 95814
Tel: (916) 657-5448

Colorado
Corporate Name Endings

The name must contain the word "Corporation," "Company," "Incorporated," "Limited," or an abbreviation thereof. The name must not imply it is organized for any purpose not stated in its chapter or Articles of Incorporation. The name must not be the same as or deceptively similar to the name of any domestic or foreign corporation, limited liability company, limited partnership, and other business entities formed in Colorado.

Corporation Requirements

Director Information

- Minimum number: One or more.

- Residence requirements: No provision.

- Age requirements: Directors must be a natural person[*] at least 18 years of age.

- Directors are not required to be listed in the Articles of Incorporation.

Officer Information. Officers are not required to be listed in the Articles of Incorporation.

Stock Information. An increase in shares or par value does not affect initial filing fees.

Corporate Records. The Articles of Incorporation, bylaws, minutes of shareholders' meetings, all written communications to shareholders for past three years, the names and addresses of directors and officers, a copy of most recent corporate report, and all financial statements for the preceding three years must be kept at the corporation's principal office.

[*] In jurisprudence, a "natural person" is a human being perceptible through the senses and subject to physical laws, as opposed to an "artificial person," i.e., an organization that the law treats for some purposes as if it were a person distinct from its members or owners.

Taxes and Fees

Annual Statements. Corporations must file an annual report called the Periodic Report. The due date is determined by the original incorporation date of the business entity. The cost for domestic corporations is $10 if e-filed or $25 for paper filings. The cost for foreign corporations is $50 if e-filed or $100 for paper filings.

Income Tax Rate. The income tax rate is 4.63 percent of Colorado net income.

S Corporation

S corporation status is recognized by the State of Colorado. A separate state election from the federal election is not required.

License Requirements

Certain types of businesses in the state are required to obtain a license and pay a fee. The following is a partial list:

- Architects
- Brokers
- Chiropractors
- Dentists
- Engineers
- Family therapists
- Geologists
- Nurses
- Optometrists
- Pharmacists
- Physical therapists
- Veterinarians

Please check with the state to make sure your business is complying with the license requirements for your particular profession.

For more information on taxes, visit www.dora.state.co.us/financial-services or www.revenue.state.co.us

For additional or updated information, visit www.sos.state.co.us

Mailing Address

Secretary of State
1560 Broadway, Suite 200
Denver, CO 80202-5169
Tel: (303) 894-2200
Fax: (303) 869-4867

Connecticut
Corporate Name Endings

The name of the corporation must be in English letters or numbers and must contain one of the following words: "Corporation," "Company," "Incorporated," "Limited," "Societa per Azioni," or contain the abbreviation "Corp.," "Inc.," "Co.," "Ltd.," or "S.p.A." The name may not imply it is organized for any purpose not permitted in its certificate. The name must be distinguishable from the name of a domestic corporation; a reserved or registered corporate name; the fictitious name of a foreign corporation; the name of a nonprofit corporation; the name of any domestic or foreign nonstock corporation; or other business entities filed with the state.

Corporation Requirements
Director Information

- Minimum number: One or more.

- Residence requirements: No provision.

- Age requirements: None.

- Directors are not required to be listed in the Articles of Incorporation.

Officer Information. Officers are not required to be listed in the Articles of Incorporation.

Stock Information. An increase in the shares may cause an increase in initial filing fees.

Corporate Records. The certificate of incorporation, bylaws, certain resolutions adopted by the board of directors, minutes of all shareholders' meetings, records of all action taken by shareholders without a meeting for the past three years, names and addresses of current directors and officers, and the most recent annual report must be kept at the principal office of the corporation.

Taxes and Fees

Annual Statements. Domestic corporations must pay a fee of $75 with each annual report. Foreign corporations must pay a $300 fee. New domestic corporations file their first report within 30 days after an organizational meeting.

Income Tax Rate. The income rate is equal to 7.5 percent of net income.

S Corporation

S corporation status is recognized by the State of Connecticut. A separate state election from the federal election is not required.

License Requirements

Certain types of businesses in the state are required to obtain a license and pay a fee. The following is partial list:

- Accountants
- Architects
- Attorneys
- Barbers
- Child day-care services
- Collection agencies
- Electrical workers
- Fund-raising organizations
- Home improvement contractors
- Insurance
- Investment
- Professional engineering services
- Real estate
- Television
- Radio, stereo, and receiving equipment service
- Repair vending machines and operators (food and drinks)

Please check with the state to make sure your business is complying with the license requirements for your particular profession.

For more information on taxes, visit www.ct.gov/drs

For additional or updated information, visit www.concord.sots.ct.gov

Mailing Address

Secretary of State
30 Trinity Street
P. O. Box 150470
Hartford, CT 06106-0470
Tel: (860) 566-4128
Fax: (860) 509-6069

Delaware
Corporate Name Endings

The corporate name ending must contain the word "Association," "Company," Corporation," "Club," "Foundation," "Fund," "Incorporated," "Institute," "Society," "Union," "Syndicate," "Limited," or the abbreviation "Co.," "Corp.," "Inc.," "Ltd.," or words or abbreviations of like import in other languages. The name must be distinguishable from the names of other corporations organized, reserved, or registered as a foreign corporation under the laws of Delaware. Use of word "Trust" is prohibited except for corporations under supervision of the Bank Commissioner.

Corporation Requirements
Director Information

- Minimum number: One or more.
- Residence requirements: No provision.
- Age requirements: None.
- Directors are not required to be listed in the Articles of Incorporation.

Officer Information. Officers are not required to be listed in the Articles of Incorporation.

Stock Information. An increase in shares or par value does affect initial filing fees.

Corporate Records. A stock ledger and basic corporate records must be kept at the principal office of the corporation.

Taxes and Fees
Annual Statements

- The annual statements for corporations are sent out to the registered agent in

December and January. The payment is due by March 1. The fee is $50, consisting of a $30 franchise tax and a $20 annual statement fee. The franchise tax is based on the number of shares and the par value, and if the number of shares is above 3,000, the annual fee may increase.

- The annual statements for LLCs are sent out to the registered agent in March and April. The payment is due June 1. The fee is $100.

Franchise Tax Rate

- Corporations that are not located in Delaware do not pay an income tax.
- A schedule of rates based on the number of authorized shares is as follows:
  - Up to and including 3,000: $30
  - Over 3,000 up to and including 5,000 shares: $50
  - Over 5,000 up to and including 10,000 shares: $90
  - Over 10,000 shares, $90 plus $50 for each 10,000 shares or part thereof over 10,000
- If your number of shares is above 3,000, the alternative method may provide a lower tax. The formula for the alternative method is:

Divide total gross assets by total issued shares carrying to six decimal places (this is your "assumed par"). If the assumed par is the same or greater than the stated par value, multiply the assumed par by the total authorized shares (this is your "assumed par value capital"). If assumed par value capital is greater than $1,000,000, round up to the next million and multiply $200 per million (e.g., $10,002,000 = 11 × $200). If less than $1,000,000 divide by $1,000,000 and multiply by $200. Should your assumed par be less than the stated par value, multiply the authorized stock by its stated par value and continue with calculation. Each no-par share must be considered as having a value of $1. The minimum tax is $30, with a maximum tax of $150,000.

Income Tax. The income tax rate for corporations actually located in Delaware is 8.7 percent.

S Corporation

S corporation status is recognized by the State of Delaware. A separate state election from the federal election is not required.

License Requirements

Delaware requires some businesses to obtain a license and pay a fee if you are operating in the state. Please check with the state to make sure your business is complying with the license requirements for your particular profession.

For more information on taxes, visit www.state.de.us/revenue/default.shtml

For additional and updated information, visit www.state.de.us/corp

Mailing Address

Secretary of State
Division of Corporations
P.O. Box 898
Dover, DE 19903
Tel: (302) 739-3073
Fax: (302) 739-3812

District of Columbia
Corporate Name Endings

The name must contain the word "Corporation," "Company," "Incorporated," "Limited," or an abbreviation thereof. The name shall not be the same as or deceptively similar to the name of a domestic corporation, authorized foreign corporation, or reserved name already existing in the District.

Corporation Requirements
Director Information

- Minimum number: One or more.
- Residence requirements: No provision.
- Age requirements: None.
- Directors are required to be listed in the Articles of Incorporation.

Officer Information. Officers are not required to be listed in the Articles of Incorporation.

Stock Information. An increase in shares or par value does not affect initial filing fees.

Corporate Records. A list of shareholders must be kept at the principal office.

Taxes and Fees

Annual Statements. Corporations must file reports with the Mayor by April 15 of the year after its incorporation and on or before April 15 of each second year thereafter. The biennial report fee is $200 for both domestic and foreign corporations.

Income Tax Rate. The District of Columbia has a tax rate of 9.975 percent on income earned in the District. The minimum tax is $100.

S Corporation

The District does not recognize the S corporation election.

License Requirements

The District of Columbia requires most businesses to obtain a license and pay a fee if operating in the District. Please check with the District to make sure your business is complying with the license requirements for your particular profession.

For more information on taxes, visit www.brc.dc.gov/tax/tax.asp

Mailing Address

John A. Wilson Buildings
1350 Pennsylvania Avenue, NW
Washington, DC 20004

Florida
Corporate Name Endings

The name must contain the word "Corporation," "Company," "Incorporated," or an abbreviation thereof. The name may not contain language stating or implying that the corporation is organized for purposes other than that permitted by Florida law or the Articles of Incorporation. The name must be such as will distinguish it from another corporation formed in the state.

Corporation Requirements
Director Information

- Minimum number: One or more.
- Residence requirements: No provision.

- Age requirements: Directors must be a natural person[*] at least 18 years of age.
- Directors are not required to be listed in the Articles of Incorporation.

Officer Information. Officers are not required to be listed in the Articles of Incorporation.

Stock Information. An increase in shares or par value does not affect initial filing fees.

Corporate Records. Corporate records must be kept; however, they are not required to be stored at a specific location.

Taxes and Fees

Annual Statements. All businesses are required to file a Uniform Business Report. The annual filing fee is $150. Reports are due January 1 and become delinquent if not filed by May 1.

Corporate Income/Franchise Taxes. Florida imposes a franchise tax on foreign and domestic corporations for the privilege of doing business in Florida. The tax rate is 5.5 percent of net income. The first $5,000 of net income for the year is exempt.

S Corporation

- S corporation status is recognized by the State of Florida. Further, Florida does not have a personal income tax; thus, shareholders would not be taxed on cor-

porate earnings. A separate state election from the federal election is not required.
- For the first year in which an entity qualifies as an S corporation, the company must file the informational portion of Form F-1120, the Florida Corporate Income/Franchise tax return. In subsequent years, S corporations are only required to file Florida Form F-1120 if the S corporation has federal taxable income.

License Requirements

Florida requires some businesses to obtain a license and pay a fee if operating in the state. Please check with the state to make sure your business is complying with the license requirements for your particular profession.

For more information on taxes, visit www.state.fl.us/dor

For additional or updated information, visit ccfcorp.dos.state.fl.us

Mailing Address

Secretary of State
Division of Corporations
P.O. Box 6327
Tallahassee, FL 32314
Tel: (850) 245-6052

Georgia
Corporate Name Endings

The name shall include the word "Corporation," "Company," "Incorporated," "Limited," or an abbreviation thereof. The name shall not exceed 80 characters, including spaces and punctuation. The name may not contain language stating or implying

[*] In jurisprudence, a "natural person" is a human being perceptible through the senses and subject to physical laws, as opposed to an "artificial person," i.e., an organization that the law treats for some purposes as if it were a person distinct from its members or owners.

the corporation is organized for a purpose other than that permitted by Georgia law or the Articles of Incorporation. The name may not contain anything that, in the reasonable judgment of the Secretary of State, is obscene. The name must be distinguishable from the other corporation names in the state.

Corporation Requirements

Director Information

- Minimum number: One or more.
- Residence requirements: No provision.
- Age requirements: Directors must be a natural person[*] at least 18 years of age.
- Directors are not required to be listed in the Articles of Incorporation.

Officer Information. Officers are not required to be listed in the Articles of Incorporation.

Stock Information. An increase in shares or par value does not affect initial filing fees.

Corporate Records. Corporate records must be kept; however, they are not required to be stored at a specific location.

Taxes and Fees

Annual Statements. All businesses must file an Annual Registration Form. The cost is $15. The form is due within 90 days of incorporating and annually by April 1.

[*] In jurisprudence, a "natural person" is a human being perceptible through the senses and subject to physical laws, as opposed to an "artificial person," i.e., an organization that the law treats for some purposes as if it were a person distinct from its members or owners.

Income Tax Rate. The income tax rate is 6 percent of net taxable income.

Net Worth Tax. Net worth, including issued capital stock, paid in surplus, is taxed by the state as listed below and earned by surplus. The net worth is presumed to be the net worth as disclosed on the corporation's books and as reflected on the return required to be filed annually by the corporation. No par value shares have the value fixed for stock by the Commissioner from the required return and any other information available to Commissioner.

Net worth over	But not over	Tax is
$ 0	$ 10,000	$ 10
10,000	25,000	20
25,000	40,000	40
40,000	60,000	60
60,000	80,000	75
80,000	100,000	100
100,000	150,000	125
150,000	200,000	150
500,000	300,000	200
300,000	500,000	250
500,000	750,000	300
750,000	1,000,000	500
1,000,000	2,000,000	750
2,000,000	4,000,000	1,000
4,000,000	6,000,000	1,250
6,000,000	8,000,000	1,500
8,000,000	10,000,000	1,750
10,000,000	12,000,000	2,000
12,000,000	14,000,000	2,500
14,000,000	16,000,000	3,000
16,000,000	18,000,000	3,500
18,000,000	20,000,000	4,000
20,000,000	22,000,000	4,500
22,000,000	over	5,000

S Corporation

S corporation status is recognized by the State of Georgia as long as all shareholders are subject to income tax in the state. Non-resident shareholders must execute a consent agreement to pay Georgia income tax on their portion of the income in order for the S corporation to be recognized for Georgia purposes. A separate state election from the federal election is not required.

License Requirements

Georgia requires most businesses to obtain a license and pay a fee if operating in the state. Please check with the state to make sure your business is complying with the license requirements for your particular profession.

For more information on taxes, visit www2.state.ga.us/departments/dor/

For additional or updated information, visit www.sos.state.ga.us/corporations

Mailing Address

Secretary of State
Corporations Division
2 Martin Luther King, Jr. Drive S.E.
Suite 315, West Tower
Atlanta, GA 30334
Tel: (404) 656-2817
Fax: (404) 657-2248

Hawaii
Corporate Name Endings

The name shall contain the word "Corporation," "Incorporated," "Limited," or an abbreviation thereof. The name shall not be the same as, or substantially identical to, the name of any other corporation, partnership, or foreign corporation or partnership existing or authorized to transact business within the state.

Corporation Requirements
Director Information

- Minimum number: Not less than three, unless there are only one or two shareholders of record; then the number of directors may be less than three but not less than the number of shareholders.
- Residence requirements: At least one director shall be a state resident.
- Age requirements: None.
- Directors are required to be listed in the Articles of Incorporation.

Officer Information. Officers are required to be listed in the Articles of Incorporation.

Stock Information. An increase in shares or par value does affect initial filing fees.

Corporate Records. Corporate records, including the index of officers and annual reports, are public information.

Taxes and Fees

Annual Statements. Domestic and foreign corporations must file an annual report with the Department of Commerce and Consumer Affairs. Domestic corporations must file by March 31 with a fee of $25. Foreign corporations must file by June 30 with a fee of $125.

Income Tax Rate. The income tax rates are 4.4 percent of the first $25,000 of taxable income, 5.4 percent of taxable income over $25,000 but not over $100,000, and 6.4 percent on all taxable income over $100,000.

S Corporation

S corporation status is recognized by the State of Hawaii. Nonresident shareholders must execute a consent agreement to pay Hawaii income tax on their portion of the income in order for the S corporation to be recognized for Hawaii purposes. A separate state election from the federal election is not required.

License Requirements

Hawaii requires most businesses to obtain a license and pay a fee if operating in the state. Please check with the state to make sure your business is complying with the license requirements for your particular profession.

For more information on taxes, visit www.state.hi.us/tax

For additional or updated information, visit www.hawaii.gov/dcca

Mailing Address

Department of Commerce and
Consumer Affairs
Business Registration Division
P.O. Box 40
Honolulu, HI 96810
Tel: (808) 586-2744
Fax: (808) 586-2733

Idaho
Corporate Name Endings

The name must contain the word "Corporation," "Company," "Incorporated," "Limited," or an abbreviation thereof, provided that if "Company" or "Co." is used, it may not be immediately preceded by the word "and" or the symbol "&." The name may not contain any word or phrase indicating or implying the corporation is organized for any pur-

pose other than one or more of the purposes contained in its Articles of Incorporation. The name may not be the same as or deceptively similar to that of a domestic corporation or a qualified foreign corporation or a reserved name, with qualified exceptions.

Corporation Requirements
Director Information

- Minimum number: One or more.
- Residence requirements: No provision.
- Age requirements: None.
- Directors are not required to be listed in the Articles of Incorporation.

Officer Information. Officers are not required to be listed in the Articles of Incorporation.

Stock Information. An increase in shares or par value does not affect initial filing fees.

Corporate Records. A corporation must keep minutes, a record of shareholders, and records of account, at its registered office.

Taxes and Fees

Annual Statements. Domestic and qualified foreign corporations must file an annual report. The reports should be filed with the Secretary of State between July 1 and November 30 of the year. The first annual report of a corporation must be filed between July 1 and November 30 of the state fiscal year (July 1 to June 30), which next succeeds the state fiscal year in which its Articles of Incorporation or its application for certificate of authority was filed. There is no filing fee if the report is filed by the due date.

Income Tax Rate. The income tax rate is 7.6 percent of taxable Idaho income. A minimum tax of $20 is imposed on all corporations.

S Corporation

S corporation status is recognized by the State of Idaho. A separate state election from the federal election is not required.

License Requirements

Idaho requires most businesses to obtain a license and pay a fee if operating in the state. Please check with the state to make sure your business is complying with the license requirements for your particular profession.

For more information on taxes, visit www.tax.idaho.gov

For additional or updated information, visit www.idsos.state.id.us

Mailing Address

Secretary of State
700 West Jefferson #203
Boise, ID 83720-0080
Tel: (208) 334-2300
Fax: (208) 334-2282

Illinois
Corporate Name Endings

The name shall contain the word "Corporation," "Company," "Incorporated," "Limited," or an abbreviation thereof. The name shall not contain any word or phrase indicating or implying it is organized to conduct the business of insurance, assurance, indemnity, acceptance of savings deposit, banking, or corporate fiduciary. The name shall be distinguishable from the name of any domestic or foreign corporation authorized to transact business or a name exclusive right to which is, at the time, reserved or registered.

Corporation Requirements
Director Information

- Minimum number: One or more.
- Residence requirements: No provision.
- Age requirements: None.
- Directors are not required to be listed in the Articles of Incorporation.

Officer Information. Officers are not required to be listed in the Articles of Incorporation.

Stock Information. An increase in shares may cause an increase in initial filing fees.

Corporate Records. The corporation must keep a record of shareholders at its registered office or principal place of business within the state.

Taxes and Fees
Annual Statements

- The annual franchise tax is computed by multiplying your corporation's paid-in capital by the franchise tax rate of 0.1 percent. The minimum tax is $25.

- An annual report form must be filed each year within 60 days immediately proceeding the first day of the anniversary month of incorporating (or in the case of a corporation that has established an extended filing month, the extended filing month of the corporation each year). The filing fee is $25.

Income Tax Rate. The income tax rate is 4.8 percent of the corporation's net income.

In addition, Illinois assesses a personal property replacement tax based on net income (2.5 percent for corporations, 1.5 percent for S corporations and all other incorporated entities) on all businesses.

S Corporations

S corporation status is recognized by the State of Illinois; however, S corporations are subject to Illinois's personal property replacement income tax of 1.5 percent. A separate state election from the federal election is not required.

License Requirements

Illinois requires many businesses to obtain a license and pay a fee if operating in the state. Please check with the state to make sure your business is complying with the license requirements for your particular profession.

For more information on taxes, visit www.revenue.state.il.us

For additional or updated information, visit www.sos.state.il.us

Mailing Address

Secretary of State
Business Services Dept.
501 S. 2nd St., Room 328
Springfield, IL 62756
Tel: (217) 782-6961

Indiana
Corporate Name Endings

The name must include the word "Corporation," "Incorporated," "Company," "Limited," or an abbreviation thereof. The name cannot imply purpose or power not possessed by corporations organized under Indiana Business Corporation Law or in the Articles of Incorporation. The name must be distinguishable from a reserved name or the name of any other corporation then existing under the laws of the state, unless consent of the other user is obtained.

Corporation Requirements
Director Information

- Minimum number: One or more.
- Residence requirements: No provision.
- Age requirements: None.
- Directors are not required to be listed in the Articles of Incorporation.

Officer Information. Officers are not required to be listed in the Articles of Incorporation.

Stock Information. An increase in shares or par value does not affect initial filing fees.

Corporate Records. The current Articles of Incorporation, the bylaws, minutes of shareholders' and directors' meetings, written communications to shareholders within the last three years, names and addresses of current directors and officers, and the most recent annual report must be kept with the corporation records.

Taxes and Fees

Biennial Statements. Every corporation must file a business entity report every two years. The filing fee is $30. The first biennial report must be filed in the second year following the calendar year in which a corporation was incorporated.

Income Tax Rate. The tax rate is 3.4 percent of Adjusted Gross Income from Indiana sources plus a 4.5 percent supplemental net income tax.

S Corporation

S corporation status is recognized by the State of Indiana; however, the corporation must withhold taxes on amounts paid to nonresidents. A separate state election from the federal election is not required.

License Requirements

Indiana requires many businesses to obtain a license and pay a fee if operating in the state. Please check with the state to make sure your business is complying with the license requirements for your particular profession.

For more information on taxes, visit www.state.in.us/dor

For additional or updated information, visit www.in.gov/sos

Mailing Address

Secretary of State
Business Services Division
302 W. Washington Street
Room E018
Indianapolis, IN 46204
Tel: (317) 232-6576
Fax: (317) 233-3387

Iowa

Corporate Name Endings

The name must contain the word "Corporation," "Incorporated," "Company," "Limited," or the abbreviation "Corp.," "Inc.," "Co.," "Ltd.," or words or abbreviations of like import in another language.

Corporation Requirements

Director Information

- Minimum number: One or more.
- Residence requirements: No provision.
- Age requirements: None.
- Directors are not required to be listed in the Articles of Incorporation.

Officer Information. Officers are not required to be listed in the Articles of Incorporation.

Stock Information. An increase in shares or par value does not affect initial filing fees.

Corporate Records. A corporation shall maintain its records in written form or in another form capable of conversion into written form within a reasonable time.

Taxes and Fees

Biennial Statements. A report must be filed with the Secretary of State every two years. The first report must be delivered to the Secretary of State between January 1 and April 1 of the year following the calendar year in which a domestic corporation was incorporated or a foreign corporation was authorized to transact business. The fee for filing the report is $45; however, online filings are discounted to $30.

Income Tax Rate

- First $25,000: 6 percent
- $25,000 to $100,000: 8 percent
- $100,000 to $250,000: 10 percent
- $250,000 or more: 12 percent

S Corporation

S corporation status is recognized by the State of Iowa. A separate state election from the federal election is not required.

License Requirements

Iowa requires many businesses to obtain a license and pay a fee if operating in the state. Please check with the state to make sure your business is complying with the license requirements for your particular profession.

For more information on taxes, visit www.state.ia.us/tax/index.html

For additional or updated information, visit www.sos.state.ia.us

Mailing Address

Secretary of State
Corporations Division
First Floor, Lucas Building
321 E. 12th Street
Des Moines, IA 50319
Tel: (515) 281-5204
Fax: (515) 242-5953

Kansas
Corporate Name Endings

The name shall contain the word "association," "Church," "College," "Company," "Corporation," "Club," "Foundation," "Fund," "Incorporated," "Institute," "Society," "Union," "Syndicate," "Limited," or the abbreviation "Co.," "Corp.," "Inc.," or "Ltd." The name shall be distinguishable upon the records of the Secretary of State from names of other corporations, limited liability companies, and limited partnerships.

Corporation Requirements
Director Information

- Minimum number: One or more.
- Residence requirements: No provision.
- Age requirements: None.
- Directors are not required to be listed in the Articles of Incorporation.

Officer Information. Officers are not required to be listed in the Articles of Incorporation.

Stock Information. An increase in shares or par value does not affect initial filing fees.

Corporate Records. The corporation's bylaws, stock register, books of account, minutes of shareholders' and directors' meetings, and other books must be available for shareholder inspection.

Taxes and Fees

Annual Statements. An annual statement must be filed each year by domestic and foreign corporations organized for profit. The tax rate is $1 per $1,000 of shareholder's equity attributable to Kansas. The minimum tax is $20, with a maximum tax of $2,500.

Income Tax Rate. The tax rate is 4 percent of taxable income, plus a surtax of 3.35 percent of Kansas's taxable income in excess of $50,000 for all tax years.

S Corporation

S corporation status is recognized by the State of Kansas. A separate state election from the federal election is not required.

License Requirements

Kansas requires that you obtain a license and pay a fee if operating certain types of businesses in the state. The following is a partial list:

- Abstracters
- Automobile clubs
- Barbers
- Beauty shops
- Engineers
- Nursery dealers
- Real estate brokers
- Security brokers
- Transient merchants

Please check with the state to make sure your business is complying with the license requirements for your particular profession.

For more information on taxes, visit www.ksrevenue.org

For additional or updated information, visit www.kssos.org

Mailing Address

Secretary of State
Memorial Hall, 1st Floor
120 SW 10th Avenue
Topeka, KS 66612-1594
Tel: (785) 296-4564

Kentucky
Corporate Name Endings

The corporate name must be distinguishable upon records of the Secretary of State from the name of existing business entities filed with the Secretary of State. The corporation may use one of these names if another corporation consents in writing or in certain other enumerated cases. The name must include the word "Corporation," "Incorporated," "Company," "Limited," or an abbreviation thereof. The name shall not contain language stating or implying the corporation is organized for a purpose other than that permitted by the act or the Articles of Incorporation.

Corporation Requirements
Director Information
- Minimum number: One or more.
- Residence requirements: No provision.
- Age requirements: None.
- Directors are not required to be listed in the Articles of Incorporation.

Officer Information. Officers are not required to be listed in the Articles of Incorporation.

Stock Information. An increase in shares may cause an increase in initial filing fees.

Corporate Records. The Articles of Incorporation, bylaws, minutes of shareholders' and directors' meetings, financial statements furnished for the past three years, a list of directors' and officers' names and addresses, and the most recent annual report must be kept with the corporation's records.

Taxes and Fees

Annual Statements. Statements must be filed with the Secretary of State by the last day of June annually, setting forth the corporation's name, the state where it is incorporated, the address of the registered office of the corporation, the registered agent's name, and the names and business addresses of directors and principal officers. The fee is $15.

Income Tax Rate. The tax rate is 4 percent of the first $25,000 of taxable net income, 5 percent of the next $25,000, 6 percent of the next $50,000, 7 percent on the next $150,000, and 8.25 percent of all income over $250,000.

S Corporation

S corporation status is recognized by the State of Kentucky. A separate state election from the federal election is not required.

License Requirements

Kentucky requires that you obtain a license and pay a fee if operating certain types of businesses in the state. The following is a partial list:

- Agents
- Architects
- Auctioneers
- Barbers
- Companies
- Driver
- Engineers
- Insurance
- Loan
- Pharmacists
- Plumbers
- Real estate
- Salespeople
- Schools
- Training

Please check with the state to make sure your business is complying with the license requirements for your particular profession.

For more information on taxes, visit www.revenue.ky.gov

For additional or updated information, visit www.sos.state.ky.us

Mailing Address

Office of Secretary of State
700 Capital Avenue, Suite 152,
State Capitol
Frankfort, KY 40601
Tel: (502) 564-3490
Fax: (502) 564-5687

Louisiana
Corporate Name Endings

The name of the corporation shall contain the word "Corporation," "Incorporated," "Limited," or an abbreviation thereof. The name may contain the word "Company" or the abbreviation "Co.," if "Company" or "Co." is not immediately preceded by the word "and" or the symbol "&." The name must not be the same, or deceptively similar to, any other reserved or registered names of another corporation. The name cannot use certain enumerated words relating to banking, savings and loans, or insurance.

Corporation Requirements

Director Information

- Minimum number: Not less than three, unless there are only one or two shareholders of record; then the number of directors may be less than three but not less than the number of shareholders.
- Residence requirements: No provision.
- Age requirements: None.
- Directors are required to be listed in the Articles of Incorporation.

Officer Information. Officers are not required to be listed in the Articles of Incorporation.

Stock Information. An increase in shares or par value does not affect initial filing fees.

Corporate Records. Books and accounts showing the amounts of the corporation's assets and liabilities, and minutes of the meetings of shareholders and directors, must be kept with the corporate records.

Taxes and Fees

Annual Statements. Annual reports must be filed with the Secretary of State by the anniversary date of the corporation's initial filing with the state. The filing fee is $25.

Income Tax Rate. The State of Louisiana taxes include components for income and franchise taxes. The income tax is based upon the rates listed below. The franchise tax is based upon capital. Franchise tax rates are 1.5 percent for the first $300,000 in capital and 3 percent for any capital thereafter. The minimum franchise tax is $10.

Louisiana taxable income over	But not over	Tax rate is
$ 0	$ 25,000	4 percent
25,000	50,000	5 percent
50,000	100,000	6 percent
100,000	200,000	7 percent
200,000	over	8 percent

S Corporation

S corporation status is recognized by the State of Louisiana. A separate state election from the federal election is not required.

License Requirements

Louisiana requires many businesses to obtain a license and pay a fee if operating in the state. Please check with the state to make sure your business is complying with the license requirements for your particular profession.

For more information on taxes, visit www.rev.state.la.us

For additional or updated information, visit www.sec.state.la.us

Mailing Address

Secretary of State
Corporations Division
P.O. Box 94125
Baton Rouge, LA 70804-9125
Tel: (225) 342-4479

Maine

Corporate Name Endings

The name cannot be any name that is the same as, or deceptively similar to, the name of any domestic corporation or qualified foreign corporation without authorization. The name cannot utilize a reserved name. The name shall not contain any word or phrase indicating it is organized for any purpose not permitted by the act.

Corporation Requirements

Director Information

- Minimum number: Not less than three, unless there are only one or two shareholders of record; then the number of directors may be less than three but not less than the number of shareholders.
- Residence requirements: No provision.
- Age requirements: None.
- Directors are required to be listed in the Articles of Incorporation.

Officer Information. Officers are not required to be listed in the Articles of Incorporation.

Stock Information. An increase in shares may cause an increase in initial filing fees.

Corporate Records. A full and complete list of shareholders must be kept at the registered office or principal place of business.

Taxes and Fees

Annual Statements. An annual report must be filed with the Secretary of State by June 1. The filing fee is $60.

Income Tax Rate. A tax is imposed on Maine net income (MNI) of taxable corporations, except insurance companies and financial institutions, equal to 3.5 percent of MNI not over $25,000; 7.93 percent of MNI over $25,000 but not over $75,000; 8.33 percent of MNI over $75,000 but not over $250,000; and 8.93 percent of MNI over $250,000.

S Corporation

S corporation status is recognized by the State of Maine. A separate state election from the federal election is not required.

License Requirements

Maine requires that you obtain a license and pay a fee if operating certain types of businesses in the state. The following is a partial list:

- Attorneys
- Auctioneers
- Commercial fishing commercial shellfish and marine worms
- Convalescent homes and nursing homes
- Electricians
- Fish cultivation
- Fish transportation
- Food establishments
- Hospitals
- Investment advisors
- Lobster and crab fishing
- Pharmacies
- Seafood (wholesale and retail)
- Security broker/dealers
- Traveler information services

Please check with the state to make sure your business is complying with the license requirements for your particular profession.

For more information on taxes, visit www.state.me.us/revenue/homepage.html
For additional or updated information, visit www.state.me.us/sos

Mailing Address

Secretary of State
Bureau of Corporation,
Elections and Commissions
101 State House Station
Augusta, ME 04333-0101
Tel: (207) 624-7736
Fax: (207) 287-5874

Maryland
Corporate Name Endings

The name must indicate the corporate status and contain the word "Corporation," "Incorporated," "Limited," or an abbreviation thereof. The name may also contain or end with the word "Company," which can never be preceded by the word "and" or the symbol "&." Names shall not imply any purpose that is not authorized by the charter. They shall not be the same as, or deceptively similar to, the name of other domestic corporations or limited partnerships, limited liability partnerships, limited liability companies, qualified foreign corporations, foreign limited partnerships, foreign limited liability partnerships, foreign limited liability companies, or names registered or reserved by any person or corporation.

Corporation Requirements
Director Information

- Minimum number: Not less than three, unless there are only one or two shareholders of record; then the number of directors may be less than three but not less than the number of shareholders.
- Residence requirements: No provision.
- Age requirements: None.
- Directors are required to be listed in the Articles of Incorporation.

Officer Information. Officers are not required to be listed in the Articles of Incorporation.

Stock Information. An increase in shares may cause an increase in initial filing fees.

Corporation Records. The stock transfer ledger and the original or a certified copy of the Articles of Incorporation must be kept at the principal office of the corporation.

Taxes and Fees

Annual Statements. Every business corporation shall submit an annual report on personal property to the Department of Assessments and Taxation. The Personal Property Return is due by April 15 with an accompanying filing fee of $100.

Income Tax Rate. The income tax rate is 7 percent.

S Corporation

S corporation status is recognized by the State of Maryland. A separate state election from the federal election is not required.

License Requirements

Maryland requires that you obtain a license and pay a fee if operating certain types of businesses in the state. The following is a partial list:

- Barbers and barber schools
- Certified public accountants
- Construction
- Counselors
- Detectives
- Electricians
- Employment
- Finance companies
- Frozen dessert manufacturers
- Hawkers and peddlers
- Home improvement contractors and salespersons
- Insurance
- Lawyers
- Pharmacies and pharmacists
- Plumbers
- Securities brokers/dealers

For more information on taxes, visit www.dat.state.md.us/

For additional or updated information, visit www.dat.state.md.us

Mailing Address

Department of Assessments and Taxation
Corporate Charter Division
301 West Preston Street
Baltimore, MD 21201-2395
Tel: (410) 767-1350
Fax: (410) 333-7097

Massachusetts
Corporate Name Endings

The corporation may assume any name indicating it is incorporated. The name may not be the same as the name or trade name of a Massachusetts corporation, foreign corporation, firm, association, person carrying on business in Massachusetts, name under reservation, nor so similar as to be mistaken for that other name, unless given the written consent of existing corporation, firm, association, or person.

Corporation Requirements
Director Information

- Minimum number: Not less than three, unless there are only one or two shareholders of record; then the number of directors may be less than three but not less than the number of shareholders.
- Residence requirements: No provision.
- Age requirements: None.
- Directors are required to be listed in the Articles of Incorporation.

Officer Information. Officers are required to be listed in the Articles of Incorporation.

Stock Information. An increase in shares may cause an increase in initial filing fees.

Corporation Records. The articles of organization, bylaws, minutes of shareholders' meetings, and the stock transfer ledger must be kept at the principal office of the corporation, corporate clerk office, or registered agent office.

Taxes and Fees

Annual Statements. Domestic and foreign corporation annual reports must be filed on or before the fifteenth day of the third month after close of the fiscal year. The filing fee is $85. Foreign corporations must file an initial certificate or report with the State Secretary within 10 days after commencing business in Massachusetts.

Income Tax Rate. Excise tax is composed of two parts: (1) (a) .26 percent of specified and allocated tangible property if a tangible property corporation, or (b) net worth if an intangible property corporation; plus (2) 9.5 percent of net income attributable to Massachusetts. The minimum tax is $456.

S Corporation

S corporation status is recognized by the State of Massachusetts; however, S corporations with total receipts of $6 million or more can be subjected to taxes at graduated rates. A separate state election from the federal election is not required.

License Requirements

Massachusetts requires that you obtain a license and pay a fee if operating certain types of businesses in the state. The following is a partial list:

- Architects
- Barbers
- Certified public accountants
- Contractors
- Hawkers and peddlers
- Opticians
- Outdoor advertising
- Real estate appraisers
- Real estate brokers and salespeople
- Water pollution control

Please check with the state to make sure your business is complying with the license requirements for your particular profession.

For more information on taxes, visit www.dor.state.ma.us

For additional or updated information, visit www.state.ma.us/sec/cor

Mailing Address

Secretary of the Commonwealth
One Ashburton Place, 17th Floor
Boston, MA 02108
Tel: (617) 727-9640
Fax: (617) 742-4538

Michigan
Corporate Name Endings

The name shall contain the word "Corporation," "Company," "Incorporated," "Limited," or an abbreviation thereof. The name shall not indicate the corporation was formed for a purpose other than one or more purposes permitted in the articles. The name shall be distinguishable from the corporate name of domestic or foreign corporations, domestic or foreign limited partnerships, or names currently reserved. The name cannot use the words "Bank," "Industrial Bank," "Deposit," "Surety," "Security," "Trust," or "Trust Company."

Corporation Requirements

Director Information

- Minimum number: One or more.
- Residence requirements: No provision.
- Age requirements: None.
- Directors are not required to be listed in the Articles of Incorporation.

Officer Information. Officers are not required to be listed in the Articles of Incorporation.

Stock Information. An increase in shares may cause an increase in initial filing fees.

Corporate Records. Corporations must keep the stock transfer ledger containing the names and addresses of all shareholders at the registered office.

Taxes and Fees

Annual Statements. Domestic and foreign corporations transacting business, employing capital or persons, or owning or managing property in Michigan must file an annual report with the Department of Commerce by May 15. The filing fee is $15.

Income Tax Rate. The business tax is 2 percent of taxable income as of 2001 and is being phased out by 2022.

S Corporation

S corporation status is recognized by the State of Michigan; however, the state subjects all corporations including S corporations to a single business tax.

License Requirements

Michigan requires that you obtain a license and pay a fee if operating certain types of businesses in the state. The following is a partial list:

- Chiropractic
- Electrical contractors
- Emigrant agents
- Gasoline retailers
- Insurance agents and solicitors
- Landscape architects
- Public accountants
- Real estate brokers or salespersons
- Transient merchants

Please check with the state to make sure your business is complying with the license requirements for your particular profession.

For more information on taxes, visit www.michigan.gov/treasury

For additional or updated information, visit www.michigan.gov/cis

Mailing Address

Michigan Department of Commerce
Corporation Division
P.O. Box 30054
Lansing, MI 48909
Tel: (517) 241-6470
Fax: (517) 241-0538

Minnesota

Corporate Name Endings

The name shall not be deceptively similar to the names of any other domestic corporation, limited partnership, limited liability partnership, limited liability company, foreign corporation, foreign limited partnership, foreign limited liability partnership, or foreign limited liability company authorized to do business in the state, unless: (1) such other corporation is about to change its name, cease business, dissolve, or withdraw, and (2) written consent therefrom is obtained. The name shall contain the word "Corporation," "Incorporated," "Limited," or the abbreviation thereof, or shall contain the word "Company" or the abbreviation "Co.," only if it is not immediately preceded by the word "and" or the character "&."

Corporation Requirements

Director Information

- Minimum number: One or more.
- Residence requirements: No provision.
- Age requirements: None.
- Directors are not required to be listed in the Articles of Incorporation.

Officer Information. Officers are not required to be listed in the Articles of Incorporation.

Stock Information. An increase in shares or par value does not affect initial filing fees.

Corporate Records. The minutes of shareholders' and directors' meetings for the last three years must be kept at the registered office. Bylaws, Articles of Incorporation, and all amendments to these documents, as well as the statement of names and addresses of its principal officers, also must be kept at this office.

Taxes and Fees

Annual Statements. An annual registration form must be filed with the Secretary of State by December 31. There is no filing fee for domestic corporations that file on a timely basis with no amendments. The filing fee for foreign corporations is $115.

Income Tax Rate. The income tax rate is 9.8 percent of taxable income.

S Corporation

S corporation status is recognized by the State of Minnesota. A separate state election from the federal election is not required; however, Minnesota does assess a minimum fee on S corporations based upon certain factors. The minimum fee ranges from $0 to $5,000.

License Requirements

Minnesota requires you obtain a license and pay a fee if operating certain types of businesses in the state. The following is a partial list:

- Collection agencies
- Driver training schools
- Dry cleaning
- Employment agencies
- Entertainment agencies
- Food handlers
- Insurance agent
- Real estate appraisers
- Vending machine operators

Please check with the state to make sure your business is complying with the license requirements for your particular profession.

For more information on taxes, visit www.taxes.state.mn.us

For additional or updated information, visit www.sos.state.mn.us

Mailing Address

Secretary of State
Division of Corporations
180 State Office Building
100 Martin Luther King Jr. Blvd.
St. Paul, MN 55155
Tel: (651) 296-2803
Fax: (651) 297-7067

Mississippi

Corporate Name Endings

The name must contain the word "Corporation," "Company," "Incorporated," "Limited," or the abbreviation "Corp.," "Co.," "Inc.," "Ltd.," or words or abbreviations of like import in another language. The name may not contain language implying the corporation is organized for any unauthorized purpose. The name must be distinguishable from that of domestic or foreign corporations entitled to do business in the state, or to reserved or registered names.

Corporation Requirements

Director Information

- Minimum number: One or more.
- Residence requirements: No provision.
- Age requirements: None.
- Directors are not required to be listed in the Articles of Incorporation.

Officer Information. Officers are not required to be listed in the Articles of Incorporation.

Stock Information. An increase in shares or par value does not affect initial filing fees.

Corporate Records. The Articles of Incorporation, bylaws, minutes of shareholders' and directors' meetings, names and addresses of current directors and officers, and the most recent annual report must be kept must be kept at the principal office of the corporation.

Taxes and Fees

Annual Statements. Annual reports are due within 60 days of each anniversary date of incorporation with respect to a domestic corporation, and within 60 days of each anniversary date of authorization to transact business in Mississippi with respect to a foreign corporation. The filing fee is $25.

Income Tax Rate. Tax rates are 3 percent of the first $5,000 of taxable income allocated to Mississippi, 4 percent on the next $5,000, and 5percent for all taxable income over $10,000.

Franchise Tax Rate

- Every domestic and foreign corporation doing business in Mississippi must pay a franchise tax. The franchise tax return is due by the fifteenth day of the third month following the accounting close of the corporation.
- The franchise tax rate is $2.50 per $1,000 or fraction thereof the value of

the capital used, invested, or employed in Mississippi. The minimum tax is $25 and is based on the corporation's capital at the close of its year preceding the filing of the return. Capital includes issued and outstanding capital stock, paid-in capital, surplus, retained earnings, and all true reserves, as well as amounts designated for payment of dividends unless irrevocably placed to the credit of stockholders. Excluded are debts, bonds, mortgages, and reserves for bad debts, depreciation, or valuation.

S Corporation

S corporation status is recognized by the State of Mississippi; however, S corporations are still required to file a franchise tax return.

License Requirements

Mississippi requires that you obtain a license and pay a fee if operating certain types of businesses in the state. The following is a partial list:

- Attorneys
- Barbers
- Child-care facilities
- Dentists
- Food-handling establishments
- Optometrists
- Pawn brokers
- Pharmacists
- Psychologists
- Real estate brokers and salespersons
- Stores

Please check with the state to make sure your business is complying with the license requirements for your particular profession.

For more information on taxes, visit www.mstc.state.ms.us

For additional or updated information, visit www.sos.state.ms.us

Mailing Address

Secretary of State
Business Services Division
P.O. Box 136
Jackson, MS 39205-0136
Tel: (601) 359-1350
Fax: (601) 356-1499

Missouri
Corporate Name Endings

The name shall contain the word "Corporation," "Company," "Incorporated," "Limited," or an abbreviation thereof. The name may not contain any word or phrase indicating or implying the corporation is a governmental agency, or that it is organized for any purpose other than the purpose for which corporations may be organized under the laws of Missouri. The name shall be distinguishable from the name of any domestic or foreign corporation authorized to do business in Missouri, or any limited partnership, limited liability company, or reserved name filed with the state.

Corporation Requirements
Director Information

- Minimum number: Not less than three, unless there are only one or two shareholders of record; then the number of directors may be less than three but not less than the number of shareholders.

- Residence requirements: No provision.
- Age requirements: Directors must be a natural person[*] at least 18 years of age.
- Directors are not required to be listed in the Articles of Incorporation.

Officer Information. Officers are not required to be listed in the Articles of Incorporation.

Stock Information. An increase in shares may cause an increase in initial filing fees.

Corporate Records. The stock transfer ledger must be kept at the principal corporate office.

Taxes and Fees

Annual Statements. An Annual Registration Report must be filed with the Secretary of State by April 15. The fee is $45.

Income Tax Rate. The tax rate is 6.25 percent of Missouri taxable income. In addition, a franchise tax is assessed on assets within the State of Missouri. The franchise tax rate is 1/30 of 1 percent of the asset base for all assets in excess of $1,000,000.

S Corporation

S corporation status is recognized by the State of Missouri. A separate state election

from the federal election is not required; however, an S corporation is subject to the franchise taxes.

License Requirements

Missouri requires that you obtain a license and pay a fee if operating certain types of businesses in the state. The following is a partial list:

- Auctioneers
- Employment agencies
- Hotels
- Insurance brokers and agents
- Merchants
- Motels
- Resorts
- Securities brokers
- Strip coal mining
- Treated timber products

Please check with the state to make sure your business is complying with the license requirements for your particular profession.

For more information on taxes, visit www.dor.state.mo.us

For additional or updated information, visit www.sos.state.mo.us

Mailing Address

Secretary of State
Business Services Division
P.O. Box 778
Jefferson City, MO 65102-0778
Tel: (573) 751-4153
Fax: (573) 751-5841

---

[*] In jurisprudence, a "natural person" is a human being perceptible through the senses and subject to physical laws, as opposed to an "artificial person," i.e., an organization that the law treats for some purposes as if it were a person distinct from its members or owners.

Montana

Corporate Name Endings

The name must be distinguishable from that of any corporation authorized to transact business in the state, a reserved or registered name, the fictitious name of a foreign corporation, or any assumed business name, limited partnership, limited liability company, trademark, or service mark. The name must contain the word "Corporation," "Company," "Incorporated," "Limited," or an abbreviation thereof.

Corporation Requirements

Director Information

- Minimum number: One or more.
- Residence requirements: No provision.
- Age requirements: None.
- Directors are not required to be listed in the Articles of Incorporation.

Officer Information. Officers are not required to be listed in the Articles of Incorporation.

Stock Information. An increase in shares may cause an increase in initial filing fees.

Corporate Records. The Articles of Incorporation, bylaws, minutes of all shareholders' and directors' meetings, names and addresses of current directors and officers, and the most recent annual report must be kept at the principal office, or at a location from which the records may be recovered within two business days.

Taxes and Fees

Annual Statements. An Annual Corporation Report must be filed with the Secretary of State between January 1 and April 15 of each year on the prescribed form. The first report is due between January 1 and April 15 of year following the calendar year in which the certificate of incorporation or certificate of authority was issued. Filing fees are $15.

Income Tax Rate. The tax is imposed at the rate of 6.75 percent of all net income. The minimum tax is $50.

S Corporation

S corporation status is recognized by the State of Montana. A separate state election from the federal election is not required.

License Requirements

Montana requires that you obtain a license and pay a fee if operating certain types of businesses in the state. The following is a partial list:

- Barbers
- Campgrounds and trailer courts
- Electricians and electrical contractors
- Engineers and land surveyors
- Food establishments
- Hotels, motels, tourist homes
- Itinerant merchants
- Motor vehicle dealers
- Pharmacies and pharmacists
- Public contractors
- Real estate brokers and salesmen
- Tourist

Please check with the state to make sure your business is complying with the license requirements for your particular profession.

For more information on taxes, visit www.state.mt.us/revenue/

For additional or updated information, visit www.sos.state.mt.us

Mailing Address

Secretary of State
Room 260, Capitol
P.O. Box 202801
Helena, MT 59620-2801
Tel: (406) 444-2034
Fax: (406) 444-3976

Nebraska

Corporate Name Endings

The name must contain the word "Corporation," "Company," "Incorporated," "Limited," or the abbreviation "Corp.," "Inc.," "Co.," or "Ltd." The name shall be distinguishable from the name of a corporation incorporated in or authorized to transact business in the state, a corporate name reserved or registered, the fictitious name of a foreign corporation, the corporate name of a not-for-profit corporation incorporated in or authorized to transact business in this state, a trade name registered in the state, the trade name of domestic or foreign corporations entitled to do business in the state, or a name that is reserved or registered. However, the similar name may be registered if corporation affected consents in writing or by court decree.

Corporation Requirements

Director Information

- Minimum number: One or more.
- Residence requirements: No provision.

- Age requirements: None.
- Directors are not required to be listed in the Articles of Incorporation.

Officer Information. Officers are not required to be listed in the Articles of Incorporation.

Stock Information. An increase in shares may cause an increase in initial filing fees.

Corporate Records. The Articles of Incorporation, bylaws, minutes of share-holders' and directors' meetings, names and addresses of current directors and officers, and the most recent annual report must be kept at the principal office of the corporation.

Taxes and Fees

Annual Statements. An annual report must be filed with the Secretary of State between January 1 and April 15 of each year on the prescribed form. The fee is based on property value, with a minimum payment of $26.

Income Tax Rate. Tax rates are 5.58 percent of the first $50,000 of taxable income and 7.81 percent of taxable income over $50,000.

S Corporation

S corporation status is recognized by the State of Nebraska. A separate state election from the federal election is not required.

License Requirements

Nebraska requires most businesses to obtain a license and pay a fee if operating in the state. Please check with the state to make sure your business is complying with the license requirements for your particular profession.

For more information on taxes, visit www.revenue.state.ne.us/index.html
For additional or updated information, visit www.sos.state.ne.us

Mailing Address

Secretary of State
Corporations Division
Room 1301, State Capitol
P.O. Box 94608
Lincoln, NE 68509-4608
Tel: (402) 471-4079
Fax: (402) 471-3666

Nevada
Corporate Name Endings

The name must not be the same, or deceptively similar to, the name of any corporation, limited partnership, limited liability company, foreign corporation, foreign limited partnership, foreign limited liability company, or a name reserved for use of any other proposed corporation, unless written consent of the person or other entity for whom the name is reserved is filed with the articles. A name appearing to be that of a natural person77 and containing a given name or initials must not be used as a corporate name, except with an additional word such as "Incorporated," "Limited," "Inc.," "Ltd.," "Company," "Co.," "Corporation," "Corp.," or other word identifying it as not being the name of a natural person. If the name implies banking, trust, or insurance powers, prior approval of the banking superintendent or insurance commissioner is needed.

Corporation Requirements
Director Information

- Minimum number: One or more.
- Residence requirements: No provision.
- Age requirements: Directors must be a natural person[*] at least 18 years of age.
- Directors are required to be listed in the Articles of Incorporation.

Officer Information. Officers are not required to be listed in the Articles of Incorporation.

Stock Information. An increase in shares may cause an increase in initial filing fees.

Corporate Records. The Articles of Incorporation, bylaws, any amendments thereto certified by the Secretary of State, and a copy of the stock ledger or statement of where it is kept, must be kept at the principal office of the corporation.

Taxes and Fees
Annual Statements

- Domestic and foreign corporations must file an Annual List of Officers, Directors, and Agents by the last day of the month in which the anniversary date

[*] In jurisprudence, a "natural person" is a human being perceptible through the senses and subject to physical laws, as opposed to an "artificial person," i.e., an organization that the law treats for some purposes as if it were a person distinct from its members or owners.

of incorporation occurs. The filing fee is $85. However, the initial list of Officers and Directors, which must be filed within 60 days of the formation of the corporation, is $165.

- In addition, all foreign corporations doing business in the state of Nevada must publish a statement of its last calendar year's business in two issues of a newspaper published in the state by March 31 of each year.

Income Tax Rate. There is no income tax in Nevada.

S Corporation

There is no income tax in Nevada, so S corporation elections have no state impact.

License Requirements

Nevada requires most businesses to obtain a license and pay a fee if operating in the state. Please check with the state to make sure your business is complying with the license requirements for your particular profession.

For more information on taxes, visit www.tax.state.nv.us

For updated or additional state specific information, visit sos.state.nv.us

Mailing Address

Secretary of State
101 North Carson Street, Suite 3
Carson City, NV 89701-3714
Tel: (775) 684-5708
Fax: (775) 684-5725

New Hampshire
Corporate Name Endings

The name must contain the word "Corporation," "Incorporated," "Limited," or the abbreviation "Inc.," "Corp.," or "Ltd." The name must not be the same, or deceptively similar to, the name of any corporation authorized to transact business in the state, any reserved or registered name, the fictitious name of a foreign corporation, domestic or foreign limited partnership, or any other business entity. The name must not contain language implying the corporation is organized for a purpose not permitted by the act or its articles.

Corporation Requirements
Director Information

- Minimum number: One or more.
- Residence requirements: No provision.
- Age requirements: None.
- Directors are not required to be listed in the Articles of Incorporation.

Officer Information. Officers are not required to be listed in the Articles of Incorporation.

Stock Information. An increase in shares or par value does not affect initial filing fees.

Corporate Records. Minutes of shareholders' and directors' meetings, a copy of the Articles of Incorporation and bylaws, the names and addresses of directors, and the most recent annual report must be kept with the corporation's records.

Taxes and Fees

Annual Statements. Annual Reports must be filed by April 1 with the Secretary of State. The filing fee is $100.

Income Tax Rate. The tax rate is 8.5 percent of taxable business profits.

Business Enterprise Tax. The tax is imposed at the rate of .75 percent of the taxable enterprise value tax base of every business enterprise. The "taxable enterprise value tax base" means the enterprise value tax base adjusted by special adjustments and further adjusted by the method of apportionment. "Enterprise value tax base" means the sum of all compensation paid or accrued, interest paid or accrued, and dividends paid by the business enterprise. This tax is imposed only on corporations with gross receipts exceeding certain thresholds.

S Corporation

S corporation status is not recognized by the State of New Hampshire.

License Requirements

New Hampshire requires most businesses to obtain a license and pay a fee if operating in the district. Please check with the district to make sure your business is complying with the license requirements for your particular profession.

For more information on taxes, visit www.state.nh.us/revenue/

For additional or updated information, visit www.sos.nh.gov

Mailing Address

Secretary of State
State House, Room 204
Concord, NH 03301
Tel: (603) 271-3242
Fax: (603) 271-6316

New Jersey
Corporate Name Endings

The name shall not contain any word, phrase, abbreviation, or derivative thereof indicating or implying it is organized for any purpose other than one or more purposes permitted by its certificate of incorporation. The name shall be distinguishable from the names of other for-profit and nonprofit domestic corporations, foreign corporations, domestic and foreign limited partnerships, and current name reservations or registrations. The name shall not contain any word, phrase, abbreviation, or derivative thereof which use is prohibited or restricted by any other statute of New Jersey. The name shall contain the word "Corporation," "Company," "Incorporated," an abbreviation thereof, or the abbreviation "Ltd."

Corporation Requirements
Director Information

- Minimum number: One or more.
- Residence requirements: No provision.
- Age requirements: Directors must be a natural person[*] at least 18 years of age.

[*] In jurisprudence, a "natural person" is a human being perceptible through the senses and subject to physical laws, as opposed to an "artificial person," i.e., an organization that the law treats for some purposes as if it were a person distinct from its members or owners.

- Directors are not required to be listed in the Articles of Incorporation.

Officer Information. Officers are not required to be listed in the Articles of Incorporation.

Stock Information. An increase in shares or par value does not affect initial filing fees.

Corporate Records. A corporation shall maintain its records in written form or in another form capable of conversion into written form within a reasonable time.

Taxes and Fees

Annual Statements. Every corporation must file an annual report within 3 ½ months after the end of the corporation's fiscal year. The filing fee is $40.

Income Tax Rate. The corporation business tax is 9 percent of taxable income. The tax rate is 7.5 percent if your entire net income is $100,000 or less. The minimum tax is $200.

S Corporation

S corporation status is recognized by the State of New Jersey. A separate state election from the federal election is required.

License Requirements

New Jersey requires that you obtain a license and pay a fee if operating certain types of businesses in the state. The following is a partial list:

- Apparel industry
- Apple growers
- Architects
- Attorneys
- Barbers
- Beauticians and hairstylists
- Certified public accountants
- Child-care centers
- Chiropractors
- Electrical contractors
- Employers
- Insurance agents, brokers, and solicitors

Please check with the state to make sure your business is complying with the license requirements for your particular profession.

For more information on taxes, visit www.state.nj.us/treasury/revenue

For additional or updated information, visit www.state.nj.us/njbgs

Mailing Address

Secretary of State
Division of Commercial Recording
Trenton, NJ 08626
Tel: (609) 530-6400

New Mexico
Corporate Name Endings

The name must contain the word "Corporation," "Incorporation," "Company," "Limited," or an abbreviation thereof. The name must not be the same as, or confusingly similar to, a name of any domestic or foreign corporation, or a name reserved by or registered by another corporation, unless written permission of other corporation is obtained. The name must not imply a purpose other than that contained in the charter.

Corporation Requirements
Director Information

- Minimum number: One or more.
- Residence requirements: No provision.
- Age requirements: None.
- Directors are required to be listed in the Articles of Incorporation.

Officer Information. Officers are not required to be listed in the Articles of Incorporation.

Stock Information. An increase in shares may cause an increase in initial filing fees.

Corporate Records. The stock transfer ledger must be kept in the principal corporate office.

Taxes and Fees

Annual Statements. A Biennial Profit Corporation Report must be filed every two years on or before the fifteenth day of the third month following the end of a corporation's fiscal year. The filing fee is $25. The first report is due within 30 days of the initial incorporation date of the corporation.

Income Tax Rate. The tax rates are 4.8 percent of net income up to $500,000, 6.4 percent of net income between $500,000 and $1,000,000, and 7.6 percent of net income over $1,000,000.

Franchise Tax. A franchise tax payment is due each year. The rate is $50 each tax year.

S Corporation

S corporation status is recognized by the State of New Mexico. A separate state election from the federal election is not required.

License Requirements

New Mexico requires most businesses to obtain a license and pay a fee if operating in the state. Please check with the state to make sure your business is complying with the license requirements for your particular profession.

For more information on taxes, visit www.state.nm.us/tax

For additional or updated information, visit www.nmprc.state.nm.us/corporations/corpshome.htm

Mailing Address

Public Regulation Commission
P.O. Box 1269
Santa Fe, NM 87504-1269
Tel: (505) 827-4502
Fax: (505) 827-4387

New York
Corporate Name Endings

The name must contain the word "Corporation," "Incorporated," "Limited," or an abbreviation thereof. The name may not be the same as, or so similar or confusing to, that of any domestic or authorized foreign corporation or reserved name. The name may not contain any word or phrase indicating the corporation is formed for any purpose other than the purpose for which the corporation may be and is formed. The use of certain enumerated words and abbreviations including banking, insurance, and various professions is prohibited or restricted.

Corporation Requirements

Director Information

- Minimum number: Not less than three, unless there are only one or two shareholders of record; then the number of directors may be less than three but not less than the number of shareholders.
- Residence requirements: No provision.
- Age requirements: Directors must be a natural person* at least 18 years of age.
- Directors are not required to be listed in the Articles of Incorporation.

Officer Information. Officers are not required to be listed in the Articles of Incorporation.

Stock Information. An increase in shares may cause an increase in initial filing fees.

Corporate Records. The stock transfer ledger must be kept in the principal corporate office.

Taxes and Fees

Annual Statements. Each domestic and foreign corporation authorized to do business in New York must file a Biennial

Statement of directors, including their addresses. The applicable filing period for a corporation is the calendar month during which its original certificate of incorporation or application for authority was filed (or the effective date thereof). A $9 filing fee must accompany each statement.

Franchise Tax Rate

- First, the tax is based on the highest of:
  - 8 percent of net income
  - 0.178 percent of capital (not to exceed $350,000), 2.5 percent of minimum taxable income, or a fixed dollar minimum tax ($1,500 maximum)
- Second, a subsidiary tax of 0.9 mill per $1 of subsidiary capital is added.
- New York has a special lower graduated tax rate for qualified small businesses. To qualify, your business cannot have net income greater than $290,000 or capital or paid-in surplus of more than $1 million. The amount of tax imposed will be 7.5 percent of net income at or below $200,000, 8 percent of net income between $200,000 and $250,000, and 2.5 percent of the net income base that exceeds $250,000.

S Corporation

S corporation status is recognized by the State of New York; however, New York imposes a franchise tax on S corporations. A separate state election from the federal election is required.

License Requirements

New York requires that you obtain a license and pay a fee if operating certain types of

---

* In jurisprudence, a "natural person" is a human being perceptible through the senses and subject to physical laws, as opposed to an "artificial person," i.e., an organization that the law treats for some purposes as if it were a person distinct from its members or owners.

businesses in the state. Please check with the state to make sure your business is complying with the license requirements for your particular profession.

LLC Publication Requirement

In New York, all LLCs formed or qualified foreign corporations are required to publish a notice of formation for six consecutive weeks in assigned newspapers. This requirement does not affect the good standing status of the LLC; however, an LLC is required to complete this requirement in order to have access to the New York State court system. The publication is made at the county level in two newspapers as assigned by the local county recorder. The cost of this requirement varies greatly, based upon the county where the business is located. In New York County, the publication costs will be higher than in the rest of the state. The reason Business Filings does not perform the publication requirement in New York is because of the great difference in price from county to county.

To comply with this requirement, please contact your local county recorder's office and they will assign the newspapers. The county recorder's phone number is located in the blue pages of your local phone book. A court in New York declared the publication requirement to be unconstitutional in November 2001; however, this case is currently under appeal. Until a decision is made in the appeal, the New York LLC publication requirement remains in effect.

For more information on taxes, visit www.tax.state.ny.us/

For additional or updated information, visit www.dos.state.ny.us

Mailing Address

Department of State
Division of Corporations, State Records, and Uniform Commercial Code
41 State Street
Albany, NY 12231-0001
Tel: (518) 473-2492
Fax: (518) 474-1418

North Carolina
Corporate Name Endings

The name must contain the word "Corporation," "Incorporated," "Company," Limited," or the abbreviation "Corp.," "Inc.," "Co.," or "Ltd." Names may not contain language stating or implying that the corporation is organized for purposes not permitted by the act and its articles. The name must be distinguishable from the name of any domestic, foreign, or nonprofit corporation, or the reserved or registered name of a limited liability company or partnership.

Corporation Requirements
Director Information

- Minimum number: One or more.
- Residence requirements: No provision.
- Age requirements: None.
- Directors are not required to be listed in the Articles of Incorporation.

Officer Information. Officers are not required to be listed in the Articles of Incorporation.

Stock Information. An increase in shares or par value does not affect initial filing fees.

Corporate Records. The Articles of Incorporation, bylaws or restated bylaws, resolutions, minutes, written communications, financial statements to shareholders, names and business addresses of current directors and officers, and most recent annual report must be kept at the principal office of the corporation.

Taxes and Fees

Annual Statements. Domestic and foreign corporations authorized to transact business in North Carolina must file a Business Corporation Annual Report with the Secretary of State within 60 days following the last day of the month in which the corporation was incorporated (or received a certificate of authority). The filing fee is $20.

Income Tax Rate. The income tax rate is 6.9 percent of net income allocated and apportioned to North Carolina. Payment must be made by the fifteenth day of the third month following the end of the corporation's tax year.

Franchise Tax. A franchise tax is also assessed on all corporations, including S corporations. The rate is $1.50 per $1,000 of issued and outstanding capital stock, surplus, and undivided profits allocable to North Carolina. The minimum tax is $35.

S Corporation

S corporation status is recognized by the State of North Carolina. A separate state election from the federal election is not required.

License Requirements

North Carolina requires most businesses to obtain a license and pay a fee if operating in the state. Please check with the state to make sure your business is complying with the license requirements for your particular profession.

For more information on taxes, visit www.dor.state.nc.us/
For additional or updated information, visit www.secstate.state.nc.us

Mailing Address

Department of Secretary of State
Corporations Division
P.O. Box 29622
Raleigh, NC 27626-0622
Tel: (919) 807-2225
Fax: (919) 807-2039

North Dakota
Corporate Name Endings

The name must contain the word "Corporation," "Incorporated," "Limited," "Company," or an abbreviation thereof. It must be in the English language or any other language expressed in English letters or characters. It may not contain words implying it is incorporated for a purpose other than business for which a company may be incorporated. The name may not be the same as, or deceptively similar to, the name of a domestic or foreign corporation, limited liability company, limited partnership, reserved name, registered fictitious name, or trade name, unless consent is given.

Corporation Requirements

Director Information

- Minimum number: One or more.
- Residence requirements: No provision.
- Age requirements: Directors must be a natural person[*] at least 18 years of age.
- Directors are required to be listed in the Articles of Incorporation.

Officer Information. Officers are not required to be listed in the Articles of Incorporation.

Stock Information. An increase in the shares may cause an increase in initial filing fees.

Corporate Records. A shareholder list and minutes of shareholders' meetings must be kept at the registered office or principal office of the corporation.

Taxes and Fees

Annual Statements. Domestic corporations and foreign corporations authorized to transact business in North Dakota must file an annual report with the Secretary of State by May 15. The filing fee is $25.

Income Tax Rate. Taxes are assessed on taxable income at the rate of 3 percent for the first $3,000. 4.5 percent of the next $5,000, 6 percent of the next $12,000, 7.5 percent of the next $10,000, 9 percent of the next $20,000, and 10.5 percent of any income that exceeds $50,000.

S Corporation

S corporation status is recognized by the State of North Dakota. A separate state election from the federal election is not required.

License Requirements

North Dakota requires most businesses to obtain a license and pay a fee if operating in the state. Please check with the state to make sure your business is complying with the license requirements for your particular profession.

For more information on taxes, visit www.state.nd.us/taxdpt

For additional or updated information, visit www.state.nd.us/sec

Mailing Address

Secretary of State
Capitol Building
600 East Boulevard Ave., Dept. 108
Bismarck, ND 58505-0500
Tel: (701) 328-2900
Fax: (701) 328-2992

Ohio

Corporate Name Endings

The name shall contain the word "Company," "Corporation," "Incorporated," or the abbreviation "Co.," "Corp.," or "Inc." The name must be distinguishable from the name of another domestic or foreign corporation authorized

---

[*] In jurisprudence, a "natural person" is a human being perceptible through the senses and subject to physical laws, as opposed to an "artificial person," i.e., an organization that the law treats for some purposes as if it were a person distinct from its members or owners.

to do business in the state, or from any trade name. The name shall not contain language implying it is connected with a government agency of the United States.

Corporation Requirements

Director Information

- Minimum number: Not less than three, unless there are only one or two shareholders of record; then the number of directors may be less than three but not less than the number of shareholders.
- Residence requirements: No provision.
- Age requirements: Must be 18 years old.
- Directors are not required to be listed in the Articles of Incorporation.

Officer Information. Officers are not required to be listed in the Articles of Incorporation.

Stock Information. An increase in the shares may cause an increase in initial filing fees.

Corporate Records. The corporation must keep books and records readily available for inspection. No particular location is required.

Taxes and Fees

Annual Statements. A domestic corporation incorporated on or after January 1, 1993, must file its first statement of continued existence on or before July 1 of the year following its year of incorporation, and each July 1 thereafter. A filing fee of $5 will be charged. There are no similar reporting requirements for foreign corporations.

Income Tax Rate. The tax rate is the greater of $50 or 5.1 percent of the first $50,000 of the value of a taxpayer's outstanding shares of stock, determined according to net income plus 8.5 percent of the value over $50,000; or .004 times the value of the taxable value of the corporation with a maximum of $150,000.

License Requirements

Ohio requires that you obtain a license and pay a fee if operating certain types of businesses in the state. The following is a partial list:

- Asbestos abatement
- Auctioneers
- Barbers
- Chiropractors
- Cosmetologists
- Fraternal benefit societies
- Hospice care provider
- Insurance agents and solicitors
- Motor vehicle salespeople
- Real estate salespeople

Please check with the state to make sure your business is complying with the license requirements for your particular profession.

For more information on taxes, visit www.tax.ohio.gov

For additional or updated information, visit www.sos.state.oh.us/sos

Mailing Address

Secretary of State
Corporations Division
180 East Broad Street, 16th Floor
Columbus, OH 43215
Tel: (614) 466-3910
Fax: (614) 485-7045

Oklahoma

Corporate Name Endings

The name must contain the word "Corporation," "Company," "Incorporated," "Limited," "Association," "Club," "Foundation," "Fund," "Institute," "Society," "Union," "Syndicate," or an abbreviation thereof. The name must be distinguishable from the name of any other corporation, limited partnership, trade name, fictitious name, reserved name, limited liability company, limited partnership, or any limited liability company name filed with the Secretary of State.

Corporation Requirements

Director Information

- Minimum number: One or more.
- Residence requirements: No provision.
- Age requirements: None.
- Directors are not required to be listed in the Articles of Incorporation.

Officer Information. Officers are not required to be listed in the Articles of Incorporation.

Stock Information. An increase in the shares may cause an increase in initial filing fees.

Corporate Records. Certain records must be kept; however, there is no provision as to the location of required records.

Taxes and Fees

Annual Statements. Domestic and foreign corporations must file a Business Registration Report. The cost of the report is $100 and is due by January 2 of the filing year.

Income Tax Rate. The income tax rate is 6 percent of taxable income.

Franchise Tax. The franchise tax rate is .0125 percent of Oklahoma capital. The minimum tax is $10. Foreign corporations are also required to pay a $100 registered agent fee. The Oklahoma Minimum/ Maximum Franchise Tax Return is due by July 1.

S Corporation

S corporation status is recognized by the State of Oklahoma. A separate state election from the federal election is not required.

License Requirements

Oklahoma requires you obtain a license and pay a fee if operating certain types of businesses in the state. The following is a partial list:

- Accountants
- Ambulatory surgical centers
- Barbers and barber instructors
- Closing-out sales
- Electrical and elevator construction
- Contractors
- Fruit and vegetable sellers
- Hospitals
- Insurance adjusters
- Pawnbrokers
- Plumbers and plumbing

- Real estate brokers
- Sales associates

Please check with the state to make sure your business is complying with the license requirements for your particular profession.

For more information on taxes, visit www.oktax.state.ok.us/oktax
For additional or updated information, visit www.sos.state.ok.us

Mailing Address

Secretary of State
2300 N. Lincoln Boulevard, Suite 101
Oklahoma City, OK 73105-4897
Tel: (405) 521-3912

Oregon
Corporate Name Endings

The name must contain the word "Corporation," "Company," "Incorporated," "Limited," or an abbreviation thereof. The name shall not contain the word "Cooperative." It must be distinguishable from the name of any corporation, reserved name, registered name, professional corporate name, nonprofit corporate name, cooperative name, limited partnership name, business trust name, or assumed business name. The name shall be in the English alphabet.

Corporation Requirements
Director Information

- Minimum number: One or more.
- Residence requirements: No provision.
- Age requirements: Directors must be a natural person[*] at least 18 years of age.

- Directors are not required to be listed in the Articles of Incorporation.

Officer Information. Officers are not required to be listed in the Articles of Incorporation.

Stock Information. An increase in shares or par value does not affect initial filing fees.

Corporate Records. The Articles of Incorporation, bylaws, all amendments currently in effect, shareholders' meeting minutes, names and addresses of directors and officers, and the corporation's most recent annual report must be kept at the principal office of the corporation.

Taxes and Fees
Annual Statements. Every domestic and foreign corporation authorized to transact business in Oregon must file an annual report with the Secretary of State and pay an annual license fee by the anniversary of the date on which the corporation's certificate of incorporation or certificate of authority to do business was issued. Domestic and foreign corporations pay a fee of $20.

Excise Tax Rate. The excise tax rate is 6.6 percent of Oregon taxable income. The minimum tax is $10.

---

[*] In jurisprudence, a "natural person" is a human being perceptible through the senses and subject to physical laws, as opposed to an "artificial person," i.e., an organization that the law treats for some purposes as if it were a person distinct from its members or owners.

S Corporation

S corporation status is recognized by the State of Oregon. A separate state election from the federal election is not required.

License Requirements

Oregon requires most businesses to obtain a license and pay a fee if operating in the state. Please check with the state to make sure your business is complying with the license requirements for your particular profession.

For more information on taxes, visit egov.oregon.gov/DOR

For additional or updated information, visit www.sos.state.or.us

Mailing Address

Secretary of State
Corporation Division
255 Capitol Street NE, Suite 151
Salem, OR 97310-1327
Tel: (503) 986-2200
Fax: (503) 378-4381

Pennsylvania
Corporate Name Endings

The name shall contain the word "Corporation," "Company," Incorporated," "Limited," or an abbreviation thereof. The name may be in any language but must be expressed in English letters or characters or Arabic or Roman numerals.

Corporation Requirements
Director Information
- Minimum number: One or more.
- Residence requirements: No provision.

- Age requirements: Directors must be a natural person[*] at least 18 years of age.
- Directors are not required to be listed in the Articles of Incorporation.

Officer Information. Officers are not required to be listed in the Articles of Incorporation.

Stock Information. An increase in shares or par value does not affect initial filing fees.

Corporate Records. The stock transfer ledger must be kept at the principal office of the corporation.

Taxes and Fees

Annual Statements. Annual statements are required for domestic or foreign limited liability partnerships, restricted professional limited liability companies, and not-for-profit corporations.

Income Tax Rate. The tax rate is 9.9 percent of taxable income. In addition, a capital stock and foreign franchise tax is assessed on Pennsylvania capital at a rate of .724 percent of capital stock value.

S Corporation

S corporation status is recognized by the State of Pennsylvania. A separate state election from the federal election is required.

---

[*] In jurisprudence, a "natural person" is a human being perceptible through the senses and subject to physical laws, as opposed to an "artificial person," i.e., an organization that the law treats for some purposes as if it were a person distinct from its members or owners.

License Requirements

Pennsylvania requires that you obtain a license and pay a fee if operating certain types of businesses in the state. The following is a partial list:

- Accountants
- Bakeries
- Charitable organizations (fund solicitation)
- Damage appraisers
- Dealers and salespersons
- Eating and drinking places
- Employment agencies
- Fishing
- Insurance agents and brokers
- Motor vehicle manufacturers
- Real estate

Please check with the state to make sure your business is complying with the license requirements for your particular profession.

For more information on taxes, visit www.revenue.state.pa.us
For additional or updated information, visit www.dos.state.pa.us/corps

Mailing Address

Department of State
Corporation Bureau
206 North Office Building
Harrisburg, PA 17120
Tel: (717) 787-1057

Rhode Island
Corporate Name Endings

The name must contain the word "Corporation," "Company," "Incorporated," "Limited," or an abbreviation thereof. The name must not be deceptively similar to any domestic or foreign corporation, limited partnership, foreign limited partnership authorized to do business in the state, or reserved or registered name, unless written consent is obtained from the holder of such name. The name may not contain any word implying that the corporation was formed for a purpose for which it is not organized.

Corporation Requirements
Director Information

- Minimum number: One or more.
- Residence requirements: No provision.
- Age requirements: None.
- Directors are not required to be listed in the Articles of Incorporation.

Officer Information. Officers are required to be listed in the Articles of Incorporation.

Stock Information. An increase in shares may cause an increase in initial filing fees.

Corporate Records. The stock transfer ledger must be kept at the principal office of the corporation.

Taxes and Fees

Annual Statements. Annual reports for domestic and foreign corporations must be filed with the Secretary of State between January 1 and March 1. The first annual report of a corporation must be filed between January 1 and March 1 of the next year succeeding the calendar year in which the certificate of incorporation or authority was issued. The filing fee is $50.

Income Tax Rate. The tax rate is 9 percent of net income. The minimum tax is $250.

Franchise Tax. The franchise tax rate is .002.5 percent of authorized stock, with a minimum tax of $250. If your corporation is liable for the business corporation tax, you pay only on the amount by which the franchise tax exceeds the business corporation tax. If your corporation has not been engaged in any business activity within the state during the preceding taxable year, you must pay the annual franchise tax based upon its authorized capital stock at the following rates: $250 where stock does not exceed $1,000,000, and $12.50 for each additional $1,000,000.

S Corporation

S corporation status is recognized by the State of Rhode Island. A separate state election from the federal election is not required; however, S corporations are still subject to the franchise tax.

License Requirements

Rhode Island requires most businesses to obtain a license and pay a fee if operating in the state. Please check with the state to make sure your business is complying with the license requirements for your particular profession.

For more information on taxes, visit www.tax.state.ri.us/

For updated or additional state specific information, visit www3.sec.state.ri.us

Mailing Address

Secretary of State
Corporations Division
100 North Main Street
Providence, RI 02903
Tel: (401) 222-3040
Fax: (401) 222-1356

South Carolina
Corporate Name Endings

The name must contain the word "Corporation," "Incorporated," "Company," "Limited," the abbreviation "Corp.," "Inc.," "Co.," or "Ltd.," or abbreviations of words with similar meanings in another language. The name cannot contain language indicating a purpose other than that permitted by state law and the articles of organization. It must be distinguishable upon records of the Secretary of State from the name of a domestic or qualified foreign corporation, reserved or registered corporate name, nonprofit corporation, or limited partnership.

Corporation Requirements
Director Information

- Minimum number: One or more.
- Residence requirements: No provision.
- Age requirements: None.
- Directors are required to be listed in the Articles of Incorporation.

Officer Information. Officers are not required to be listed in the Articles of Incorporation.

Stock Information. An increase in shares or par value does not affect initial filing fees.

Corporate Records. The Articles of Incorporation, bylaws, current amendments, board resolutions creating classes or series of shares, minutes of shareholders' meetings from the last 10 years, written communications to shareholders from the last three years, names and addresses of current directors and officers, most recent annual report, and federal and state income tax returns for the last 10 years must be kept at the principal office of the corporation.

Taxes and Fees

Annual Statements. The annual license fee is $15 plus $1 for each $1,000 (or fraction thereof) of capital stock and paid-in surplus, as shown by corporate records on the first day of the income year next preceding the date of filing the report. The license fee is included on the income tax return filed by each corporation. The minimum tax is $25.

Income Tax Rate. The tax rate is 5 percent of South Carolina net income.

S Corporation

S corporation status is recognized by the State of South Carolina. A separate state election from the federal election is not required.

License Requirements

South Carolina requires most businesses to obtain a license and pay a fee if operating in the state. Please check with the state to make sure your business is complying with the license requirements for your particular profession.

For more information on taxes, visit www.dor.state.sc.us/

For additional or updated information, visit www.scsos.com

Mailing Address

Secretary of State
P.O. Box 11350
Columbia, SC 29211
Tel: (803) 734-2158
Fax: (803) 734-1614

South Dakota
Corporate Name Endings

The name must contain the word "Corporation," "Company," "Incorporated," "Limited," or an abbreviation thereof. It may not be the same as, or descriptively similar to, the name of any domestic or qualified foreign corporation, reserved or registered name, or any limited partnership, unless consent is obtained. The name must not imply it is organized for any purpose other than that stated in the Articles of Incorporation. The name may not be the same as, or deceptively similar to, a name in use by any other domestic corporation or authorized foreign corporation in South Dakota.

Corporation Requirements
Director Information
- Minimum number: One or more.
- Residence requirements: No provision.
- Age requirements: Directors must be a natural person* at least 18 years of age.

---

* In jurisprudence, a "natural person" is a human being perceptible through the senses and subject to physical laws, as opposed to an "artificial person," i.e., an organization that the law treats for some purposes as if it were a person distinct from its members or owners.

- Directors are required to be listed in the Articles of Incorporation.

Officer Information. Officers are not required to be listed in the Articles of Incorporation.

Stock Information. An increase in shares may cause an increase in initial filing fees.

Corporate Records. A stock transfer ledger must be kept at the principal corporate office.

Taxes and Fees

Annual Statements. An annual report is due to the Secretary of State by the first day of the second month following the anniversary month of the corporation each year. The filing fee is $25.

Income Tax Rate. There is no income tax in South Dakota.

S Corporation

S corporation status is recognized by the State of South Dakota. A separate state election from the federal election is not required; South Dakota imposes neither a corporate income tax nor a personal income tax.

License Requirements

South Dakota requires most businesses to obtain a license and pay a fee if operating in the state. Please check with the state to make sure your business is complying with the license requirements for your particular profession.

For more information on taxes, visit www.state.sd.us/drr2

For additional or updated information, visit www.state.sd.us/sos

Mailing Address

Secretary of State
Capitol Building
500 East Capitol Avenue, Suite 204
Pierre, SD 57501-5070
Tel: (605) 773-4845
Fax: (605) 773-6580

Tennessee
Corporate Name Endings

The name must include the word "Corporation," Incorporated," "Company," or an abbreviation thereof, including words or abbreviations in a foreign language. The name must be distinguishable in the Secretary of State's records from any corporate or assumed name of a domestic or qualified foreign corporation, a reserved or registered name under Tennessee law, or the name of a not-for-profit corporation, limited partnership, or limited liability company.

Corporation Requirements
Director Information

- Minimum number: One or more.
- Residence requirements: No provision.
- Age requirements: None.
- Directors are required to be listed in the Articles of Incorporation.

Officer Information. Officers are not required to be listed in the Articles of Incorporation.

Stock Information. An increase in shares or par value does not affect initial filing fees.

Corporate Records. The charter, bylaws, all amendments currently in effect, shareholders' meeting minutes, a list of current directors and officers including their addresses, and the corporation's most recent annual report must be kept at the principal office of the corporation.

Taxes and Fees

Annual Statements. Every domestic and foreign corporation authorized to transact business in Tennessee (except state and national banks) must file an annual report with the Secretary of State by the first day of the fourth month following the close of the corporation's fiscal year. The filing fee is $20.

Income Tax Rate. The excise tax is 6 percent of Tennessee income subject to excise tax.

Franchise Tax. Corporations must pay a franchise tax based on the amount of stock of the corporation. The tax rate is .25 percent of issued and outstanding capital stock, surplus, and undivided profits as shown on the corporation's books and records at the close of its last fiscal year preceding the making of the required report. The minimum tax is $100.

S Corporation

S corporation status is not recognized by the State of Tennessee.

License Requirements

Tennessee requires most businesses to obtain a license and pay a fee if operating in the district. Please check with the district to make sure your business is complying with the license requirements for your particular profession.

For more information on taxes, visit www.state.tn.us/revenue

For additional or updated information, visit www.state.tn.us/sos

Mailing Address

Department of State
Business Services
312 8th Avenue North
6th Floor, Snodgrass Tower
Nashville, TN 37243
Tel: (615) 741-2286

Texas
Corporate Name Endings

The name must contain the word "Corporation," "Company," "Incorporated," or an abbreviation thereof. The name must not imply a purpose other than that stated in the Articles of Incorporation. It may not be the same as, or deceptively similar to, the name of any domestic or foreign corporation, or reserved or registered name. However, a name already in use may be used if the corporation or LLC gets written consent from the user filed with the Secretary of State. The name may not contain the word "Lottery."

Corporation Requirements
Director Information
- Minimum number: One or more.
- Residence requirements: No provision.

- Age requirements: Directors must be a natural person[*] at least 18 years of age.
- Directors are not required to be listed in the Articles of Incorporation.

Officer Information. Officers are not required to be listed in the Articles of Incorporation.

Stock Information. An increase in shares or par value does not affect initial filing fees.

Corporate Records. The stock transfer records must be kept with the principal corporate office.

Taxes and Fees

Annual Statements. Corporations must complete and file a franchise tax return. (See below.)

Income/Franchise Tax Rate. The franchise tax is computed at the rate of: (1) .25 percent of net taxable capital and (2) 4.5 percent of net taxable earned surplus. If the amount computed under either part of the basis formula is zero or less, the tax is zero. If the amount of tax computed is less than $100, the corporation is not required to pay such amount and is not considered to owe any franchise tax for the period.

S Corporation

S corporation status is not recognized by the State of Texas.

---

[*] In jurisprudence, a "natural person" is a human being perceptible through the senses and subject to physical laws, as opposed to an "artificial person," i.e., an organization that the law treats for some purposes as if it were a person distinct from its members or owners.

License Requirements

Texas requires that you obtain a license and pay a fee if operating certain types of businesses in the state. Please check with the state to make sure your business is complying with the license requirements for your particular profession.

For more information on taxes, visit www.window.state.tx.us/m23taxes.html

For additional or update information, visit www.sos.state.tx.us

Mailing Address

Secretary of State
Corporations Section
P.O. Box 13697
Austin, TX 78711
Tel: (512) 463-5555
Fax: (512) 463-5709

Utah
Corporate Name Endings

The name must contain the word "Corporation," "Incorporated," "Company," or an abbreviation thereof, or words or abbreviations with the same meaning in another language. It must be distinguishable from the name of any domestic corporation, authorized foreign corporation, domestic or foreign limited liability company or partnership, or reserved or registered name in the state of Utah.

Corporation Requirements
Director Information

- Minimum number: Not less than three, unless there are only one or two shareholders of record; then the number of directors may be less than three but not less than the number of shareholders.

- Residence requirement: No provision.
- Age requirements: Directors must be a natural person* at least 18 years of age.
- Directors are not required to be listed in the Articles of Incorporation.

Officer Information. Officers are not required to be listed in the Articles of Incorporation.

Stock Information. An increase in shares or par value does not affect initial filing fees.

Corporate Records. The Articles of Incorporation, bylaws, minutes of all share-holders' meetings, records of actions taken without meeting for the past three years, the names and addresses of current directors and officers, the most recent annual report, and financial statements prepared for periods ending during the last three years must be kept at the principal office of the corporation.

Taxes and Fees

Annual Statements. An Application for Renewal must be filed with the Division of Corporations and Commercial Code no later than the end of the second month following the month in which the report form is mailed by the division. The annual report fee is $10.

---

* In jurisprudence, a "natural person" is a human being perceptible through the senses and subject to physical laws, as opposed to an "artificial person," i.e., an organization that the law treats for some purposes as if it were a person distinct from its members or owners.

Income Tax Rate. The tax rate is 5 percent of net income. The minimum tax is $100.

S Corporation

S corporation status is recognized by the State of Utah. A separate state election from the federal election is not required.

License Requirements

Utah requires most businesses to obtain a license and pay a fee if operating in the state. Please check with the state to make sure your business is complying with the license requirements for your particular profession.

For more information on taxes, visit www.tax.utah.gov

For additional or updated information, visit www.commerce.state.ut.us

Mailing Address

Department of Commerce
Division of Corporations and
Commercial Code
P.O. Box 146705
Salt Lake City, UT 84114-6705
Tel: (801) 530-4849
Fax: (801) 530-6438

Vermont
Corporate Name Endings

The name must contain the word "Corporation," "Incorporated," "Company," "Limited," or an abbreviation thereof. The name may not contain language stating or implying that the corporation is organized for purposes other than those permitted by state law. The name shall not have the word

"Cooperative" or any abbreviation thereof. The name shall be distinguishable from, and not the same as, deceptively similar to, or likely to be confused with or mistaken for any name granted, registered, or reserved under chapter or with the Secretary of State.

Corporation Requirements

Director Information
- Minimum number: Not less than three, unless there are only one or two shareholders of record; then the number of directors may be less than three but not less than the number of shareholders.
- Residence requirements: No provision.
- Age requirements: None.
- Directors are not required to be listed in the Articles of Incorporation.

Officer Information. Officers are not required to be listed in the Articles of Incorporation.

Stock Information. An increase in shares or par value does not affect initial filing fees.

Corporate Records. The Articles of Incorporation, bylaws, resolutions, minutes, all written communications to shareholders within the past three years, a list of names and business addresses of its current directors and officers, and the company's most recent annual report must be kept at the corporation's principal office.

Taxes and Fees

Annual Statements. Every domestic and foreign corporation authorized to do business in Vermont must file an annual report with the Secretary of State within 2½ months after the expiration of its fiscal year (March 15 for calendar year companies). The annual fee for a domestic corporation is $25. The annual fee for a foreign corporation is $150.

Income Tax Rate. Income tax rates are 7 percent on Vermont net income of $10,000 or less, 8.10 percent of net income between $10,001 and $25,000, 9.20 percent of net income between $25,001 and $250,000, 9.75 percent of net income in excess of $250,000. The minimum tax is $250.

S Corporation

S corporation status is recognized by the State of Vermont. A separate state election from the federal election is not required; although, some S corporations are required to pay a minimum entity level tax of $250.

License Requirements

Vermont requires most businesses to obtain a license and pay a fee if operating in the state. Please check with the state to make sure your business is complying with the license requirements for your particular profession.

For more information on taxes, visit www.state.vt.us/tax

For additional or updated information, visit www.sec.state.vt.us

Mailing Address

Secretary of State
Corporations Division
81 River Street
Montpelier, VT 05609-1104
Tel: (802) 828-2386
Fax: (802) 828-2853

Virginia
Corporate Name Endings
The name shall contain the word "Corporation," "Incorporated," "Company," "Limited," or an abbreviation thereof. The name shall not contain any prohibited word or phrase implying it is organized for any purpose other than that stated in the Articles of Incorporation. The name may not be confusingly similar to that of any domestic or qualified foreign corporation.

Corporation Requirements
Director Information
- Minimum number: One or more.
- Residence requirements: No provision.
- Age requirements: None.
- Directors are not required to be listed in the Articles of Incorporation.

Officer Information. Officers are not required to be listed in the Articles of Incorporation.

Stock Information. An increase in shares may cause an increase in initial filing fees.

Corporate Records. Corporate records must be kept, but no location is specified.

Taxes and Fees
Annual Statements. Domestic and qualified foreign corporations must file an annual report with the State Corporation Commission on the first day of the second month in which the business was incorporated or authorized to transact business. The annual registration fee is $100 if the number of authorized shares is 5,000 shares or less. If the corporation has authorized shares of more than 5,000, the annual fee is $50 plus $30 for each additional 5,000 shares, up to a maximum of $1,700.

Income Tax Rate. The tax rate is 6 percent of Virginia taxable income.

S Corporation
S corporation status is recognized by the State of Virginia. A separate state election from the federal election is not required.

License Requirements
Virginia requires most businesses to obtain a license and pay a fee if operating in the state. Please check with the state to make sure your business is complying with the license requirements for your particular profession.

For more information on taxes, visit www.tax.virginia.gov

For additional or updated information, visit www.state.va.us/scc

Mailing Address
State Corporation Commission
P.O. Box 1197
Richmond, VA 23218
Tel: (804) 371-9967

Washington
Corporate Name Endings
The corporate name must include the word "Corporation," "Incorporated," "Company,"

"Limited," or the abbreviation "Corp.," "Inc.," "Co.," or "Ltd." The name must not imply a purpose other than the purpose stated in the charter. The name must be distinguishable from the name of any other domestic corporation or of any foreign corporation authorized to do business in the state. The name must not include certain enumerated words indicating it is a bank or savings and loan, or any other words or phrases prohibited by any state statute.

Corporation Requirements

Director Information

- Minimum number: One or more.
- Residence requirements: No provision.
- Age requirements: None.
- Directors are not required to be listed in the Articles of Incorporation.

Officer Information. Officers are not required to be listed in the Articles of Incorporation.

Stock Information. An increase in shares or par value does not affect initial filing fees.

Corporate Records. Articles of incorporation, bylaws, minutes of shareholders' meetings, financial statements for the past three years, all written communications to shareholders within the past three years, a list of names and addresses of current directors and officers, and the most recent annual report delivered to the Secretary of State must be kept at the principal office of the corporation.

Taxes and Fees

Annual Statements. A Corporation License Renewal and annual report must be filed with the Department of Licensing on or before the expiration of the corporation's corporate license, or not less than 30 days or more than 90 days prior to the expiration date of any staggered yearly license. The license fee is $50, with a renewal fee of $9.

Income Tax Rate. There is no income tax in the State of Washington.

S Corporation

The State of Washington has no corporate income tax, so S corporation elections have no impact.

License Requirements

Washington requires most businesses to obtain a license and pay a fee if operating in the state. Please check with the state to make sure your business is complying with the license requirements for your particular profession.

For more information on taxes, visit dor.wa.gov

For additional or updated information, visit www.secstate.wa.gov

Mailing Address

Secretary of State
Corporations Division
P.O. Box 40234
Olympia, WA 98504-0234
Tel: (360) 753-7115

West Virginia

Corporate Name Endings

The name must contain the word "Company," "Corporation," "Incorporated," "Limited," or a form thereof. The name must not be the same as or deceptively similar to a name already in use by another existing corporation or foreign corporation qualified to do business in West Virginia, without written consent of the other corporation, or by a court order establishing the right of the applicant to use the name. The name must not imply a purpose other than that stated in the Articles of Incorporation. The words "Engineer" or "Engineering" cannot be used unless the corporate purpose is professional engineering and one or more of the incorporators is a registered professional engineer.

Director Information

- Minimum number: One or more.
- Residence requirements: No provision.
- Age requirements: None.
- Directors are required to be listed in the Articles of Incorporation.

Officer Information. Officers are not required to be listed in the Articles of Incorporation.

Stock Information. An increase in shares may cause an increase in the initial filing fees.

Corporate Records. The stock transfer ledger must be kept at the principal corporate office.

Taxes and Fees

Annual Statements. A business registration certificate must be filed every two years. The filing fee is $30.

Income Tax Rate. The tax rate is 9.0 percent of taxable income.

Corporate Franchise Tax

- The Corporate License Tax is due based upon capital stock. The franchise tax rate is the greater of: (a) $50 or (b) 0.7 percent of the value of the corporation's capital for domestic corporations.
- No par stock is valued at $25 per share unless it was originally issued for a greater consideration.
- The Corporate License Tax for foreign corporations ranges from $250 to $4,375, based upon capital stock values.

S Corporation

S corporation status is recognized by the State of West Virginia provided the S corporation files an Informational Return. A separate state election from the federal election is not required; however, S corporations are subject to the business franchise tax.

License Requirements

West Virginia requires most businesses to obtain a license and pay a fee if operating in the state. Please check with the state to make sure your business is complying with the license requirements for your particular profession.

For more information on taxes, visit www.wvrevenue.gov

For additional or updated information, visit www.wvsos.org

Mailing Address

Secretary of State
Bldg. 1, Suite 157-K
1900 Kanawha Blvd. East
Charleston, WV 25305-0770
Tel: (304) 558-8000
Fax: (304) 558-5758

Wisconsin
Corporate Name Endings

The name of the corporation shall contain the word "Corporation," "Incorporated," "Company," "Limited," or an abbreviation thereof, or words or abbreviations of words with similar meanings in another language. The name may not contain language stating or implying the corporation is organized for a purpose other than as permitted. The corporate name must be distinguishable upon the records of the Secretary of State from other corporations, LLCs, and other business entities authorized to use the name in the state.

Corporation Requirements
Director Information

- Minimum number: One or more.
- Residence requirements: No provision.
- Age requirements: None.
- Directors are required to be listed in the Articles of Incorporation.

Officer Information. Officers are not required to be listed in the Articles of Incorporation.

Stock Information An increase in shares may cause an increase in initial filing fees.

Corporate Records. The corporation is required to kept records; however, no location is specified.

Taxes and Fees

Annual Statements. Annual reports for domestic and foreign corporations are due each year following the year in which the corporation was incorporated, during the quarter in which the anniversary date of the incorporation occurs. The filing fee is $25 for online filing or $40 for paper reports.

Income Tax Rate. The income tax rate is 7.9 percent of Wisconsin net income.

S Corporation

S corporation status is recognized by the State of Wisconsin. A separate state election from the federal election is not required.

License Requirements

Wisconsin requires most businesses to obtain a license and pay a fee if operating in the state. The following is a partial list:

- Collection agencies
- Dairy products
- Detectives

- Employment agents
- Fishermen
- Food processing plants
- Insurance agents
- Interior designers
- Landscape architects
- Pharmacies
- Real estate brokers
- Restaurants

Please check with the state to make sure your business is complying with the license requirements for your particular profession.

For more information on taxes, visit www.dor.state.wi.us

For additional or updated information, visit www.wdfi.org

Mailing Address

Secretary of State
Division of Corporate and
Consumer Services
Corporations Bureau, 3rd Floor
P.O. Box 7846
Madison, WI 53707-7846
Tel: (608) 261-7577
Fax: (608) 267-6813

Wyoming
Corporate Name Endings

The name of the corporation may not contain language implying a different purpose from the purpose or purposes in the Articles of Incorporation. The name shall not be the same as or similar to the name of any domestic or foreign profit or non-

profit corporation, trade name, trademark, or service mark registered in this state, limited liability company, statutory trust company, or limited partnership or other business entity.

Corporation Requirements
Director Information
- Minimum number: One or more.
- Residence requirements: No provision.
- Age requirements: None.
- Directors are required to be listed in the Articles of Incorporation.

Officer Information. Officers are not required to be listed in the Articles of Incorporation.

Stock Information. An increase in shares or par value does not affect the initial filing fees.

Corporate Records. The Articles of Incorporation, bylaws, board resolutions creating classes or series of shares, minutes of all shareholders' meetings, records of all actions taken by shareholders without meeting for the past three years, all written communications to shareholders within the past three years, a list of names and business addresses of current directors and officers, and the most recent annual report must be kept at the principal office of the corporation.

Taxes and Fees
Annual Statements. Annual statements are due by December 1. The tax is based on the corporate property and assets located

and employed in Wyoming. The license tax is $50, or two-tenths of one million on the dollar ($.0002) of corporate assets, whichever is greater.

Income Tax Rate. The State of Wyoming has no corporate income tax.

S Corporation

The State of Wyoming has no corporate income tax, so S corporation elections have no impact.

License Requirements

Wyoming requires most businesses to obtain a license and pay a fee if operating in the state. Please check with the state to make sure your business is complying with the license requirements for your particular profession.

For more information on taxes, visit revenue.state.wy.us/

For additional or updated information, visit soswy.state.wy.us

Mailing Address

Secretary of State
Corporations Division
The Capitol Building, Room 110
200 West 24th Street
Cheyenne, WY 82002-0020
Tel: (307) 777-7311
Fax: (307) 777-5339

Appendix **B**

Articles of Incorporation

Don't Be Intimidated by Your Articles of Incorporation

This step of incorporating may not be as complicated as you imagine. Some states are very particular about the format your Articles of Incorporation must take, and a generic template does not apply. But if you follow a few simple steps, you can save time and money.

Step 1

Many Secretary of State Web sites provide a link that allows you to create and submit your Articles of Incorporation online. Check out Appendix A and look up the state in which you are going to incorporate. Look toward the bottom of the state information and find the link that says "For additional or updated information." Go to this link and look around for a place to fill out your information online. If you can't find it, call the phone number supplied and ask if there is a place where you can submit your Articles of Incorporation online.

Many of these online submissions don't cost you money. Also, many of the online links will only ask you a limited number of questions and then you will be on your way. This is by far the easiest and preferred way to create your Articles of Incorporation.

Step 2

If you were not able to find a way to submit your information online to form your corporation, then check for a supplied template. This template would be on the same site that you search above (the Secretary of State Web site).

Step 3

If your chosen state does not provide a manner in which to submit or create your Articles of Incorporation online, or an online template, then you can use the generic template we supply in this appendix.

While requirements vary from state to state, the generic template covers the requirements for most states. We have also provided some different templates for a few of the states for which this generic template will not work. These additional templates are provided so that you can get a feel for how minor the changes from state to state really are.

Articles of Incorporation
of
[Corporate Name]

THE UNDERSIGNED, in order to form a corporation for the purposes hereinafter stated, under and pursuant to the provisions of General Corporation Law of the State of _____, hereby certifies as follows:

ARTICLE I
CORPORATE NAME

The name of the Corporation is _____.

ARTICLE II
INITIAL OFFICE AND AGENT

The address of this Corporation's initial registered office and the name of its original registered agent at such address is:

Address of Corporation, and County   Registered Agent, Title, and Address

_____   _____

_____   _____

_____   _____

I hereby acknowledge and accept appointment as corporation registered agent:

_____

Signature

ARTICLE III
PURPOSES

[Describe the purpose of your corporation. If you are unsure as to the exact purpose of the corporation at this time, then state something like: "The purpose of the corporation is to engage in any lawful act or activity for which a corporation may be organized under the General Corporation Laws of the State of _____."]

ARTICLE IV
DURATION

[For example: "The duration of this Corporation is 'perpetual.'" Or "The term for which this Corporation is to exist until _____."]

ARTICLE V
STOCK

The aggregate number of shares that this Corporation shall have authority to issue is 1,000 shares of $1.00 per value stock.

ARTICLE VI
CORPORATION BYLAWS

The Board of Directors is authorized and empowered to make, alter, amend, and rescind the Bylaws of the corporation, but Bylaws made by the Board may be altered or repealed and new Bylaws made by the stockholders.

ARTICLE VII
LIABILITY OF DIRECTORS

Pursuant to the general corporation laws of the State of _____ any and all directors of this Corporation shall not be liable to the Corporation, its shareholders, or any third party for breach of duty of care; such potential liability is hereby eliminated.

ARTICLE VIII
BOARD OF DIRECTORS

The name and address of each person serving as a member of the initial Board of Directors is:

_____

_____

_____

_____

_____

_____

_____

_____

_____

_____

_____

ARTICLE IX
INCORPORATORS

The name(s) and address(es) of the Incorporator(s) is (are):

_____

_____

_____

_____

IN WITNESS WHEREOF, the incorporator(s) has hereunto set his hand this _____ day of _____, _____.

That they are all incorporators herein; that they have read the above and foregoing Articles of Incorporation; know the contents thereof and that the same is true to the best of their knowledge and belief, excepting as to matters herein alleged upon information and belief and as to those matters they believe to be true.

INCORPORATORS:

_____   _____
Signature   Signature

_____   _____
Signature   Signature

STATE OF   )
                                             :§
COUNTY OF   )

On the _____ day of _____, _____ personally appeared before me _____, the signer of the within instrument, who duly acknowledged to me he executed the same.

_____
Notary Public

_____
Residing at:

_____
My commission expires:

CALIFORNIA ARTICLES OF INCORPORATION

I

The name of this corporation is _____.

II

The purpose of the corporation is to engage in any lawful act or activity for which a corporation may be organized under the **GENERAL CORPORATION LAW** of California other than the banking business, the trust company business or the practice of a profession permitted to be incorporated by the California Corporations Code.

III

The name and address in the State of California of this corporation's initial agent for service of process is:

Name _____

Address _____

City, State _____

IV

This corporation is authorized to issue only one class of shares of stock; and the total number of shares which this corporation is authorized to issue is _____.

_____

, Incorporator

New York State
Department of State
Division of Corporations, State Records
and Uniform Commercial Code
Albany, NY 12231

(This form must be printed or typed in black ink)

CERTIFICATE OF INCORPORATION
OF

_____

(Insert Corporate Name)

Under Section 402 of the Business Corporation Law

FIRST: The name of the corporation is: _____

SECOND: This corporation is formed to engage in any lawful act or activity for which a corporation may be organized under the Business Corporation Law, provided that it is not formed to engage in any act or activity requiring the consent or approval of any state official, department, board, agency or other body without such consent or approval first being obtained.

THIRD: The county, within this state, in which the office of the corporation is to be located is: _____

FOURTH: The total number of shares which the corporation shall have authority to issue and a statement of the par value of each share or a statement that the shares are without par value are: _____ [e.g., 200 No Par Value]

FIFTH: The secretary of state is designated as agent of the corporation upon whom process against the corporation may be served. The address to which the Secretary of State shall mail a copy of any process accepted on behalf of the corporation is:

_____

_____

_____

SIXTH: (optional) The name and street address in this state of the registered agent upon whom process against the corporation may be served is:

_____

_____

_____

SEVENTH: (*optional*—the existence of the corporation begins on the date the certificate of incorporation is filed by the Department of State. Corporate existence may begin on a date, not to exceed 90 days, after the date of filing by the Department of State. Complete this paragraph only if you wish to have the corporation's existence to begin on a later date, which is not more than 90 days after the date of filing by the Department of State.) The date the corporate existence shall begin is: _____ .

Incorporator Information Required

_____
(Signature)

_____
(Type or print name)

_____
(Address)

_____
(City, State, Zip code)

- -

CERTIFICATE OF INCORPORATION
OF

_____
(Insert Corporate Name)

Under Section 402 of the Business Corporation Law

- -

Filed by: _____
                      (Name)

                      _____
                      (Mailing address)

                      _____
                      (City, State, and Zip code)

Note: This form was prepared by the New York State Department of State for filing a certificate of incorporation for a business corporation. It does not contain all optional provisions under the law. You are not required to use this form. You may draft your own form or use forms available at legal stationery stores. The Department of State recommends that legal documents be prepared under the guidance of an attorney. The fee for a certificate of incorporation is $125 plus the applicable tax on shares required by Section 180 of the Tax Law. The minimum tax on shares is $10. The tax on 200 no par value shares is $10 (total $135). Checks should be made payable to the Department of State for the total amount of the filing fee and tax.

Another example where the default template does not apply. Maine requires the additional page below to be submitted as well.

**DOMESTIC
BUSINESS CORPORATION**

STATE OF MAINE
**ACCEPTANCE OF APPOINTMENT
AS CLERK OF**

_____

(Name of domestic business corporation)

Pursuant to 13-A MRSA §304.2-A, the undersigned hereby accepts the appointment as clerk for the above-named domestic business corporation.

CLERK   **DATED** _____

_____   _____
            (Signature)   (Type or print name)

Appendix C

IRS Form SS-4 and Instructions

Form SS-4
(Rev. December 2001)
Department of the Treasury
Internal Revenue Service

Application for Employer Identification Number

(For use by employers, corporations, partnerships, trusts, estates, churches,
government agencies, Indian tribal entities, certain individuals, and others.)

▶ See separate instructions for each line.   ▶ Keep a copy for your records.

EIN

OMB No. 1545-0003

Type or print clearly.		
1 Legal name of entity (or individual) for whom the EIN is being requested		
2 Trade name of business (if different from name on line 1)	**3** Executor, trustee, "care of" name	
4a Mailing address (room, apt., suite no. and street, or P.O. box)	**5a** Street address (if different) (Do not enter a P.O. box.)	
4b City, state, and ZIP code	**5b** City, state, and ZIP code	
6 County and state where principal business is located		
7a Name of principal officer, general partner, grantor, owner, or trustor	**7b** SSN, ITIN, or EIN	

8a Type of entity (check only one box)

☐ Sole proprietor (SSN) _____
☐ Partnership
☐ Corporation (enter form number to be filed) ▶ _____
☐ Personal service corp.
☐ Church or church-controlled organization
☐ Other nonprofit organization (specify) ▶ _____
☐ Other (specify) ▶

☐ Estate (SSN of decedent) _____
☐ Plan administrator (SSN) _____
☐ Trust (SSN of grantor) _____
☐ National Guard   ☐ State/local government
☐ Farmers' cooperative   ☐ Federal government/military
☐ REMIC   ☐ Indian tribal governments/enterprises
Group Exemption Number (GEN) ▶ _____

8b If a corporation, name the state or foreign country (if applicable) where incorporated

State	Foreign country

9 Reason for applying (check only one box)

☐ Started new business (specify type) ▶_____
☐ Hired employees (Check the box and see line 12.)
☐ Compliance with IRS withholding regulations
☐ Other (specify) ▶

☐ Banking purpose (specify purpose) ▶ _____
☐ Changed type of organization (specify new type) ▶ _____
☐ Purchased going business
☐ Created a trust (specify type) ▶ _____
☐ Created a pension plan (specify type) ▶ _____

10 Date business started or acquired (month, day, year) | **11** Closing month of accounting year

12 First date wages or annuities were paid or will be paid (month, day, year). **Note:** *If applicant is a withholding agent, enter date income will first be paid to nonresident alien. (month, day, year)* . . . . ▶

13 Highest number of employees expected in the next 12 months. **Note:** *If the applicant does not expect to have any employees during the period, enter "-0-."* . . . . ▶

Agricultural	Household	Other

14 Check **one** box that best describes the principal activity of your business.
☐ Construction ☐ Rental & leasing ☐ Transportation & warehouse ☐ Health care & social assistance ☐ Wholesale–agent/broker
☐ Real estate ☐ Manufacturing ☐ Finance & insurance ☐ Accommodation & food service ☐ Wholesale–other ☐ Retail
☐ Other (specify)

15 Indicate principal line of merchandise sold; specific construction work done; products produced; or services provided.

16a Has the applicant ever applied for an employer identification number for this or any other business? . . . . . ☐ Yes ☐ No
Note: *If "Yes," please complete lines 16b and 16c.*

16b If you checked "Yes" on line 16a, give applicant's legal name and trade name shown on prior application if different from line 1 or 2 above.
Legal name ▶   Trade name ▶

16c Approximate date when, and city and state where, the application was filed. Enter previous employer identification number if known.

Approximate date when filed (mo., day, year)	City and state where filed	Previous EIN

Third Party Designee	Complete this section **only** if you want to authorize the named individual to receive the entity's EIN and answer questions about the completion of this form.	
	Designee's name	Designee's telephone number (include area code) ( )
	Address and ZIP code	Designee's fax number (include area code) ( )

Under penalties of perjury, I declare that I have examined this application, and to the best of my knowledge and belief, it is true, correct, and complete.

Applicant's telephone number (include area code) ( )

Name and title (type or print clearly) ▶

Applicant's fax number (include area code) ( )

Signature ▶   Date ▶

For Privacy Act and Paperwork Reduction Act Notice, see separate instructions.   Cat. No. 16055N   Form **SS-4** (Rev. 12-2001)

Form SS-4 (Rev. 12-2001)

Do I Need an EIN?

File Form SS-4 if the applicant entity does not already have an EIN but is required to show an EIN on any return, statement, or other document.[1] **See also the separate instructions for each line on Form SS-4.**

IF the applicant...	AND...	THEN...
Started a new business	Does not currently have (nor expect to have) employees	Complete lines 1, 2, 4a- 6, 8a, and 9- 16c.
Hired (or will hire) employees, including household employees	Does not already have an EIN	Complete lines 1, 2, 4a- 6, 7a- b (if applicable), 8a, 8b (if applicable), and 9- 16c.
Opened a bank account	Needs an EIN for banking purposes only	Complete lines 1- 5b, 7a- b (if applicable), 8a, 9, and 16a- c.
Changed type of organization	Either the legal character of the organization or its ownership changed (e.g., you incorporate a sole proprietorship or form a partnership)[2]	Complete lines 1- 16c (as applicable).
Purchased a going business[3]	Does not already have an EIN	Complete lines 1- 16c (as applicable).
Created a trust	The trust is other than a grantor trust or an IRA trust[4]	Complete lines 1- 16c (as applicable).
Created a pension plan as a plan administrator[5]	Needs an EIN for reporting purposes	Complete lines 1, 2, 4a- 6, 8a, 9, and 16a- c.
Is a foreign person needing an EIN to comply with IRS withholding regulations	Needs an EIN to complete a Form W-8 (other than Form W-8ECI), avoid withholding on portfolio assets, or claim tax treaty benefits[6]	Complete lines 1- 5b, 7a- b (SSN or ITIN optional), 8a- 9, and 16a- c.
Is administering an estate	Needs an EIN to report estate income on Form 1041	Complete lines 1, 3, 4a- b, 8a, 9, and 16a- c.
Is a withholding agent for taxes on non-wage income paid to an alien (i.e., individual, corporation, or partnership, etc.)	Is an agent, broker, fiduciary, manager, tenant, or spouse who is required to file **Form 1042,** Annual Withholding Tax Return for U.S. Source Income of Foreign Persons	Complete lines 1, 2, 3 (if applicable), 4a- 5b, 7a- b (if applicable), 8a, 9, and 16a- c.
Is a state or local agency	Serves as a tax reporting agent for public assistance recipients under Rev. Proc. 80-4, 1980-1 C.B. 581[7]	Complete lines 1, 2, 4a- 5b, 8a, 9, and 16a- c.
Is a single-member LLC	Needs an EIN to file **Form 8832,** Classification Election, for filing employment tax returns, **or** for state reporting purposes[8]	Complete lines 1- 16c (as applicable).
Is an S corporation	Needs an EIN to file **Form 2553,** Election by a Small Business Corporation[9]	Complete lines 1- 16c (as applicable).

[1] For example, a sole proprietorship or self-employed farmer who establishes a qualified retirement plan, or is required to file excise, employment, alcohol, tobacco, or firearms returns, must have an EIN. **A partnership, corporation, REMIC (real estate mortgage investment conduit), nonprofit organization (church, club, etc.), or farmers' cooperative must use an EIN for any tax-related purpose even if the entity does not have employees.**

[2] However, **do not** apply for a new EIN if the existing entity only **(a)** changed its business name, **(b)** elected on Form 8832 to change the way it is taxed (or is covered by the default rules), or **(c)** terminated its partnership status because at least 50% of the total interests in partnership capital and profits were sold or exchanged within a 12-month period. (The EIN of the terminated partnership should continue to be used. See Regulations section 301.6109-1(d)(2)(iii).)

[3] Do not use the EIN of the prior business unless you became the "owner" of a corporation by acquiring its stock.

[4] However, IRA trusts that are required to file **Form 990-T,** Exempt Organization Business Income Tax Return, must have an EIN.

[5] A plan administrator is the person or group of persons specified as the administrator by the instrument under which the plan is operated.

[6] Entities applying to be a Qualified Intermediary (QI) need a QI-EIN even if they already have an EIN. **See Rev. Proc. 2000-12.**

[7] See also *Household employer* on page 4. **(Note:** State or local agencies may need an EIN for other reasons, e.g., hired employees.)

[8] Most LLCs **do not** need to file Form 8832. See **Limited liability company (LLC)** on page 4 for details on completing Form SS-4 for an LLC.

[9] An existing corporation that is electing or revoking S corporation status should use its previously-assigned EIN.

Instructions for Form SS-4

Department of the Treasury
Internal Revenue Service

(Rev. September 2003)

For use with Form SS-4 (Rev. December 2001)
Application for Employer Identification Number.
Section references are to the Internal Revenue Code unless otherwise noted.

General Instructions

Use these instructions to complete **Form SS-4,** Application for Employer Identification Number. Also see **Do I Need an EIN?** on page 2 of Form SS-4.

Purpose of Form

Use Form SS-4 to apply for an employer identification number (EIN). An EIN is a nine-digit number (for example, 12-3456789) assigned to sole proprietors, corporations, partnerships, estates, trusts, and other entities for tax filing and reporting purposes. The information you provide on this form will establish your business tax account.

*An EIN is for use in connection with your business activities only. Do **not** use your EIN in place of your social security number (SSN).*

Items To Note

Apply online. You can now apply for and receive an EIN online using the internet. See **How To Apply** below.

File only one Form SS-4. Generally, a sole proprietor should file only one Form SS-4 and needs only one EIN, regardless of the number of businesses operated as a sole proprietorship or trade names under which a business operates. However, if the proprietorship incorporates or enters into a partnership, a new EIN is required. Also, each corporation in an affiliated group must have its own EIN.

EIN applied for, but not received. If you do not have an EIN by the time a return is due, write "Applied For" and the date you applied in the space shown for the number. **Do not** show your SSN as an EIN on returns.

If you do not have an EIN by the time a tax deposit is due, send your payment to the Internal Revenue Service Center for your filing area as shown in the instructions for the form that you are filing. Make your check or money order payable to the "United States Treasury" and show your name (as shown on Form SS-4), address, type of tax, period covered, and date you applied for an EIN.

How To Apply

You can apply for an EIN online, by telephone, by fax, or by mail depending on how soon you need to use the EIN. Use only one method for each entity so you do not receive more than one EIN for an entity.

Online. You can receive your EIN by internet and use it immediately to file a return or make a payment. Go to the

IRS website at **www.irs.gov/businesses** and click on **Employer ID Numbers** under **topics.**

Telephone. You can receive your EIN by telephone and use it immediately to file a return or make a payment. Call the IRS at **1-800-829-4933**. (International applicants must call 215-516-6999.) The hours of operation are 7:00 a.m. to 10:00 p.m. The person making the call must be authorized to sign the form or be an authorized designee. See **Signature** and **Third Party Designee** on page 6. Also see the **TIP** below.

If you are applying by telephone, it will be helpful to complete Form SS-4 before contacting the IRS. An IRS representative will use the information from the Form SS-4 to establish your account and assign you an EIN. Write the number you are given on the upper right corner of the form and sign and date it. Keep this copy for your records.

If requested by an IRS representative, mail or fax (facsimile) the signed Form SS-4 (including any Third Party Designee authorization) within 24 hours to the IRS address provided by the IRS representative.

*Taxpayer representatives can apply for an EIN on behalf of their client and request that the EIN be faxed to their **client** on the same day.*
Note: *By using this procedure, you are authorizing the IRS to fax the EIN without a cover sheet.*

Fax. Under the Fax-TIN program, you can receive your EIN by fax within 4 business days. Complete and fax Form SS-4 to the IRS using the Fax-TIN number listed on page 2 for your state. A long-distance charge to callers outside of the local calling area will apply. Fax-TIN numbers can only be used to apply for an EIN. **The numbers may change without notice.** Fax-TIN is available 24 hours a day, 7 days a week.

Be sure to provide your fax number so the IRS can fax the EIN back to you. **Note:** By using this procedure, you are authorizing the IRS to fax the EIN without a cover sheet.

Mail. Complete Form SS-4 at least 4 to 5 weeks before you will need an EIN. Sign and date the application and mail it to the service center address for your state. You will receive your EIN in the mail in approximately 4 weeks. See also **Third Party Designee** on page 6.

Call 1-800-829-4933 to verify a number or to ask about the status of an application by mail.

Cat. No. 62736F

Where To Fax or File

If your principal business, office or agency, or legal residence in the case of an individual, is located in:	Call the Fax-TIN number shown or file with the "Internal Revenue Service Center" at:
Connecticut, Delaware, District of Columbia, Florida, Georgia, Maine, Maryland, Massachusetts, New Hampshire, New Jersey, New York, North Carolina, Ohio, Pennsylvania, Rhode Island, South Carolina, Vermont, Virginia, West Virginia	Attn: EIN Operation P. 0. Box 9003 Holtsville, NY 11742-9003 Fax-TIN 631-447-8960
Illinois, Indiana, Kentucky, Michigan	Attn: EIN Operation Cincinnati, OH 45999 Fax-TIN 859-669-5760
Alabama, Alaska, Arizona, Arkansas, California, Colorado, Hawaii, Idaho, Iowa, Kansas, Louisiana, Minnesota, Mississippi, Missouri, Montana, Nebraska, Nevada, New Mexico, North Dakota, Oklahoma, Oregon, Puerto Rico, South Dakota, Tennessee, Texas, Utah, Washington, Wisconsin, Wyoming	Attn: EIN Operation Philadelphia, PA 19255 Fax-TIN 215-516-3990
If you have no legal residence, principal place of business, or principal office or agency in any state:	Attn: EIN Operation Philadelphia, PA 19255 Telephone 215-516-6999 Fax-TIN 215-516-3990

How To Get Forms and Publications

Phone. You can order forms, instructions, and publications by phone 24 hours a day, 7 days a week. Call 1-800-TAX-FORM (1-800-829-3676). You should receive your order or notification of its status within 10 workdays.

Personal computer. With your personal computer and modem, you can get the forms and information you need using the IRS website at **www.irs.gov** or File Transfer Protocol at **ftp.irs.gov.**

CD-ROM. For small businesses, return preparers, or others who may frequently need tax forms or publications, a CD-ROM containing over 2,000 tax products (including many prior year forms) can be purchased from the National Technical Information Service (NTIS).

To order **Pub. 1796,** Federal Tax Products on CD-ROM, call **1-877-CDFORMS** (1-877-233-6767) toll free or connect to **www.irs.gov/cdorders.**

Tax Help for Your Business

IRS-sponsored Small Business Workshops provide information about your Federal and state tax obligations.

For information about workshops in your area, call 1-800-829-4933.

Related Forms and Publications

The following **forms** and **instructions** may be useful to filers of Form SS-4:
- **Form 990-T,** Exempt Organization Business Income Tax Return
- **Instructions for Form 990-T**
- **Schedule C (Form 1040),** Profit or Loss From Business
- **Schedule F (Form 1040),** Profit or Loss From Farming
- **Instructions for Form 1041 and Schedules A, B, D, G, I, J, and K-1,** U.S. Income Tax Return for Estates and Trusts
- **Form 1042,** Annual Withholding Tax Return for U.S. Source Income of Foreign Persons
- **Instructions for Form 1065,** U.S. Return of Partnership Income
- **Instructions for Form 1066,** U.S. Real Estate Mortgage Investment Conduit (REMIC) Income Tax Return
- **Instructions for Forms 1120 and 1120-A**
- **Form 2553,** Election by a Small Business Corporation
- **Form 2848,** Power of Attorney and Declaration of Representative
- **Form 8821,** Tax Information Authorization
- **Form 8832,** Entity Classification Election
   For more **information** about filing Form SS-4 and related issues, see:
- **Circular A,** Agricultural Employer's Tax Guide (Pub. 51)
- **Circular E,** Employer's Tax Guide (Pub. 15)
- **Pub. 538,** Accounting Periods and Methods
- **Pub. 542,** Corporations
- **Pub. 557,** Exempt Status for Your Organization
- **Pub. 583,** Starting a Business and Keeping Records
- **Pub. 966,** Electronic Choices for Paying ALL Your Federal Taxes
- **Pub. 1635,** Understanding Your EIN
- **Package 1023,** Application for Recognition of Exemption Under Section 501(c)(3) of the Internal Revenue Code
- **Package 1024,** Application for Recognition of Exemption Under Section 501(a)

Specific Instructions

Print or type all entries on Form SS-4. Follow the instructions for each line to expedite processing and to avoid unnecessary IRS requests for additional information. Enter "N/A" (nonapplicable) on the lines that do not apply.

Line 1—Legal name of entity (or individual) for whom the EIN is being requested. Enter the legal name of the entity (or individual) applying for the EIN exactly as it appears on the social security card, charter, or other applicable legal document.

Individuals. Enter your first name, middle initial, and last name. If you are a sole proprietor, enter your individual name, not your business name. Enter your business name on line 2. Do not use abbreviations or nicknames on line 1.

> **Trusts.** Enter the name of the trust.

> **Estate of a decedent.** Enter the name of the estate.

> **Partnerships.** Enter the legal name of the partnership as it appears in the partnership agreement.

> **Corporations.** Enter the corporate name as it appears in the corporation charter or other legal document creating it.

> **Plan administrators.** Enter the name of the plan administrator. A plan administrator who already has an EIN should use that number.

Line 2—Trade name of business. Enter the trade name of the business if different from the legal name. The trade name is the "doing business as " (DBA) name.

> *Use the full legal name shown on line 1 on all tax returns filed for the entity. (However, if you enter a trade name on line 2 and choose to use the trade name instead of the legal name, enter the trade name on **all returns** you file.) To prevent processing delays and errors, **always** use the legal name only (or the trade name only) on **all** tax returns.*

Line 3—Executor, trustee, "care of" name. Trusts enter the name of the trustee. Estates enter the name of the executor, administrator, or other fiduciary. If the entity applying has a designated person to receive tax information, enter that person's name as the "care of" person. Enter the individual's first name, middle initial, and last name.

Lines 4a-b—Mailing address. Enter the mailing address for the entity's correspondence. If line 3 is completed, enter the address for the executor, trustee or "care of" person. Generally, this address will be used on all tax returns.

> *File **Form 8822**, Change of Address, to report any subsequent changes to the entity's mailing address.*

Lines 5a-b—Street address. Provide the entity's physical address **only** if different from its mailing address shown in lines 4a-b. **Do not** enter a P.O. box number here.

Line 6—County and state where principal business is located. Enter the entity's primary **physical** location.

Lines 7a-b—Name of principal officer, general partner, grantor, owner, or trustor. Enter the first name, middle initial, last name, and SSN of **(a)** the principal officer if the business is a corporation, **(b)** a general partner if a partnership, **(c)** the owner of an entity that is disregarded as separate from its owner (disregarded entities owned by a corporation enter the corporation's name and EIN), or **(d)** a grantor, owner, or trustor if a trust.

If the person in question is an **alien individual** with a previously assigned individual taxpayer identification number (ITIN), enter the ITIN in the space provided and submit a copy of an official identifying document. If

necessary, complete **Form W-7,** Application for IRS Individual Taxpayer Identification Number, to obtain an ITIN.

You are **required** to enter an SSN, ITIN, or EIN unless the only reason you are applying for an EIN is to make an entity classification election (see Regulations sections 301.7701-1 through 301.7701-3) and you are a nonresident alien with no effectively connected income from sources within the United States.

Line 8a—Type of entity. Check the box that best describes the type of entity applying for the EIN. If you are an alien individual with an ITIN previously assigned to you, enter the ITIN in place of a requested SSN.

> *This is not an election for a tax classification of an entity. See **Limited liability company (LLC)** on page 4.*

> **Other.** If not specifically listed, check the "Other" box, enter the type of entity and the type of return, if any, that will be filed (for example, "Common Trust Fund, Form 1065" or "Created a Pension Plan"). Do not enter "N/A." If you are an alien individual applying for an EIN, see the **Lines 7a-b** instructions above.
> - **Household employer.** If you are an individual, check the "Other" box and enter "Household Employer" and your SSN. If you are a state or local agency serving as a tax reporting agent for public assistance recipients who become household employers, check the "Other" box and enter "Household Employer Agent." If you are a trust that qualifies as a household employer, you do not need a separate EIN for reporting tax information relating to household employees; use the EIN of the trust.
> - **QSub.** For a qualified subchapter S subsidiary (QSub) check the "Other" box and specify "QSub."
> - **Withholding agent.** If you are a withholding agent required to file Form 1042, check the "Other" box and enter "Withholding Agent."

> **Sole proprietor.** Check this box if you file Schedule C, C-EZ, or F (Form 1040) and have a qualified plan, or are required to file excise, employment, alcohol, tobacco, or firearms returns, or are a payer of gambling winnings. Enter your SSN (or ITIN) in the space provided. If you are a nonresident alien with no effectively connected income from sources within the United States, you do not need to enter an SSN or ITIN.

> **Corporation.** This box is for any corporation **other than a personal service corporation.** If you check this box, enter the income tax form number to be filed by the entity in the space provided.

> *If you entered **"1120S"** after the "Corporation" checkbox, the corporation **must** file Form 2553 **no later than the 15th day of the 3rd month of the tax year the election is to take effect.** Until Form 2553 has been received and approved, you will be considered a Form 1120 filer. See the Instructions for Form 2553.*

> **Personal service corp.** Check this box if the entity is a personal service corporation. An entity is a personal service corporation for a tax year only if:

- The principal activity of the entity during the testing period (prior tax year) for the tax year is the performance of personal services substantially by employee-owners, and
- The employee-owners own at least 10% of the fair market value of the outstanding stock in the entity on the last day of the testing period.

Personal services include performance of services in such fields as health, law, accounting, or consulting. For more information about personal service corporations, see the Instructions for Forms 1120 and 1120-A and Pub. 542.

Other nonprofit organization. Check this box if the nonprofit organization is other than a church or church-controlled organization and specify the type of nonprofit organization (for example, an educational organization).

 *If the organization also seeks tax-exempt status, you **must** file either Package 1023 or Package 1024. See Pub. 557 for more information.*

If the organization is covered by a group exemption letter, enter the four-digit **group exemption number (GEN).** (Do not confuse the GEN with the nine-digit EIN.) If you do not know the GEN, contact the parent organization. Get Pub. 557 for more information about group exemption numbers.

Plan administrator. If the plan administrator is an individual, enter the plan administrator's SSN in the space provided.

REMIC. Check this box if the entity has elected to be treated as a real estate mortgage investment conduit (REMIC). See the Instructions for Form 1066 for more information.

Limited liability company (LLC). An LLC is an entity organized under the laws of a state or foreign country as a limited liability company. For Federal tax purposes, an LLC may be treated as a partnership or corporation or be disregarded as an entity separate from its owner.

By **default,** a domestic LLC with only one member is **disregarded** as an entity separate from its owner and must include all of its income and expenses on the owner's tax return (e.g., **Schedule C (Form 1040)).** Also by default, a domestic LLC with two or more members is treated as a partnership. A domestic LLC may file Form 8832 to avoid either default classification and elect to be classified as an association taxable as a corporation. For more information on entity classifications (including the rules for foreign entities), see the instructions for Form 8832.

 *Do not file Form 8832 if the LLC accepts the default classifications above. **However, if the LLC will be electing S Corporation status, it must timely file both Form 8832 and Form 2553.***

Complete Form SS-4 for LLCs as follows:
- A single-member domestic LLC that accepts the default classification (above) does not need an EIN and generally should not file Form SS-4. Generally, the LLC

should use the name and EIN of its **owner** for all Federal tax purposes. However, the reporting and payment of employment taxes for employees of the LLC may be made using the name and EIN of **either** the owner or the LLC as explained in Notice 99-6. You can find Notice 99-6 on page 12 of Internal Revenue Bulletin 1999-3 at **www.irs.gov/pub/irs-irbs/irb99-03.pdf. (Note:** If the LLC applicant indicates in box 13 that it has employees or expects to have employees, the owner (whether an individual or other entity) of a single-member domestic LLC will also be assigned its own EIN (if it does not already have one) even if the LLC will be filing the employment tax returns.)
- A single-member, domestic LLC that accepts the default classification (above) and wants an EIN for filing employment tax returns (see above) or non-Federal purposes, such as a state requirement, must check the "Other" box and write "Disregarded Entity" or, when applicable, "Disregarded Entity—Sole Proprietorship" in the space provided.
- A multi-member, domestic LLC that accepts the default classification (above) must check the "Partnership" box.
- A domestic LLC that will be filing Form 8832 to elect corporate status must check the "Corporation" box and write in "Single-Member" or "Multi-Member" immediately below the "form number" entry line.

Line 9—Reason for applying. Check only **one** box. Do not enter "N/A."

Started new business. Check this box if you are starting a new business that requires an EIN. If you check this box, enter the type of business being started. **Do not** apply if you already have an EIN and are only adding another place of business.

Hired employees. Check this box if the existing business is requesting an EIN because it has hired or is hiring employees and is therefore required to file employment tax returns. **Do not** apply if you already have an EIN and are only hiring employees. For information on employment taxes (e.g., for family members), see Circular E.

 You may be required to make electronic deposits of all depository taxes (such as employment tax, excise tax, and corporate income tax) using the Electronic Federal Tax Payment System (EFTPS). See section 11, Depositing Taxes, of Circular E and Pub. 966.

Created a pension plan. Check this box if you have created a pension plan and need an EIN for reporting purposes. Also, enter the type of plan in the space provided.

 Check this box if you are applying for a trust EIN when a new pension plan is established. In addition, check the "Other" box in line 8a and write "Created a Pension Plan" in the space provided.

Banking purpose. Check this box if you are requesting an EIN for banking purposes only, and enter the banking purpose (for example, a bowling league for depositing dues or an investment club for dividend and interest reporting).

Changed type of organization. Check this box if the business is changing its type of organization. For example, the business was a sole proprietorship and has been incorporated or has become a partnership. If you check this box, specify in the space provided (including available space immediately below) the type of change made. For example, "From Sole Proprietorship to Partnership."

Purchased going business. Check this box if you purchased an existing business. **Do not** use the former owner's EIN unless you became the "owner" of a corporation by acquiring its stock.

Created a trust. Check this box if you created a trust, and enter the type of trust created. For example, indicate if the trust is a nonexempt charitable trust or a split-interest trust.

Exception. Do **not** file this form for certain grantor-type trusts. The trustee does not need an EIN for the trust if the trustee furnishes the name and TIN of the grantor/owner and the address of the trust to all payors. See the Instructions for Form 1041 for more information.

 Do not *check this box if you are applying for a trust EIN when a new pension plan is established. Check "Created a pension plan."*

Other. Check this box if you are requesting an EIN for any other reason; and enter the reason. For example, a newly-formed state government entity should enter "Newly-Formed State Government Entity" in the space provided.

Line 10—Date business started or acquired. If you are starting a new business, enter the starting date of the business. If the business you acquired is already operating, enter the date you acquired the business. If you are changing the form of ownership of your business, enter the date the new ownership entity began. Trusts should enter the date the trust was legally created. Estates should enter the date of death of the decedent whose name appears on line 1 or the date when the estate was legally funded.

Line 11—Closing month of accounting year. Enter the last month of your accounting year or tax year. An accounting or tax year is usually 12 consecutive months, either a calendar year or a fiscal year (including a period of 52 or 53 weeks). A calendar year is 12 consecutive months ending on December 31. A fiscal year is either 12 consecutive months ending on the last day of any month other than December or a 52-53 week year. For more information on accounting periods, see Pub. 538.

Individuals. Your tax year generally will be a calendar year.

Partnerships. Partnerships must adopt one of the following tax years:
- The tax year of the majority of its partners,
- The tax year common to all of its principal partners,
- The tax year that results in the least aggregate deferral of income, or
- In certain cases, some other tax year.

See the Instructions for Form 1065 for more information.

REMICs. REMICs must have a calendar year as their tax year.

Personal service corporations. A personal service corporation generally must adopt a calendar year unless:
- It can establish a business purpose for having a different tax year, or
- It elects under section 444 to have a tax year other than a calendar year.

Trusts. Generally, a trust must adopt a calendar year except for the following:
- Tax-exempt trusts,
- Charitable trusts, and
- Grantor-owned trusts.

Line 12—First date wages or annuities were paid or will be paid. If the business has or will have employees, enter the date on which the business began or will begin to pay wages. If the business does not plan to have employees, enter "N/A."

Withholding agent. Enter the date you began or will begin to pay income (including annuities) to a nonresident alien. This also applies to individuals who are required to file Form 1042 to report alimony paid to a nonresident alien.

Line 13—Highest number of employees expected in the next 12 months. Complete each box by entering the number (including zero ("-0-")) of "Agricultural," "Household," or "Other" employees expected by the applicant in the next 12 months. For a definition of agricultural labor (farmwork), see Circular A.

Lines 14 and 15. Check the **one** box in line 14 that best describes the principal activity of the applicant's business. Check the "Other" box (and specify the applicant's principal activity) if none of the listed boxes applies.

Use line 15 to describe the applicant's principal line of business in more detail. For example, if you checked the "Construction" box in line 14, enter additional detail such as "General contractor for residential buildings" in line 15.

Construction. Check this box if the applicant is engaged in erecting buildings or other structures, (e.g., streets, highways, bridges, tunnels). The term "Construction" also includes special trade contractors, (e.g., plumbing, HVAC, electrical, carpentry, concrete, excavation, etc. contractors).

Real estate. Check this box if the applicant is engaged in renting or leasing real estate to others; managing, selling, buying or renting real estate for others; or providing related real estate services (e.g., appraisal services).

Rental and leasing. Check this box if the applicant is engaged in providing tangible goods such as autos, computers, consumer goods, or industrial machinery and equipment to customers in return for a periodic rental or lease payment.

Manufacturing. Check this box if the applicant is engaged in the mechanical, physical, or chemical transformation of materials, substances, or components into new products. The assembling of component parts of manufactured products is also considered to be manufacturing.

Transportation & warehousing. Check this box if the applicant provides transportation of passengers or cargo; warehousing or storage of goods; scenic or sight-seeing transportation; or support activities related to these modes of transportation.

Finance & insurance. Check this box if the applicant is engaged in transactions involving the creation, liquidation, or change of ownership of financial assets and/or facilitating such financial transactions; underwriting annuities/insurance policies; facilitating such underwriting by selling insurance policies; or by providing other insurance or employee-benefit related services.

Health care and social assistance. Check this box if the applicant is engaged in providing physical, medical, or psychiatric care using licensed health care professionals or providing social assistance activities such as youth centers, adoption agencies, individual/family services, temporary shelters, etc.

Accommodation & food services. Check this box if the applicant is engaged in providing customers with lodging, meal preparation, snacks, or beverages for immediate consumption.

Wholesale–agent/broker. Check this box if the applicant is engaged in arranging for the purchase or sale of goods owned by others or purchasing goods on a commission basis for goods traded in the wholesale market, usually between businesses.

Wholesale–other. Check this box if the applicant is engaged in selling goods in the wholesale market generally to other businesses for resale on their own account.

Retail. Check this box if the applicant is engaged in selling merchandise to the general public from a fixed store; by direct, mail-order, or electronic sales; or by using vending machines.

Other. Check this box if the applicant is engaged in an activity not described above. Describe the applicant's principal business activity in the space provided.

Lines 16a-c. Check the applicable box in line 16a to indicate whether or not the entity (or individual) applying for an EIN was issued one previously. Complete lines 16b and 16c **only** if the "Yes" box in line 16a is checked. If the applicant previously applied for **more than one** EIN, write "See Attached" in the empty space in line 16a and attach a separate sheet providing the line 16b and 16c information for each EIN previously requested.

Third Party Designee. Complete this section **only** if you want to authorize the named individual to receive the entity's EIN and answer questions about the completion of Form SS-4. The designee's authority terminates at the time the EIN is assigned and released to the designee. **You must complete the signature area for the authorization to be valid.**

Signature. When required, the application must be signed by **(a)** the individual, if the applicant is an individual, **(b)** the president, vice president, or other

principal officer, if the applicant is a corporation, **(c)** a responsible and duly authorized member or officer having knowledge of its affairs, if the applicant is a partnership, government entity, or other unincorporated organization, or **(d)** the fiduciary, if the applicant is a trust or an estate. Foreign applicants may have any duly-authorized person, (e.g., division manager), sign Form SS-4.

Privacy Act and Paperwork Reduction Act Notice. We ask for the information on this form to carry out the Internal Revenue laws of the United States. We need it to comply with section 6109 and the regulations thereunder which generally require the inclusion of an employer identification number (EIN) on certain returns, statements, or other documents filed with the Internal Revenue Service. If your entity is required to obtain an EIN, you are required to provide all of the information requested on this form. Information on this form may be used to determine which Federal tax returns you are required to file and to provide you with related forms and publications.

We disclose this form to the Social Security Administration for their use in determining compliance with applicable laws. We may give this information to the Department of Justice for use in civil and criminal litigation, and to the cities, states, and the District of Columbia for use in administering their tax laws. We may also disclose this information to Federal and state agencies to enforce Federal nontax criminal laws and to combat terrorism.

We will be unable to issue an EIN to you unless you provide all of the requested information which applies to your entity. Providing false information could subject you to penalties.

You are not required to provide the information requested on a form that is subject to the Paperwork Reduction Act unless the form displays a valid OMB control number. Books or records relating to a form or its instructions must be retained as long as their contents may become material in the administration of any Internal Revenue law. Generally, tax returns and return information are confidential, as required by section 6103.

The time needed to complete and file this form will vary depending on individual circumstances. The estimated average time is:

Recordkeeping	6 min.
Learning about the law or the form	22 min.
Preparing the form	46 min.
Copying, assembling, and sending the form to the IRS	20 min.

If you have comments concerning the accuracy of these time estimates or suggestions for making this form simpler, we would be happy to hear from you. You can write to the Tax Products Coordinating Committee, Western Area Distribution Center, Rancho Cordova, CA 95743-0001. **Do not** send the form to this address. Instead, see **How To Apply** on page 1.

IRS Form 2553
and Instructions
(S Corporation Election)

Form **2553**
(Rev. December 2002)
Department of the Treasury
Internal Revenue Service

Election by a Small Business Corporation
(Under section 1362 of the Internal Revenue Code)
▶ See Parts II and III on back and the separate instructions.
▶ The corporation may either send or fax this form to the IRS. See page 2 of the instructions.

OMB No. 1545-0146

Notes:
1. *Do not file Form 1120S, U.S. Income Tax Return for an S Corporation, for any tax year before the year the election takes effect.*
2. *This election to be an S corporation can be accepted only if all the tests are met under Who May Elect on page 1 of the instructions; all shareholders have signed the consent statement; and the exact name and address of the corporation and other required form information are provided.*
3. *If the corporation was in existence before the effective date of this election, see Taxes an S Corporation May Owe on page 1 of the instructions.*

Part I   Election Information

**Please
Type
or Print**

Name of corporation (see instructions)	**A** Employer identification number
Number, street, and room or suite no. (If a P.O. box, see instructions.)	**B** Date incorporated
City or town, state, and ZIP code	**C** State of incorporation

D Check the applicable box(es) if the corporation, after applying for the EIN shown in **A** above, changed its name ☐ or address ☐

E Election is to be effective for tax year beginning (month, day, year) . . . . ▶   /   /

F Name and title of officer or legal representative who the IRS may call for more information

G Telephone number of officer or legal representative
(   )

H If this election takes effect for the first tax year the corporation exists, enter month, day, and year of the **earliest** of the following: (1) date the corporation first had shareholders, (2) date the corporation first had assets, or (3) date the corporation began doing business . . . . ▶   /   /

I Selected tax year: Annual return will be filed for tax year ending (month and day) ▶ ....

If the tax year ends on any date other than December 31, except for a 52–53-week tax year ending with reference to the month of December, you **must** complete Part II on the back. If the date you enter is the ending date of a 52–53-week tax year, write "52–53-week year" to the right of the date.

J Name and address of each shareholder; shareholder's spouse having a community property interest in the corporation's stock; and each tenant in common, joint tenant, and tenant by the entirety. (A husband and wife (and their estates) are counted as one shareholder in determining the number of shareholders without regard to the manner in which the stock is owned.)	**K** Shareholders' Consent Statement. Under penalties of perjury, we declare that we consent to the election of the above-named corporation to be an S corporation under section 1362(a) and that we have examined this consent statement, including accompanying schedules and statements, and to the best of our knowledge and belief, it is true, correct, and complete. We understand our consent is binding and may not be withdrawn after the corporation has made a valid election. (Shareholders sign and date below.)		**L** Stock owned		**M** Social security number or employer identification number (see instructions)	**N** Share-holder's tax year ends (month and day)
	Signature	Date	Number of shares	Dates acquired		

Under penalties of perjury, I declare that I have examined this election, including accompanying schedules and statements, and to the best of my knowledge and belief, it is true, correct, and complete.

Signature of officer ▶   Title ▶   Date ▶

For Paperwork Reduction Act Notice, see page 4 of the instructions.   Cat. No. 18629R   Form **2553** (Rev. 12-2002)

Form 2553 (Rev. 12-2002)　　　　　　　　　　　　　　　　　　　　　　　　　　　　　　　Page **2**

Part II　Selection of Fiscal Tax Year (All corporations using this part must complete item O and item P, Q, or R.)

O　Check the applicable box to indicate whether the corporation is:

　　1. ☐ A new corporation adopting the tax year entered in item I, Part I.

　　2. ☐ An existing corporation retaining the tax year entered in item I, Part I.

　　3. ☐ An existing corporation changing to the tax year entered in item I, Part I.

P　Complete item P if the corporation is using the automatic approval provisions of Rev. Proc. 2002-38, 2002-22 I.R.B. 1037, to request **(1)** a natural business year (as defined in section 5.05 of Rev. Proc. 2002-38) or **(2)** a year that satisfies the ownership tax year test (as defined in section 5.06 of Rev. Proc. 2002-38). Check the applicable box below to indicate the representation statement the corporation is making.

　　1. Natural Business Year ▶ ☐ I represent that the corporation is adopting, retaining, or changing to a tax year that qualifies as its natural business year as defined in section 5.05 of Rev. Proc. 2002-38 and has attached a statement verifying that it satisfies the 25% gross receipts test (see instructions for content of statement). I also represent that the corporation is not precluded by section 4.02 of Rev. Proc. 2002-38 from obtaining automatic approval of such adoption, retention, or change in tax year.

　　2. Ownership Tax Year ▶ ☐ I represent that shareholders (as described in section 5.06 of Rev. Proc. 2002-38) holding more than half of the shares of the stock (as of the first day of the tax year to which the request relates) of the corporation have the same tax year or are concurrently changing to the tax year that the corporation adopts, retains, or changes to per item I, Part I, and that such tax year satisfies the requirement of section 4.01(3) of Rev. Proc. 2002-38. I also represent that the corporation is not precluded by section 4.02 of Rev. Proc. 2002-38 from obtaining automatic approval of such adoption, retention, or change in tax year.

Note: *If you do not use item P and the corporation wants a fiscal tax year, complete either item Q or R below. Item Q is used to request a fiscal tax year based on a business purpose and to make a back-up section 444 election. Item R is used to make a regular section 444 election.*

Q　Business Purpose- To request a fiscal tax year based on a business purpose, you must check box Q1. See instructions for details including payment of a user fee. You may also check box Q2 and/or box Q3.

　　1. Check here ▶ ☐ if the fiscal year entered in item I, Part I, is requested under the prior approval provisions of Rev. Proc. 2002-39, 2002-22 I.R.B. 1046. Attach to Form 2553 a statement describing the relevant facts and circumstances and, if applicable, the gross receipts from sales and services necessary to establish a business purpose. See the instructions for details regarding the gross receipts from sales and services. If the IRS proposes to disapprove the requested fiscal year, do you want a conference with the IRS National Office?　☐ Yes　☐ No

　　2. Check here ▶ ☐ to show that the corporation intends to make a back-up section 444 election in the event the corporation's business purpose request is not approved by the IRS. (See instructions for more information.)

　　3. Check here ▶ ☐ to show that the corporation agrees to adopt or change to a tax year ending December 31 if necessary for the IRS to accept this election for S corporation status in the event (1) the corporation's business purpose request is not approved and the corporation makes a back-up section 444 election, but is ultimately not qualified to make a section 444 election, or (2) the corporation's business purpose request is not approved and the corporation did not make a back-up section 444 election.

R　Section 444 Election- To make a section 444 election, you must check box R1 and you may also check box R2.

　　1. Check here ▶ ☐ to show the corporation will make, if qualified, a section 444 election to have the fiscal tax year shown in item I, Part I. To make the election, you must complete **Form 8716,** Election To Have a Tax Year Other Than a Required Tax Year, and either attach it to Form 2553 or file it separately.

　　2. Check here ▶ ☐ to show that the corporation agrees to adopt or change to a tax year ending December 31 if necessary for the IRS to accept this election for S corporation status in the event the corporation is ultimately not qualified to make a section 444 election.

Part III　Qualified Subchapter S Trust (QSST) Election Under Section 1361(d)(2)*

Income beneficiary's name and address	Social security number
Trust's name and address	Employer identification number

Date on which stock of the corporation was transferred to the trust (month, day, year) . . . . ▶ 　 / 　 /

In order for the trust named above to be a QSST and thus a qualifying shareholder of the S corporation for which this Form 2553 is filed, I hereby make the election under section 1361(d)(2). Under penalties of perjury, I certify that the trust meets the definitional requirements of section 1361(d)(3) and that all other information provided in Part III is true, correct, and complete.

_____　_____

Signature of income beneficiary or signature and title of legal representative or other qualified person making the election　　　Date

*Use Part III to make the QSST election only if stock of the corporation has been transferred to the trust on or before the date on which the corporation makes its election to be an S corporation. The QSST election must be made and filed separately if stock of the corporation is transferred to the trust after the date on which the corporation makes the S election.

⊛　　　　　　　　　　　　　　　　　　　　　　　　　　　Form **2553** (Rev. 12-2002)

Instructions for Form 2553

Department of the Treasury
Internal Revenue Service

(Rev. December 2002)
Election by a Small Business Corporation
Section references are to the Internal Revenue Code unless otherwise noted.

General Instructions

Purpose

To elect to be an S corporation, a corporation must file Form 2553. The election permits the income of the S corporation to be taxed to the shareholders of the corporation rather than to the corporation itself, except as noted below under **Taxes an S Corporation May Owe.**

Who May Elect

A corporation may elect to be an S corporation only if it meets all of the following tests:

1. It is a domestic corporation.

Note: *A limited liability company (LLC) **must** file **Form 8832**, Entity Classification Election, to elect to be treated as an association taxable as a corporation in order to elect to be an S corporation.*

2. It has no more than 75 shareholders. A husband and wife (and their estates) are treated as one shareholder for this requirement. All other persons are treated as separate shareholders.

3. Its only shareholders are individuals, estates, exempt organizations described in section 401(a) or 501(c)(3), or certain trusts described in section 1361(c)(2)(A). See the instructions for Part III regarding qualified subchapter S trusts (QSSTs).

A trustee of a trust wanting to make an election under section 1361(e)(3) to be an electing small business trust (ESBT) should see Notice 97-12, 1997-1 C.B. 385. However, in general, for tax years beginning after May 13, 2002, Notice 97-12 is superseded by Regulations section 1.1361-1(c)(1). Also see Rev. Proc. 98-23, 1998-1 C.B. 662, for guidance on how to convert a QSST to an ESBT. However, in general, for tax years beginning after May 13, 2002, Rev. Proc. 98-23 is superseded by Regulations section 1.1361-1(j)(12). If there was an inadvertent failure to timely file an ESBT election, see the relief provisions under Rev. Proc. 98-55, 1998-2 C.B. 643.

4. It has no nonresident alien shareholders.

5. It has only one class of stock (disregarding differences in voting rights). Generally, a corporation is treated as having only one class of stock if all outstanding shares of the corporation's stock confer identical rights to distribution and liquidation proceeds. See Regulations section 1.1361-1(l) for details.

6. It is not one of the following ineligible corporations:

a. A bank or thrift institution that uses the reserve method of accounting for bad debts under section 585,

b. An insurance company subject to tax under the rules of subchapter L of the Code,

c. A corporation that has elected to be treated as a possessions corporation under section 936, or

d. A domestic international sales corporation (DISC) or former DISC.

7. It has a permitted tax year as required by section 1378 or makes a section 444 election to have a tax year other than a permitted tax year. Section 1378 defines a permitted tax year as a tax year ending December 31, or any other tax year for which the corporation establishes a business purpose to the satisfaction of the IRS. See Part II for details on requesting a fiscal tax year based on a business purpose or on making a section 444 election.

8. Each shareholder consents as explained in the instructions for column K.

See sections 1361, 1362, and 1378 for additional information on the above tests.

A parent S corporation can elect to treat an eligible wholly-owned subsidiary as a qualified subchapter S subsidiary (QSub). If the election is made, the assets, liabilities, and items of income, deduction, and credit of the QSub are treated as those of the parent. To make the election, get **Form 8869,** Qualified Subchapter S Subsidiary Election. If the QSub election was not timely filed, the corporation may be entitled to relief under Rev. Proc. 98-55.

Taxes an S Corporation May Owe

An S corporation may owe income tax in the following instances:

1. If, at the end of any tax year, the corporation had accumulated earnings and profits, and its passive investment income under section 1362(d)(3) is more than 25% of its gross receipts, the corporation may owe tax on its excess net passive income.

2. A corporation with net recognized built-in gain (as defined in section 1374(d)(2)) may owe tax on its built-in gains.

3. A corporation that claimed investment credit before its first year as an S corporation will be liable for any investment credit recapture tax.

4. A corporation that used the LIFO inventory method for the year immediately preceding its first year as an S corporation may owe an additional tax due to LIFO recapture. The tax is paid in four equal installments, the first of which must be paid by the due date (not including extensions) of the corporation's income tax return for its last tax year as a C corporation.

For more details on these taxes, see the Instructions for Form 1120S.

Cat. No. 49978N

Where To File

Send the original election (no photocopies) or fax it to the Internal Revenue Service Center listed below. If the corporation files this election by fax, keep the original Form 2553 with the corporation's permanent records.

If the corporation's principal business, office, or agency is located in 	Use the following Internal Revenue Service Center address or fax number
Connecticut, Delaware, District of Columbia, Illinois, Indiana, Kentucky, Maine, Maryland, Massachusetts, Michigan, New Hampshire, New Jersey, New York, North Carolina, Ohio, Pennsylvania, Rhode Island, South Carolina, Vermont, Virginia, West Virginia, Wisconsin	Cincinnati, OH 45999 (859) 669-5748
Alabama, Alaska, Arizona, Arkansas, California, Colorado, Florida, Georgia, Hawaii, Idaho, Iowa, Kansas, Louisiana, Minnesota, Mississippi, Missouri, Montana, Nebraska, Nevada, New Mexico, North Dakota, Oklahoma, Oregon, South Dakota, Tennessee, Texas, Utah, Washington, Wyoming	Ogden, UT 84201 (801) 620-7116

When To Make the Election

Complete and file Form 2553 **(a)** at any time before the 16th day of the 3rd month of the tax year, if filed during the tax year the election is to take effect, or **(b)** at any time during the preceding tax year. An election made no later than 2 months and 15 days after the beginning of a tax year that is less than 2½ months long is treated as timely made for that tax year. **An election made after the 15th day of the 3rd month but before the end of the tax year is effective for the next year.** For example, if a calendar tax year corporation makes the election in April 2002, it is effective for the corporation's 2003 calendar tax year.

However, an election made after the due date will be accepted as timely filed if the corporation can show that the failure to file on time was due to reasonable cause. To request relief for a late election, the corporation generally must request a private letter ruling and pay a user fee in accordance with Rev. Proc. 2002-1, 2002-1 I.R.B. 1 (or its successor). But if the election is filed within 12 months of its due date and the original due date for filing the corporation's initial Form 1120S has not passed, the ruling and user fee requirements do not apply. To request relief in this case, write "FILED PURSUANT TO REV. PROC. 98-55" at the top of page 1 of Form 2553, attach a statement explaining the reason for failing to file the election on time, and file Form 2553 as otherwise instructed. See Rev. Proc. 98-55 for more details.

See Regulations section 1.1362-6(b)(3)(iii) for how to obtain relief for an inadvertent invalid election if the corporation filed a timely election, but one or more shareholders did not file a timely consent.

Acceptance or Nonacceptance of Election

The service center will notify the corporation if its election is accepted and when it will take effect. The corporation will also be notified if its election is not accepted. The corporation should generally receive a determination on its election within 60 days after it has filed Form 2553. If box Q1 in Part II is checked on page 2, the corporation will receive a ruling letter from the IRS in Washington, DC, that either approves or denies the selected tax year. When box Q1 is checked, it will generally take an additional 90 days for the Form 2553 to be accepted.

Care should be exercised to ensure that the IRS receives the election. If the corporation is not notified of acceptance or nonacceptance of its election within 3 months of the date of filing (date mailed), or within 6 months if box Q1 is checked, take follow-up action by corresponding with the service center where the corporation filed the election.

If the IRS questions whether Form 2553 was filed, an acceptable proof of filing is **(a)** certified or registered mail receipt (timely postmarked) from the U.S. Postal Service, or its equivalent from a designated private delivery service (see Notice 2002-62, 2002-39 I.R.B. 574 (or its successor)); **(b)** Form 2553 with accepted stamp; **(c)** Form 2553 with stamped IRS received date; or **(d)** IRS letter stating that Form 2553 has been accepted.

 *Do not file Form 1120S for any tax year before the year the election takes effect. If the corporation is now required to file **Form 1120**, U.S. Corporation Income Tax Return, or any other applicable tax return, continue filing it until the election takes effect.*

End of Election

Once the election is made, it stays in effect until it is terminated. If the election is terminated in a tax year beginning after 1996, IRS consent is generally required for another election by the corporation (or a successor corporation) on Form 2553 for any tax year before the 5th tax year after the first tax year in which the termination took effect. See Regulations section 1.1362-5 for details.

Specific Instructions

Part I (*All corporations must complete.*)

Name and Address of Corporation

Enter the true corporate name as stated in the corporate charter or other legal document creating it. If the corporation's mailing address is the same as someone else's, such as a shareholder's, enter "c/o" and this person's name following the name of the corporation. Include the suite, room, or other unit number after the street address. If the Post Office does not deliver to the street address and the corporation has a P.O. box, show the box number instead of the street address. If the corporation changed its name or address after applying for its employer identification number, be sure to check the box in item D of Part I.

Item A. Employer Identification Number (EIN)

If the corporation has applied for an EIN but has not received it, enter "applied for." If the corporation does not have an EIN, it should apply for one on **Form SS-4,** Application for Employer Identification Number. You can order Form SS-4 by calling 1-800-TAX-FORM (1-800-829-3676) or by accessing the IRS Web Site **www.irs.gov**.

Item E. Effective Date of Election

Enter the beginning effective date (month, day, year) of the tax year requested for the S corporation. Generally, this will be the beginning date of the tax year for which the ending effective date is required to be shown in item I, Part I. For a new corporation (first year the corporation exists) it will generally be the date required to be shown in item H, Part I. The tax year of a new corporation starts on the date that it has shareholders, acquires assets, or begins doing business, whichever happens first. If the effective date for item E for a newly formed corporation is later than the date in item H, the corporation should file Form 1120 or Form 1120-A for the tax period between these dates.

Column K. Shareholders' Consent Statement

Each shareholder who owns (or is deemed to own) stock at the time the election is made must consent to the election. If the election is made during the corporation's tax year for which it first takes effect, any person who held stock at any time during the part of that year that occurs before the election is made, must consent to the election, even though the person may have sold or transferred his or her stock before the election is made.

An election made during the first 2½ months of the tax year is effective for the following tax year if any person who held stock in the corporation during the part of the tax year before the election was made, and who did not hold stock at the time the election was made, did not consent to the election.

Note: *Once the election is made, a new shareholder is not required to consent to the election; a new Form 2553 will not be required.*

Each shareholder consents by signing and dating in column K or signing and dating a separate consent statement described below. The following special rules apply in determining who must sign the consent statement.
- If a husband and wife have a community interest in the stock or in the income from it, both must consent.
- Each tenant in common, joint tenant, and tenant by the entirety must consent.
- A minor's consent is made by the minor, legal representative of the minor, or a natural or adoptive parent of the minor if no legal representative has been appointed.
- The consent of an estate is made by the executor or administrator.
- The consent of an electing small business trust is made by the trustee.
- If the stock is owned by a trust (other than an electing small business trust), the deemed owner of the trust must consent. See section 1361(c)(2) for details regarding trusts that are permitted to be shareholders and rules for determining who is the deemed owner.

Continuation sheet or separate consent statement. If you need a continuation sheet or use a separate consent statement, attach it to Form 2553. The separate consent statement must contain the name, address, and EIN of the corporation and the shareholder information requested in columns J through N of Part I. If you want, you may combine all the shareholders' consents in one statement.

Column L

Enter the number of shares of stock each shareholder owns and the dates the stock was acquired. If the election is made during the corporation's tax year for which it first takes effect, do not list the shares of stock for those shareholders who sold or transferred all of their stock before the election was made. However, these shareholders must still consent to the election for it to be effective for the tax year.

Column M

Enter the social security number of each shareholder who is an individual. Enter the EIN of each shareholder that is an estate, a qualified trust, or an exempt organization.

Column N

Enter the month and day that each shareholder's tax year ends. If a shareholder is changing his or her tax year, enter the tax year the shareholder is changing to, and attach an explanation indicating the present tax year and the basis for the change (e.g., automatic revenue procedure or letter ruling request).

Signature

Form 2553 must be signed by the president, treasurer, assistant treasurer, chief accounting officer, or other corporate officer (such as tax officer) authorized to sign.

Part II

Complete Part II if you selected a tax year ending on any date other than December 31 (other than a 52-53-week tax year ending with reference to the month of December).

Note: *In certain circumstances the corporation may not obtain automatic approval of a fiscal year under the natural business year (Box P1) or ownership tax year (Box P2) provisions if it is under examination, before an area office, or before a federal court with respect to any income tax issue and the annual accounting period is under consideration. For details, see section 4.02 of Rev. Proc. 2002-38, 2002-22 I.R.B. 1037.*

Box P1

Attach a statement showing separately for each month the amount of gross receipts for the most recent 47 months. A corporation that does not have a 47-month period of gross receipts cannot automatically establish a natural business year.

Box Q1

For examples of an acceptable business purpose for requesting a fiscal tax year, see section 5.02 of Rev. Proc. 2002-39, 2002-22 I.R.B. 1046, and Rev. Rul. 87-57, 1987-2 C.B. 117.

Attach a statement showing the relevant facts and circumstances to establish a business purpose for the requested fiscal year. For details on what is sufficient to establish a business purpose, see section 5.02 of Rev. Proc. 2002-39.

If your business purpose is based on one of the natural business year tests provided in section 5.03 of Rev. Proc. 2002-39, identify if you are using the 25% gross receipts, annual business cycle, or seasonal business test. For the 25% gross receipts test, provide a schedule showing the amount of gross receipts for each month for the most recent 47 months. For either the annual business cycle or seasonal business test, provide the gross receipts from sales and services (and inventory costs, if applicable) for each month of the short period, if any, and the three immediately preceding tax years. If the corporation has been in existence for less than three tax years, submit figures for the period of existence.

If you check box Q1, you will be charged a user fee of up to $600 (subject to change—see Rev. Proc. 2002-1 or its successor). Do not pay the fee when filing Form 2553. The service center will send Form 2553 to the IRS in Washington, DC, who, in turn, will notify the corporation that the fee is due.

Box Q2

If the corporation makes a back-up section 444 election for which it is qualified, then the election will take effect in the event the business purpose request is not approved. In some cases, the tax year requested under the back-up section 444 election may be different than the tax year requested under business purpose. See **Form 8716,** Election To Have a Tax Year Other Than a Required Tax Year, for details on making a back-up section 444 election.

Boxes Q2 and R2

If the corporation is not qualified to make the section 444 election after making the item Q2 back-up section 444 election or indicating its intention to make the election in item R1, and therefore it later files a calendar year return, it should write "Section 444 Election Not Made" in the top left corner of the first calendar year Form 1120S it files.

Part III

Certain qualified subchapter S trusts (QSSTs) may make the QSST election required by section 1361(d)(2) in Part III. Part III may be used to make the QSST election only if corporate stock has been transferred to the trust on or before the date on which the corporation makes its election to be an S corporation. However, a statement can be used instead of Part III to make the election. If there was an inadvertent failure to timely file a QSST election, see the relief provisions under Rev. Proc. 98-55.

Note: *Use Part III **only** if you make the election in Part I (i.e., Form 2553 cannot be filed with only Part III completed).*

The deemed owner of the QSST must also consent to the S corporation election in column K, page 1, of Form 2553. See section 1361(c)(2).

Paperwork Reduction Act Notice. We ask for the information on this form to carry out the Internal Revenue laws of the United States. You are required to give us the information. We need it to ensure that you are complying with these laws and to allow us to figure and collect the right amount of tax.

You are not required to provide the information requested on a form that is subject to the Paperwork Reduction Act unless the form displays a valid OMB control number. Books or records relating to a form or its instructions must be retained as long as their contents may become material in the administration of any Internal Revenue law. Generally, tax returns and return information are confidential, as required by section 6103.

The time needed to complete and file this form will depend on individual circumstances. The estimated average time is:

Recordkeeping	9 hr., 34 min.
Learning about the law or the form	3 hr., 28 min.
Preparing, copying, assembling, and sending the form to the IRS	3 hr., 47 min.

If you have comments concerning the accuracy of these time estimates or suggestions for making this form simpler, we would be happy to hear from you. You can write to the Tax Forms Committee, Western Area Distribution Center, Rancho Cordova, CA 95743-0001. **Do not** send the form to this address. Instead, see **Where To File** on page 2.

Appendix E

Bylaws Template

Bylaws
of

ARTICLE I
OFFICES

The office of the Corporation shall be located in the city and state designated in the Articles of Incorporation. The Corporation may also maintain offices at such other places within or without the United States as the Board of Directors may, from time to time, determine.

ARTICLE II
MEETING OF SHAREHOLDERS

Section 1. Annual Meetings. The annual meeting of the shareholders of the Corporation shall be held within five months after the close of the fiscal year of the Corporation for the purpose of electing directors and transacting such other business as may properly come before the meeting.

Section 2. Special Meetings. Special meetings of the shareholders may be called at any time by the Board of Directors or by the President and shall be called by the President or the Secretary at the written request of the holders of ten percent (10%) of the shares then outstanding and entitled to vote thereat, or as otherwise required under the provisions of the General Corporation Laws of the State of _____ (hereinafter, the business Corporation Act).

Section 3. Place of Meetings.   All meetings of shareholders shall be held at the principal office of the Corporation or at such other places as shall be designated in the notices or waivers of notice of such meetings.

Section 4. Notice of Meetings

a.   Written notice of each meeting of shareholders, whether annual or special, stating the time when and place where it is to be held, shall be served either personally or by mail, not less than ten (10) or more than fifty (50) days before the meeting, upon each shareholder of record entitled to vote at such meeting and to any other shareholder to whom the giving of notice may be required by law. Notice of a special meeting shall also state the purpose or purposes for which the meeting is called and shall indicate that it is being issued by, or at the direction of, the person or persons calling the meeting. If, at any meeting, action is proposed to be taken that would, if taken, entitle shareholders to receive payment for their shares pursuant to the business

Corporation Act, the notice of such meeting shall include a statement of that purpose and to that effect. If mailed, such notice shall be directed to each such shareholder at his address as it appears on the records of the shareholders of the corporation, unless he shall have previously filed with the Secretary of the Corporation a written request that notices intended for him be mailed to some other address, in which case it shall be mailed to the address designated in such request.

b. Notice of any meeting need not be given to any person who may become a Shareholder of record after the mailing of such notice and prior to the meeting, or to any shareholder who attends such meeting, in person or by proxy, to any shareholder who, in person or by proxy submits a signed waiver of notice either before or after such meeting. Notice of any adjourned meeting of shareholders need not be given unless otherwise required by statute.

Section 5. Quorum

a. Except as otherwise provided herein or by statute, or in the Articles of Incorporation (such Articles and any amendments thereof being hereinafter collectively referred to as the "Articles of Incorporation"), at all meetings of shareholders of the Corporation, the presence at the commencement of such meetings in person or by proxy of shareholders holding of record a majority of the total number of shares of the Corporation then issued and outstanding and entitled to vote shall be necessary and sufficient to constitute a quorum for the transaction of any business. The withdrawal of any shareholder after the commencement of a meeting shall have no effect on the existence of a quorum after a quorum has been established at such meeting.

b. Despite the absence of a quorum at any annual or special meeting of shareholders, the shareholders, by a majority of the votes cast by the holders of shares entitled to vote thereon, may adjourn the meeting. At any such adjourned meeting at which a quorum is present, any business may be transacted which might have been transacted at the meeting as originally called if a quorum had been present.

Section 6. Voting

a. Except as otherwise provided by statute or by the Articles of Incorporation, any corporate action, other than the election of directors, to be taken by vote of the shareholders by the holders of shares entitled to vote thereon.

b. Except as otherwise provided by statute or by the Articles of Incorporation at each meeting of shareholders, each holder of record of shares of the Corporation entitled to vote thereat shall be entitled to one vote for each share registered in his name on the books of the Corporation.

c. Each shareholder entitled to vote or to express consent or dissent without a meeting may do so by proxy; provided, however, that the instrument authorizing such proxy to act shall have been executed in writing by the shareholder himself or by his attorney-in-fact thereunto duly authorized in writing. No proxy shall be valid after the expiration of eleven (11) months from the date of its execution unless the persons executing it shall have specified therein the length of time it is to continue in force. Such instrument shall be exhibited to the Secretary at the meeting and shall be filed with the records of the Corporation.

ARTICLE III
BOARD OF DIRECTORS

Section 1. Number, Election, and Term of Office

a.   The number of the directors of the Corporation shall be one (1) unless and until otherwise determined by vote of a majority of the entire Board of Directors. The number of directors shall not be less than one.

b.   Except as may otherwise be provided herein or in the Articles of Incorporation, the members of the Board of Directors of the Corporation shall be elected by a majority of the votes cast at a meeting of shareholders by the holders of shares entitled to vote in the election.

c.   Each director shall hold office until the annual meeting of the shareholders next succeeding his election and until his successor is elected and qualified or until his prior death, resignation, or removal.

Section 2. Duties and Powers.   The Board of Directors shall be responsible for the control and management of the affairs, property, and interests of the Corporation and may exercise all powers of the Corporation, except as are in the Articles of Incorporation or by statute expressly conferred upon or reserved to the shareholders.

Section 3. Annual and Regular Meetings; Notice

a.   A regular annual meeting of the Board of Directors shall be held immediately following the annual meeting of the shareholders at the place of such annual meeting of shareholders.

b.   The Board of Directors, from time to time, may provide by resolution for the holding of other regular meetings of the Board of Directors and may fix the time and place thereof.

c.   Notice of any regular meeting of the Board of Directors shall not be required to be given and, if given, need not specify the purpose of the meeting; provided, however, that in case the Board of Directors shall fix or change the time or place of any regular meeting, notice of such action shall be given to each director who shall not have been present at the meeting at which such action was taken within the time limited and in the manner set forth in paragraph (b) of Section 4 of the Article III with respect to special meetings, unless such notice shall be waived in the manner set forth in paragraph (c) of such Section 4.

Section 4. Special Meetings; Notice

a. Special meetings of the Board of Directors shall be held whenever called specified in the respective notices or waivers of notice thereof.

b. Notice of special meetings shall be mailed directly to each director, addressed to him at his residence or usual place of business, at least two (2) days before the day on which the meeting is to be held or shall be sent to him at such place by telegram, radio, or cable, or shall be delivered to him personally or given to him orally not later than the day before the day on which the meeting is to be held. A notice, or waiver of notice, except as required by Section 8 of this Article III, need not specify the purpose of the meeting.

c. Notice of any special meeting shall not be required to be given to any director who shall attend such meeting without protesting prior thereto or at its commencement, the lack of notice to him, or who submits a signed, adjourned meeting shall not be required to be given.

Section 5. Chairman

At all meetings of the Board or Directors, the Chairman of the Board, if any and if present, shall preside. If there shall be no Chairman or he shall be absent, then the President shall preside, and in his absence a Chairman chosen by the directors shall preside.

Section 6. Quorum and Adjournments

a. At all meetings of the Board or Directors, the presence of a majority of the entire Board shall be necessary and sufficient to constitute a quorum for the transaction of business except as otherwise provided by law, by the Articles of Incorporation, or by these Bylaws.

b. A majority of the directors present at the time and place of any regular or special meeting, although less than a quorum, may adjourn the same from time to time without notice until a quorum shall be present.

Section 7. Manner of Acting

a. At all meetings of the Board of Directors, each director present shall have one vote, irrespective of the number of shares of stock, if any, which he may hold.

b. Except as otherwise provided by statute, by the Articles of Incorporation, or by these Bylaws, the action of a majority of the directors present at any meeting at which a quorum is present shall be the act of the Board of Directors. Any action authorized, in writing, by all of the directors entitled to vote thereon and filed with the minutes of the Corporation shall be the act of the Board of Directors with the same force and effect as if the same had been passed by unanimous vote at a duly called meeting of the Board.

Section 8. Vacancies. Any vacancy in the Board of Directors occurring by reason of an increase in the number of directors or by reason of the death, resignation, disqualification, removal (unless a vacancy created by the removal of a director by the shareholders shall be filled by the shareholders at the meeting at which the removal was effected), or inability to act of any director or otherwise shall be filled for the unexpired portion of the term by a majority vote of the remaining directors, though less than a quorum, at any regular meeting or special meeting of the Board of Directors called for that purpose.

Section 9. Resignation.   Any director may resign at any time by giving written notice to the Board of Directors, the President, or the Secretary of the corporation. Unless otherwise specified in such written notice, such resignation shall take effect upon receipt thereof by the Board of Directors or such officer and the acceptance of such resignation shall not be necessary to make it effective.

Section 10. Removal.   Any director may be removed with or without cause at any time by the shareholders, at a special meeting of the shareholders called for that purpose, and may be removed for cause by action of the Board.

Section 11. Salary.   No stated salary shall be paid to directors, as such, for their services but, by resolution of the Board of Directors, a fixed sum and expenses of attendance, if any, may be allowed for attendance at each regular or special meeting of the Board; provided, however, that nothing herein contained shall be construed to preclude any director from serving the Corporation in any other capacity and receiving compensation therefore.

Section 12. Contracts

   a.   No contract or other transaction between this Corporation and any other Corporation shall be impaired, affected, or invalidated, nor shall any director be liable in any way by reason of the fact that any one or more of the directors of this Corporation is or are interested in, or is a director or officer, or are directors or officers of such other corporation, provided that such facts are disclosed or made known to the Board of Directors.

   b.   Any director, personally and individually, may be a party to or may be interested in any contract or transaction of this Corporation and no director shall be liable in any way by reason of such interest, provided that the fact of such interest be disclosed or made known to the Board of Directors, and provided that the Board of Directors shall authorize, approve, or ratify such contract or transaction by the vote (not counting the vote of any such director) of a majority of a quorum, notwithstanding the presence of any such director at the meeting at which such action is taken. Such director or directors may be counted in determining the presence of a quorum at such meeting. This Section shall not be construed to impair or invalidate or in any way affect any contract or other transaction which would otherwise be valid under the law (common, statutory, or otherwise) applicable thereto.

Section 13. Committees.   The Board of Directors, by resolution adopted by a majority of the entire Board, may from time to time designate from among its members an executive committee and such other committees, and alternate members thereof, as they deem desirable, each consisting of three or more members, with such powers and authority (to the extent permitted by law) as may be provided in such resolution. Each such committee shall serve at the pleasure of the Board.

ARTICLE IV
OFFICERS

Section 1. Number, Qualifications, Election, and Term of Office

a.   The officers of the Corporation shall consist of a President, a Secretary, a Treasurer, and such other officers, including a Chairman of the Board of Directors and one or more Vice Presidents, as the Board of Directors may from time to time deem advisable. Any officer, other than the Chairman of the Board of Directors, may be, but is not required to be, a director of the Corporation. Any two or more offices may be held by the same person, unless state law—present or future—otherwise dictates.

b.   The officers of the Corporation shall be elected by the Board of Directors at the regular annual meeting of the Board following the annual meeting of shareholders.

c.   Each officer shall hold office until the annual meeting of the Board of Directors next succeeding his election and until his successor shall have been elected and qualified or until his death, resignation, or removal.

Section 2. Resignation.   Any officer may resign at any time by giving written notice of such resignation to the Board or Directors or to the President or the Secretary of the Corporation. Unless otherwise specified in such written notice, such resignation shall take effect upon receipt thereof by the Board of Directors or by such officer, and the acceptance of such resignation shall not be necessary to make it effective.

Section 3. Removal.   Any officer may be removed, either with or without cause, and a successor elected by the Board at any time.

Section 4. Vacancies.   A vacancy in any office by reason of death, resignation, inability to act, disqualification, or any other cause may at any time be filled for the unexpired portion of the term by the Board of Directors.

Section 5. Duties of Officers.   Officers of the Corporation shall, unless otherwise provided by the Board of Directors, each have such powers and duties as generally pertain to their respective offices as well as such powers and duties as may be set forth in these Bylaws or may, from time to time, be specifically conferred or imposed by the Board of Directors. The President shall be the chief executive officer of the Corporation.

Section 6. Sureties and Bonds.   In case the Board of Directors shall so require, any officer, employee, or agent of the Corporation shall execute to the Corporation a bond in such sum and with such surety or sureties as the Board of Directors may direct, conditioned on the faithful performance of his duties to the Corporation, including responsibility for negligence and for the accounting for all property, funds, or securities of the Corporation which may come into his hands.

Section 7. Shares of Other Corporations.   Whenever the Corporation is the holder of shares of any other corporation, any right or power of the Corporation as such shareholder (including the attendance, acting, and voting at shareholders' meetings and execution of waivers, consents, proxies, or other instruments) may be exercised on behalf of the Corporation by the President, any Vice President, or such other person as the Board of Directors may authorize.

ARTICLE V
SHARES OF STOCK

Section 1. Certificate of Stock

a.   The certificates representing shares of the Corporation shall be in such form as shall be adopted by the Board of Directors and shall be numbered and registered in the order issued. They shall bear the holder's name and the number of shares and shall be signed by (i) the Chairman of the Board or the President or a Vice President and (ii) the Secretary or any Assistant Secretary and may bear the corporate seal.

b.   No certificate representing shares shall be issued until the full amount of consideration therefore has been paid, except as otherwise permitted by law.

c.   The Board of Directors may authorize the issuance of certificates for fractions of a share which shall entitle the holder to exercise voting rights, receive dividends and participate in liquidating distributions in proportion to the fractional holdings; or it may authorize the payment in cash of the fair market value of fractions of a share as of the time when those entitled to receive such fractions are determined; or it may authorize the issuance, subject to such conditions as may be permitted by law, of scrip in registered or bearer form over the signature of an officer or agent of the Corporation, exchangeable as therein provided for full shares, but such scrip shall not entitle the holder to any rights of a shareholder, except as therein provided.

Section 2. Lost or Destroyed Certificates.   The holder of any certificate representing shares of the Corporation shall immediately notify the Corporation of any loss or destruction of the certificate representing the same. The Corporation may issue a new certificate in the place of any certificate theretofore issued by it, alleged to have been lost or destroyed. On production of such evidence, the Board of Directors may, in its discretion, require the owner of the lost or destroyed certificate, or his legal representatives, to give the Corporation a bond in such sum as the Board may direct and with such surety or sureties as may be satisfactory to the Board to indemnify the corporation against any claims, loss, liability, or damage it may suffer on account of the issuance or the new certificate. A new certificate may be issued without requiring any such evidence or bond when, in the judgment of the Board of Directors, it is proper so to do.

Section 3. Transfers of Shares

a. Transfers of shares of the Corporation shall be made on the share records of the Corporation only by the holder of record thereof, in person or by his duly authorized attorney, upon surrender for cancellation of the certificate or certificates representing such shares, with an assignment or power of transfer endorsed thereon or delivered therewith duly executed, with such proof of the authenticity of the signature and of authority to transfer and of payment of transfer taxes as the Corporation or its agents may require.

b. The Corporation shall be entitled to treat the holder of record of any share or shares as the absolute owner thereof for all purposes and, accordingly, shall not be bound to recognize any legal, equitable, or other claim to, or interest in, such share or shares on the part of any other person, whether or not it shall have express or other notice thereof, except as otherwise expressly provided by law.

Section 4. Record Date. In lieu of closing the share records of the Corporation, the Board of Directors may fix, in advance, a date not exceeding fifty (50) days, nor less than ten (10) days, as the record date for the determination of shareholders entitled to receive notice of, or to vote at, any meeting of shareholders, or to consent to any proposal without a meeting or for the purpose of determining shareholders entitled to receive payment of any dividends, or allotment of any rights, or for the purpose of any other action. If no record date is fixed, the record date for the determination of stockholders entitled to notice of or to vote at a meeting of shareholders shall be at the close of business on the day next preceding the day on which notice is given or, if no notice is given, the day on which the meeting is held; the record dated for determining shareholders for any other purpose shall be at the close of business on the day on which the resolution of the directors relating thereto is adopted. When a determination of shareholders of record entitled to notice of or to vote at any meeting or shareholders has been made as provided for herein, such determination shall apply to any adjournment thereof, unless the directors fix a new record date for the adjourned meeting.

ARTICLE VI
DIVIDENDS

Subject to applicable law, dividends may be declared and paid out of any funds available therefore as often, in such amounts, and at such time as the Board of Directors may determine.

ARTICLE VII
FISCAL YEAR

The Fiscal year of the Corporation shall be fixed by the Board of Directors from time to time, subject to applicable law.

ARTICLE VIII
CORPORATE SEAL

The Corporate Seal, if any, shall be in such form as shall be approved from time to time by the Board of Directors.

ARTICLE IX
AMENDMENTS

Section 1. By Shareholders. All Bylaws of the Corporation shall be subject to alteration or repeal and new Bylaws may be made by a majority vote of the shareholders at the time entitled to vote in the election of directors.

Section 2. By Directors. The Board of Directors shall have power to make, adopt, alter, amend, and repeal, from time to time, Bylaws of the Corporation; provided, however, that the shareholders entitled to vote with respect thereto as in this Article IX above-provided may alter, amend, or repeal Bylaws made by the Board of Directors, except that the Board of Directors shall have no power to change the quorum for meetings of shareholders or of the Board of Directors or to change any provisions of the Bylaws with respect to the removal of directors or the filling of vacancies in the Board resulting from the removal by the shareholders. If any Bylaws regulating an impending election of directors is adopted, amended or repealed by the Board of Directors, there shall be set forth in the notice of the next meeting of shareholders for the election of directors, the Bylaws so adopted, amended or repealed, together with a concise statement of the changes made.

The Undersigned certify the foregoing Bylaws have been adopted as the first Bylaws of the Corporation in accordance with the requirements of the Business Corporation Act this _____ day of _____,_____.

Secretary

_____
(Signature)

Appendix **F**

Minutes of
Annual Meeting
of Shareholders

Minutes of Annual Meeting of Shareholders of

_____

Pursuant to legal and lawful notice, the Annual Meeting of Stockholders of the Corporation was held at _____, on _____ day of _____, _____.

The meeting was called to order by the _____ of the Corporation.

The Secretary then reported that the meeting had been called pursuant to a notice of meeting and/or waiver of notice thereof in accordance with the bylaws. It was ordered that a copy of the notice and waiver of notice be appended to the minutes of the meeting.

The Secretary then read the roll of stockholders from the stock transfer ledger. The following stockholders were present in person or by proxy:

STOCKHOLDER	SHARES	IN PERSON	BY PROXY

The Chairman stated that a majority of the total number of shares issued and outstanding was represented and that the meeting was complete and ready to transact any business before it. It was ordered that proxies be appended to the minutes of the meeting.

The President then gave a general report of the business and finances of the Corporation and the Secretary reported the following changes of stockholders since the last such report:

The Chairman then stated that the election of directors of the Corporation was now in order. The following were nominated as directors and then so elected to serve until the next annual meeting of the stockholders:

There being no further business, the meeting was adjourned.

_____, Secretary

Minutes of Annual Meeting of Board of Directors

Minutes of Annual
Meeting of Board of Directors
of

_____

DATE:

IN ATTENDANCE:

MATTERS DISCUSSED/DECISIONS MADE:

MEETING ADJOURNED AT:

_____, _Secretary_

Appendix H

Sample Business Plan

Let's take a look at how you can best organize your business.

Your Business Plan

In business, a written plan is essential. Not only will it give you the perspective to uncover potential strengths and weaknesses, but it will allow you to focus your thinking and set goals. You can also use the business plan to brainstorm and develop new marketing ideas.

Your business plan should be an ongoing project, not a onetime strategy. As you learn more, your business will naturally change and evolve; your business plan should reflect this inherent flexibility.

Here's an example of a business plan. Use it as a guide, but be sure to modify your own business plan to suit your particular needs. Most likely, you will not need as much detail as shown in the example; keep your business plan as simple as you can.

Business Plan Outline

    I. Cover Page

   II. Table of Contents

  III. Statement of Purpose

  IV. Section 1: Business Description

      A. Introduction

      B. Business philosophy

IX. Appendixes
  A. Store layout
  B. Marketing studies
  C. Sales catalog/other inventory information
  D. Advertising layout
  E. Copy of store lease
  F. Licensing information

While creating your plan, don't be afraid to seek expert help. Lots of people will be willing to offer sound advice, such as recently retired professionals or a local businessperson of your acquaintance. You can also find valuable information at your local civic clubs, the Chamber of Commerce, the Small Business Administration, or even by attending a seminar. The best way to jump-start your business is to hire a small business coach. He or she will work with you to overcome your weaknesses and help your business get on the right track. Public libraries also offer a wealth of free information.

Index

About the Authors

Jeffery A. Jensen, CPA, and **Brian Radford** are the founders of American Business Solutions, Inc., a small-business consulting firm.

Stephen Bulpitt is the founder of United Financial Solutions, an e-publishing and small-business consulting firm.